# Advanced
# Bookkeeping

**British library cataloguing-in-publication data**

A catalogue record for this book is available from the British Library.

Published by:
Kaplan Publishing UK
Unit 2 The Business Centre
Molly Millars Lane
Wokingham
Berkshire
RG41 2QZ

ISBN 978-0-85732-038-4

© Kaplan Financial Limited, 2013

Printed and bound in Great Britain.

# Contents

# Chapter 1

# THE REGULATORY FRAMEWORK

This chapter discusses the conceptual framework that underpins modern financial reporting.

---

## CONTENTS

---

## LEARNING OUTCOMES

At the end of this chapter you should be able to:

- explain the need for, and objectives of, financial statements

- identify the users of financial statements and their particular interests in the statements

- describe and explain the following elements of the financial statements and their interaction: assets, liabilities, ownership interest, gains, losses, contributions from owners and distributions to owners

- identify the three stages of recognising elements for inclusion in financial statements

- discuss the nature and purpose of a conceptual framework

- explain the potential benefits and drawbacks of an agreed conceptual framework

- explain the role and general issues covered by the Statement of Principles

- identify and explain the qualitative characteristics of financial information

- discuss and apply accounting concepts and policies

- discuss the shortcomings of historical cost accounting and how they might be overcome

- explain the standard setting process and the role of the Financial Reporting Council, Accounting Standards Board, Urgent Issues Task Force and Financial Reporting Review Panel.

# 1 USERS OF FINANCIAL STATEMENTS

## 1.1 THE PURPOSE OF ACCOUNTING

The purpose of accounting is to provide information to users of financial statements. Legally, company financial statements are drawn up for the benefit of the shareholders, so that they can assess the performance of their Board of Directors. However, in practice many other groups will use these financial statements, and these groups will all have different needs. These groups, and their needs, are described below.

## 1.2 MANAGEMENT

Management will be interested in an analysis of revenues and expenses which will provide information that is useful when plans are formulated and decisions made. Once the budget for a business is complete, the accountant can produce figures for what actually happens as the budget period unfolds, so that they can be compared with the budget. Management will also need to know the cost consequences of a particular course of action to aid their decision making.

## 1.3 SHAREHOLDERS AND POTENTIAL SHAREHOLDERS

This group includes the investing public at large and the stockbrokers and commentators who advise them. The shareholders should be informed of the manner in which management has used their funds which have been invested in the business. This is a matter of reporting on past events. However, both shareholders and potential shareholders are also interested in the future performance of the business and use past figures as a guide to the future if they have to vote on proposals or decide whether to sell their shares.

Financial analysts advising investors such as insurance companies, pension funds, unit trusts and investment trusts are among the most sophisticated users of accounting information, and a company contemplating a takeover bid is yet another type of potential shareholder.

## 1.4 EMPLOYEES AND THEIR TRADE UNION REPRESENTATIVES

These use accounting information to assess the potential performance of the business. This information is relevant to the employee, who wishes to discover whether the company can offer him safe employment and promotion through growth over a period of years, and also to the trade unionist, who uses past profits and potential profits in his calculations and claims for higher wages or better conditions. The viability of different divisions of a company is of interest to this group.

## 1.5 LENDERS

This group includes some who have financed the business over a long period by lending money which is to be repaid at the end of a number of years, as well as short-term creditors such as a bank which allows a company to overdraw its bank account for a number of months, and suppliers of raw materials, which permit a company to buy goods from them and pay, for example, in four to twelve weeks' time.

Lenders are interested in the security of their loan, so they will look at financial statements to ensure that the company will be able to make their repayment on the due date and meet the interest requirements before that date. The amount of cash available and the value of assets which form a security for the debt are of importance to this group. Credit rating agencies are interested in the accounts for similar reasons.

## 1.6 GOVERNMENT AGENCIES

These use accounting information, either when collecting statistical information to reveal trends within the economy as a whole or, in the case of the Inland Revenue, to assess the profit on which the company's tax liability is to be computed.

## 1.7 THE BUSINESS CONTACT GROUP

Customers of a business may use accounting data to assess the viability of a company if a long-term contract is soon to be placed. Competitors will also use the accounts for purposes of comparison.

## 1.8 THE PUBLIC

From time to time, other groups not included above may have an interest in the company e.g. members of a local community where the company operates, environmental pressure groups, and so on.

## 1.9 CONCLUSION

Financial statements serve a wide variety of user groups, who have different interests and also different levels of financial sophistication. This makes it particularly difficult to produce accounts which are intelligible to the layman but sufficiently comprehensive for the expert.

The next section looks at how standards have been developed to try to meet these diverse needs.

# 2 THE REGULATORY SYSTEM

## 2.1 INTRODUCTION

The regulatory framework of accounting is made up of a number of legislative and quasi-legislative influences. This section provides an overview of these influences which can be listed as:

(a)     Company Law

(b)     Accounting Standards issued by the Accounting Standards Board (ASB)

(c)     EU Directives

(d)     The Stock Exchange.

All four of these sources combine to form what is known as UK GAAP, Generally Accepted Accounting Practice.

The first three are briefly considered below.

## 2.2   COMPANY LAW

The regulatory framework of accounting is affected by company law in a number of areas.

(a)     Financial statements of companies must show a 'true and fair view'.

(b)     Accounting standards issued by the ASB have quasi-legal authority.

(c)     Prescribed formats for the profit and loss account and balance sheet are required.

(d)     Detailed disclosures of information are required.

(e)     A company is limited in the amount of profits it can distribute to its shareholders.

(f)     Changes in share capital are regulated by law.

Items (c) to (f) are covered in the chapters on limited company accounts, to the extent that knowledge is required at this level of accounting.  Items (a) and (b) are dealt with below.

## 2.3   THE TRUE AND FAIR VIEW

Since 1948, statutory financial statements have been required to show a 'true and fair view'.  However, there is no universal definition of a 'true and fair view'.  A simple, unofficial, definition could be as follows:

- 'True' means that the accounts are arithmetically correct and in compliance with all relevant regulations.

- 'Fair' means that the accounts are unbiased and not misleading.

The meaning of the phrase has changed over time.  In 1948, there was a great deal of leeway as to how a set of accounts should be drawn up.  With the introduction of accounting standards, the choices available for preparing a set of accounts have been restricted, and so there is a much stricter interpretation of a 'true and fair view' today than there was 50 years ago.

## 2.4   ACCOUNTING STANDARDS

The Companies Act is mainly designed to deal with the problem of inadequate information.  Accounting standards set out to tackle a different problem: that of the diversity of treatment of certain items in published accounts.

**Definition**    **Accounting standards** are authoritative statements of how particular types of transactions and other events should be reflected in financial statements.

There are many areas of accounting where there is more than one generally accepted method of dealing with particular transactions. Because types of businesses often vary so much between one another, what is suitable as an accounting policy for one business may be unsuitable for another. It is, however, important for a given business to follow its accounting policies from one year to the next, so that valid comparisons of performance may be made.

The following are examples of the areas where variations in accounting practices are recognised:

(a)    depreciation of fixed assets

(b)    research and development expenditure

(c)    hire purchase or instalment transactions

(d)    stock and work-in-progress.

## 2.5    THE ROLES OF THE FRC, ASB, UITF AND REVIEW PANEL

### The Financial Reporting Council (FRC)

The FRC comprises around 25 members drawn from the users and preparers of accounts and auditors. It was originally set up to oversee the accounting standard setting process and the quality of published financial information. In July 2003 it was announced that the FRC would also take on the responsibility for supervising the audit profession, audit practice and corporate governance

The FRC guides the standard setting process and ensures that the ASB's work is properly funded.

The FRC has two operating bodies responsible for accounting standards and financial reporting. These are the Accounting Standards Board (ASB) and the Financial Reporting Review Panel (FRRP).

The standard setting bodies are shown below:

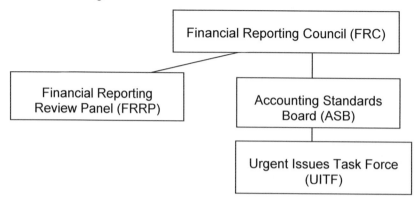

### The Accounting Standards Board (ASB)

The ASB has 10 members, including a full-time chairman and a full-time technical director. The aims of the ASB are to establish and improve standards of financial accounting and reporting for the benefit of users, preparers and auditors of financial information.

The ASB works to achieve its aims by:

- developing principles to guide it in establishing standards and to provide a framework within which others can exercise judgement in resolving accounting issues. The ASB's *Statement of Principles for Financial Reporting* is covered later in this chapter

- issuing new accounting standards, or amending existing ones, in response to evolving business practices, new economic developments and deficiencies being identified in current practice

- addressing urgent issues promptly

- working with the International Accounting Standards Board (IASB), with national standards-setters and relevant European Union Institutions to encourage high quality in the IASB's standards and their adoption in the EU.

The ASB issues Financial Reporting Standards (FRSs). A few Statements of Standard Accounting Practice (SSAPs) are still in force; these were issued by the Accounting Standards Committee (ASC) which was the predecessor of the ASB.

### The Financial Reporting Review Panel (FRRP)

The Review Panel has about 15 members. It examines apparent departures from the accounting requirements of the Companies Act and relevant accounting standards.

The Review Panel investigates specific matters about a company's financial statements when these are reported. It also actively monitors company financial statements, concentrating on industry sectors where the risk of defective financial statements is believed to be high.

The Review Panel has the power to seek a court order requiring companies to re-draft their financial statements. In practice, it normally attempts to persuade directors to revise defective accounts voluntarily. To date, no court orders have been sought.

### The Urgent Issues Task Force (UITF)

The UITF is a committee of the ASB. Its function is to address areas where an accounting standard or a Companies Act provision exists, but where unsatisfactory or conflicting interpretations have developed or seem likely to develop. The normal standard setting process is not normally practicable in these cases because of their urgency.

Once an issue has been identified, the UITF operates by seeking general agreement about the accounting treatment to be adopted. It issues UITF Abstracts which set out its pronouncements. UITF Abstracts have the same authority as accounting standards. They must be followed if financial statements are to give a true and fair view.

### The standard setting process

Once a topic has been identified, ASB staff carry out research. The members of the ASB debate the issues and then normally proceed as follows:

- A Discussion Paper is issued and interested parties are invited to comment. A Discussion Paper explores the issues involved, discusses possible accounting treatments and sets out the ASB's preliminary conclusions.

- A Financial Reporting Exposure Draft (FRED) is then issued. A FRED is the proposed accounting standard in draft form. FREDs are widely circulated and all interested parties are invited to comment.

- The ASB then considers the comments received. The new FRS is then issued.

## 2.6 EU DIRECTIVES

It is the aim of the EU that its member states will eventually become parts of a single economic entity. To achieve this goal businesses must operate under the same legal and accounting requirements. As a result two EU Directives have been incorporated into UK Law (and into the law of the other member states). These are:

- the Fourth Directive governing formats and disclosure requirements

- the Seventh Directive relates to group accounts, and is included in the Companies Act.

## 2.7 2005 AND INTERNATIONAL ACCOUNTING STANDARDS

The European Union has required all publicly quoted companies to apply International Accounting Standards (now known as International Financial Reporting Standards) since January 2005.

## 2.8 ADVANTAGES AND DISADVANTAGES OF ACCOUNTING STANDARDS

There are obvious advantages of accounting standards. Without them, an entity would be free to adopt any accounting treatment that it chose.

- Accounting standards result in consistency of accounting treatment; this means that (in theory) it is possible to compare the financial statements of different entities in a meaningful way.

- Accounting standards also mean that similar transactions are treated in the same way over time, making it possible to evaluate an entity's performance over time.

- Accounting standards make it more difficult (although not impossible) for entities to adopt accounting treatments that deliberately mislead users of the financial statements.

- The increasing use of international accounting standards means that it is now becoming easier to compare the financial statements of entities that operate in different countries.

- Accounting standards generally improve the quality of the information provided to users of financial statements; (in theory) they ensure that the information in financial statements is relevant to the needs of users and reliable.

However, there are also some disadvantages:

- It can be argued that the selection of accounting policies is a matter of judgement and should be left to individual entities. Different organisations operate under different conditions; an accounting policy that is appropriate for some entities may not be appropriate for others and may actually reduce the usefulness of the financial statements.

- Some preparers will view accounting standards as a set of rules to be circumvented and so standards do not necessarily prevent 'creative accounting'. (However, note that UK accounting standards are based on principles, rather than a set of rules; this makes abuse less likely.)

- Some accounting standards may change the commercial decisions made by entities. An entity could avoid actions that would benefit it in the long term if a standard required a treatment that would (for example) reduce profits in the short term.

- Many recent accounting standards have been drawn up primarily to meet the information needs of large institutional investors in public companies. For many smaller companies, the cost of complying (in time and effort, as well as money) may outweigh the benefits to users and preparers.

- Where accounting standards require complex treatments and extensive disclosures, it can be argued that these make the financial statements harder to understand and therefore less useful.

Most of the disadvantages apply to particular situations, rather than to accounting standards in themselves. Most preparers and users of financial statements accept that the advantages of accounting standards far outweigh the disadvantages.


## 2.9   CONCLUSION

In the UK, the regulatory framework for accounting is made up of the legal framework set out in the Companies Act and the requirements of the accountancy profession set out in SSAPs and FRSs. In the future, international standards will be the most important influence on UK accounting.

## 3　A CONCEPTUAL FRAMEWORK

The UK conceptual framework is known as the *Statement of Principles*. The basic objective of the conceptual framework is to provide a logical and sensible guide for preparing accounting standards and applying them.  In effect it will be the constitution within which accountants work, while the standards themselves will be the detailed laws enacted to apply these constitutional principles.

## 4　STATEMENT OF PRINCIPLES

### 4.1　INTRODUCTION

In December 1999, the ASB published its Statement of Principles for Financial Reporting.  This sets out the principles that the ASB believes should underlie the preparation and presentation of general purpose financial statements.  It aims to provide a coherent framework to assist the ASB in the development and review of accounting standards.

There are eight chapters in the Statement of Principles:

1　　The objective of financial statements

2　　The reporting entity

3　　The qualitative characteristics of financial information

4　　The elements of financial statements

5　　Recognition in financial statements

6　　Measurement in financial statements

7　　Presentation of financial information

8　　Accounting for interests in other entities

### 4.2　PURPOSE AND STATUS OF STATEMENT

The purpose of the Statement of Principles is to:

(a)　　Assist the ASB in the development and review of accounting standards.

(b)　　Provide a basis for reducing the number of accounting treatments allowed.

(c)　　Assist accountants in applying accounting standards and in dealing with topics that do not form the subject of an accounting standard.

(d)　　Assist auditors in deciding whether financial statements conform with accounting standards.

(e)　　Assist users in interpreting financial statements.

(f)　　Explain the ASB's approach to the formulation of accounting standards.

The Statement of Principles will not become an accounting standard.  Nothing in the Statement overrides a specific accounting standard.

## 4.3   CHAPTER 1 – THE OBJECTIVE OF FINANCIAL STATEMENTS

The objective of financial statements is to provide information about the reporting entity's financial performance and financial position that is useful to a wide range of users for assessing the stewardship of the entity's management and for making economic decisions.

## 4.4   CHAPTER 2 – THE REPORTING ENTITY

If there is legitimate demand for an entity to produce financial statements, then they should.  An entity is any cohesive economic unit under single control.  For our purposes, this means that individual limited companies must produce financial statements, and that also groups of companies under common control must produce group financial statements.

## 4.5   CHAPTER 3 – THE QUALITATIVE CHARACTERISTICS OF FINANCIAL INFORMATION

Information provided by financial statements needs to be **relevant** and **reliable**.  If there is a choice of approach then the one chosen is the one that maximises the relevance of the information.

The information provided by the financial statements also needs to be **comparable** and **understandable**.

Information is **relevant** if it has the ability to influence the economic decisions of users and is provided in time to influence those decisions.

Information is **reliable** if:

(a)     it can be depended upon by users to represent faithfully what it either purports to represent or could reasonably be expected to represent, and therefore reflects the substance of the transactions and other events that have taken place

(b)     it is free from deliberate or systematic bias and material error and is complete; and

(c)     in its preparation under conditions of uncertainty, a degree of caution has been applied in exercising the necessary judgements.

Information is **comparable** if it enables users to discern and evaluate similarities in, and differences between, the nature and effects of transactions and other events over time and across different reporting entities.

Information is **understandable** if its significance can be appreciated by users that have a reasonable knowledge of business and economic activities and accounting and a willingness to study, with reasonable diligence, the information provided.

The Statement also considers materiality.  Only information that is **material** needs to be given in the financial statements.

Information is **material** if its misstatement or omission might reasonably be expected to influence the economic decisions of users.

The relationship between these characteristics is shown in the diagram below.

The qualitative characteristics of financial information

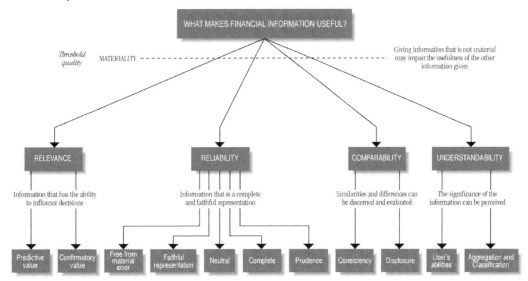

The overriding requirement for financial statements is that they should give a true and fair view of the financial position, performance and financial adaptability of an entity.

## 4.6    CHAPTER 4 – THE ELEMENTS OF FINANCIAL STATEMENTS

(a)    **Assets**

**Definition**    **Assets** are rights or other access to future economic benefits controlled by an entity as a result of past transactions or events.

**Rights or other access to future economic benefits**

At its simplest this means that the asset will eventually generate cash.  For example:

*    A machine will make goods.

*    These goods will be sold, generating cash or creating debtors.

*    Trade debtors will pay up in cash.

The machine, the goods and the trade debtors all help to generate cash, and so they are all assets.

**Controlled by an entity**

An entity does not have to own an asset in order to get the economic benefits from it.  For example, a leased asset will generate the same economic benefits as an identical asset that is owned by the business.

Past transactions or events

The transaction or event must be 'past' before an asset can arise.  For example:

*    Trade debtors only arise as a result of past sales.

*    Stocks are normally valued at their historic cost (past), not at their hoped for sales price (future).

(b) **Liabilities**

**Definition**     **Liabilities** are the obligations of an entity to transfer economic benefits as a result of past transactions or events.

**Obligations**

An obligation implies that the outflow of resources is **unavoidable**. Planned expenditure (such as future repairs) are avoidable, and so they do not create liabilities.

**Transfer economic benefits**

This could be a transfer of cash, or other property, the provision of a service, or the refraining from activities which would otherwise be profitable.

**Past transactions or events**

Similar points are made here to those under assets.

(c) **Ownership interest**

**Definition**     **Ownership interest** is the residual amount found by deducting all of the entity's liabilities from all of the entity's assets.

The above describes the residual nature of ownership interest. Owners' wealth can be increased whether or not a distribution is made. The sharing may be in different proportions.

Ownership interest is usually analysed in financial statements to distinguish that arising from owners' contributions from that resulting from other events. The latter is split into different reserves which may have different applications or legal status.

(d) **Gains and losses**

These are counted as two of the seven elements.

**Definition**     **Gains** are increases in ownership interest not resulting from contributions from owners.

**Definition**     **Losses** are decreases in ownership interest not resulting from distributions to owners.

(e) **Contributions from owners**

**Definition**     **Contributions from owners** are increases in ownership interest resulting from transfers from owners in their capacity as owners.

These will usually be in cash but they could be in other forms of property, by accepting equity in satisfaction of liabilities or by performing services.

The consideration is the granting of rights in the ownership interest.

(f)     **Distributions to owners**

**Definition**     **Distributions to owners** are decreases in ownership interest resulting from transfers made to owners in their capacity as owners.

Distributions include dividends and purchase of own shares but not bonus issues since ownership interest remains constant.

## 4.7   CHAPTER 5 – RECOGNITION IN FINANCIAL STATEMENTS

**Definition**     **Recognition** involves depiction of the item in words and by a monetary amount and the inclusion of that amount in the financial statement totals.

Only items which meet the definition of an element of the financial statements should be recognised. The definitions are set out in Chapter 4 of the Statement as explained above.

## 4.8   CHAPTER 6 – MEASUREMENT IN FINANCIAL STATEMENTS

**Definition**     **Measurement** is concerned with the monetary amount of the depiction of an element in the financial statements.

(a)     A measurement basis – either historic cost or current value – needs to be selected for each category of assets or liabilities. The basis selected should be the one that best meets the objective of financial statements.

(b)     An asset or liability being measured using the historical cost basis is recognised initially at transaction cost. An asset or liability being measured using the current value basis is recognised initially at its current value at the time it was acquired or assumed.

(c)     Subsequent remeasurement will occur if it is necessary to ensure that:

(i)      assets measured at historical cost are carried at the lower of cost and recoverable amount; and

(ii)     assets and liabilities measured on the current value basis are carried at up-to-date current values.

(d)     Such remeasurements will be recognised only if:

(i)      there is sufficient evidence that the monetary amount of the asset or liability has changed; and

(ii)     the new amount of the asset or liability can be measured with sufficient reliability.

## 4.9   CHAPTER 7   PRESENTATION OF FINANCIAL INFORMATION

This part of the Statement of Principles explores the way in which information should be presented in financial statements in order to meet the objective described in Chapter 1. The presentation decision is taken in the context of a structured set of financial statements comprising **primary statements** and **supporting notes**.

(a) **The primary statements**

| | |
|---|---|
| Profit and loss account | (financial performance) |
| Statement of total recognised gains and losses | (financial performance) |
| Balance sheet | (financial position) |
| Cash flow statement | |

(b) **Notes to financial statements**

The notes to financial statements should amplify and explain the primary statements giving more detailed information on items and in certain instances provide an alternative view of a particular transaction or event from that included in those primary statements. The notes and primary statements form an integrated whole.

(c) **Accompanying information**

Accompanying information is information which is positioned outside the primary statements and notes. This may include voluntary or evolutionary disclosures and information that, perhaps because it is too subjective, is not suitable for inclusion in the primary financial statements and the notes.

Accompanying information may include:

(i) a business review as required by the Companies Act 2006

(ii) information prepared from a different perspective from that adopted in the financial statements

(iii) statistical information

(iv) highlights and summary indicators.

## 4.10 CHAPTER 8 – ACCOUNTING FOR INTERESTS IN OTHER ENTITIES

Financial statements need to reflect the effect on the reporting entity's financial performance and position of its interests in other entities.

Consolidated financial statements are the financial statements of a group of companies – the reporting entity plus the other entities that it controls.

## 5 THE POTENTIAL BENEFITS AND DRAWBACKS OF AN AGREED CONCEPTUAL FRAMEWORK

**Potential benefits**

The potential benefits of a conceptual framework are related to the purposes stated by the ASB for the Statement of Principles. In summary, the benefits are:

- a framework for setting accounting standards

- a basis for resolving disputes

- fundamental principles do not have to be repeated in accounting standards

- there should be a reduction in pressure from vested interests who wish to pursue a particular policy out of self-interest rather than satisfying the general needs of users.

**Potential drawbacks**

Drawbacks to a conceptual framework include:

- due to their general nature the principles may not, in practice, reduce the options available

- there may be further disagreement as to the contents of the framework in addition to disagreement over the contents of standards.

**Conclusion**

There is widespread support for a conceptual framework, but aspects of the Statement of Principles have proved to be controversial, particularly the emphasis on the use of current values.

# 6    FRS 18 *ACCOUNTING POLICIES*

## 6.1    INTRODUCTION

FRS 18 restates the Statement of Principles.  It also describes the difference between accounting policies and accounting estimates, and outlines two accounting concepts; going concern and accruals.  These accounting concepts are the basis of all other accounting standards.  The Companies Act mentions five accounting principles; these are going concern and accruals (as in FRS 18) plus three more: prudence, consistency and separate valuation.  These are also discussed in this section.

## 6.2    POLICIES

Entities should select the most appropriate accounting policies and apply them consistently.  **Accounting policies** are the principles applied by an entity to report transactions, assets, and liabilities in the financial statements.  Accounting policies should be based upon all relevant SSAPs and FRSs.  If there are no relevant standards then the Statement of Principles should provide some guidance.

The accounting policies chosen by an entity should be disclosed in the financial statements.  Any changes should be highlighted, and their effect on profits and net assets disclosed.

## 6.3    ESTIMATES

Estimation techniques are used to measure monetary amounts.  For example, depreciation of assets (spreading out the cost of acquiring an asset over its estimated useful life) is an accounting policy, but the choice between depreciating over five years or 15 years is an estimate.

## 6.4    GOING CONCERN CONCEPT

The going concern concept assumes that a business (or entity) will **continue in operational existence for the foreseeable future**.

This means that the financial statements are drawn up on the assumption that there is no **intention or necessity to liquidate or curtail significantly the scale of operation**.

Circumstances where the going concern assumption would not be justified would include:

(i) where there is a specific intention to liquidate the business in the near future

(ii) where there is a strong possibility that shortage of finance will force the business into liquidation. This may be revealed by preparing a cash flow forecast for the next 12 months where a month-by-month comparison of expected cash inflows and outflows indicates financing requirements that are unlikely to be satisfied by the bank or by outside lenders

(iii) where there is a strong possibility that shortage of finance will result in the sale of a significant part of the business.

In the above circumstances the going concern assumption would not be valid, and the financial statements would be prepared on a basis which takes the likely consequences into account.

In most cases, however, financial statements will be prepared on a going concern basis and the directors will be able to justify the idea that such a basis is valid. The directors and auditors of a company both have a responsibility to ensure that the company is indeed a going concern if the going concern basis is adopted.

## 6.5 ACCRUALS (OR MATCHING) CONCEPT

The accruals or matching concept states that costs and revenues should be matched one with the other and dealt with in the accounting period to which they relate.

The starting position should be to use the concept to determine the accounting period in which revenue (i.e. sales) is recognised.

Revenue is usually recognised when it is realised. The realisation of revenue is usually taken to occur on the date of sale rather than on the date when the cash relating to the sale is received.

The efforts of expenditure in the past have led to the revenues accruing now. It is thus logical to match the costs or expenses of earning revenue with the revenue reported in any particular period. The operating profit determined in this way is supposed to indicate how efficiently the resources of the business have been utilised.

Although the accruals or matching principle is conceptually simple, it does run into practical difficulties.

For example, expenditure on fixed assets will provide benefits extending over several accounting periods. When a fixed asset is acquired it is necessary to estimate its useful life. The **service potential** of a fixed asset will diminish over its useful life, and this reduction is a cost or expense to be matched against the revenue of each period and is called **depreciation**.

## 6.6 PRUDENCE CONCEPT

Prudence states that revenues and profits are not reported and recognised in the financial statements unless realised. Revenues and profits are not deemed realised until the likelihood of conversion to cash is high. In most cases, this means the date of sale. By way of contrast, immediate provision is made for anticipated losses, even if such losses are not yet realised.

An example of the prudence concept is the situation in which a liability has been estimated to be between £500 and £600. Some accountants will make provision for the highest estimate on the grounds of prudence. Modern accounting thought though would make provision for the most likely value, high or low.

## 6.7 CONSISTENCY CONCEPT

A business should be consistent in its accounting treatment of similar items, both **within** a particular accounting period and **between** one accounting period and the next.

For example, in the case of depreciation of fixed assets, there is more than one accepted accounting treatment. One business may use one method, another business may use another. As far as the consistency concept is concerned, once a business has selected a method, it should use this method consistently for all assets in that class and for all accounting periods. Only in this way can users of financial statements draw meaningful conclusions from reported results. If a business were to change any of its accounting policies (e.g. the basis of depreciation) it must have a good reason for doing so and in addition, the financial effect of such a change should be quantified and, if material, reported to the shareholders.

## 6.8 SEPARATE VALUATION

Each item in the financial statements should be valued separately. In particular, assets should not be netted off against liabilities, and profits should not be netted off against losses.

## 6.9 HISTORICAL COST CONVENTION

The historical cost accounting system is a system of accounting in which all values are based on the historical costs incurred. This is the basis of accounting prescribed by the Companies Act (although the Act does allow Alternative Accounting Rules that enable certain assets to be revalued and stated at their revalued amounts).

## 6.10 MATERIALITY

This is the principle that financial statements should separately disclose items which are significant enough to affect evaluation or decisions.

The significance of an item stems from its importance in the overall context of the financial statements.

This convention ensures that only significant items are included in the financial statements in order to improve their clarity. The materiality test i.e. what is and is not significant, will differ from organisation to organisation.

Materiality may be considered in the context of the financial statements as a whole or individual items within them. It may also be considered in relative or absolute terms depending upon the item concerned.

## 6.11 DUALITY

The duality concept underpins double entry and the balance sheet. For each entry in the accounting records, there is an equal and opposite entry.

## 6.12 SUBSTANCE OVER FORM

Financial statements should reflect the economic substance of a transaction, rather than its legal form, where these are different.

A good example of this convention is that of assets acquired on hire purchase terms or under certain types of lease agreement. Despite the fact that such assets are not owned by the user until the final instalment has been paid, a fixed asset is recorded in the accounts at the start of the agreement. This is because the user has the benefit of the fixed asset, as if he or she owned it. The hire purchase agreement (or the lease) is simply a way of financing the purchase.

---

### ACTIVITY 1

---

State the accounting concept(s) being applied in each of these situations:

(1)     Plant and machinery has a net book value of £24m, but it would only fetch £15m if it were to be sold.

(2)     The plant and machinery is being depreciated over five years.

(3)     Stock is valued at £23m, even though it will probably sell for £35m.

(4)     John Ltd has just bought the trade and assets of  Sally, a rival unincorporated business.  John has changed Sally's accounting policies, bringing them into line with the rest of the business.

*For a suggested answer, see the 'Answers' section at the end of the book.*

## 7     HISTORICAL COST ACCOUNTING AND ITS SHORTCOMINGS

### 7.1     INTRODUCTION

Under historical cost accounting, assets are measured at their original cost throughout their lives, regardless of any changes in their market value.

This is the normal method of accounting. It has many advantages, but it also has serious disadvantages.

### 7.2     ADVANTAGES OF HISTORICAL COST ACCOUNTING

The advantages of historical cost accounting include:

*   records are based on objectively verifiable amounts (actual cost of assets, etc.)

*   it is simple and cheap

*   the profit concept is well understood

*   within limits, historical cost figures provide a basis for comparison with the results of other companies for the same period or similar periods, with the results of the same company for previous periods and with budgets

*   lack of competition – no acceptable alternative has been developed.

## 7.3 DISADVANTAGES OF HISTORICAL COST ACCOUNTING

The disadvantages of historical cost accounting include:

- It overstates profits when prices are rising through inflation. Several factors contribute to this. For example, if assets are maintained at their original cost, depreciation is based on that cost. As inflation pushes prices up, the true value to the business of the use of the asset becomes progressively more than the depreciation charge. This disadvantage can be overcome by revaluing fixed assets. Depreciation is then based on the revalued amount.

- It maintains financial capital but does not maintain physical capital. If a business makes a profit it must necessarily have more net assets. If the whole of that profit is distributed as dividend by a company, or withdrawn from the business by a sole trader, the business has the same capital at the end of the year as it had at the beginning. In other words, it has maintained its financial capital. However, it will not have maintained its physical capital if prices have risen through inflation during the year, because the financial capital will not buy the same stock and other assets to enable the business to continue operating at the same level.

- The balance sheet does not show the value of the business. A balance sheet summarises the assets and liabilities of the business, but there are several reasons why it does not represent the true value of the business. One reason for this could be that the use of historical cost accounting means that assets are included at cost less depreciation based on that cost rather than at current value. (Another reason is, of course, that not all the assets are included in the balance sheet – for example, internally generated goodwill will not appear.)

- It provides a poor basis for assessing performance. The profit is overstated, as explained above, while assets are understated. The result is that return on capital employed is doubly distorted and exaggerated.

- It does not recognise the loss suffered through holding monetary assets while prices are rising. A business holding cash or debtors through a period of inflation suffers a loss as its purchasing power declines.

## 7.4 ALTERNATIVES TO HISTORICAL COST ACCOUNTING

There are two main alternatives to historical cost accounting.

**Current purchasing power accounting**

Current purchasing power accounting (CPP) involves adjusting the historical cost accounts using a general price index (the Retail Price Index) so that all items are expressed in £s of year-end purchasing power.

The method has been rejected, most notably because many accountants felt it misleading to adjust specific assets such as stock and fixed assets by means of a general price index which was far more relevant to the spending power of a family than that of a trader.

### Current cost accounting

Current cost accounting (CCA) involves taking account of specific price changes as they affect a particular business and will result in a separate set of financial statements, distinct from the historical cost financial statements.

Although accountants generally believe CCA is superior to CPP, the profession has as yet to agree on any single method of accounting for inflation (or indeed, some people would even argue, on the need to do so).

## 7.5 CONCLUSION

It is largely accepted that historical cost accounts have very severe limitations, but so far the accounting profession has not devised any acceptable alternative. At present there is no requirement to prepare either CPP accounts or CCA accounts.

In practice many organisations overcome the limitations of historical cost accounts by revaluing certain fixed assets (normally land and buildings) and including these valuations in the financial statements. This is sometimes known as 'modified historic cost accounting' and is allowed by the Companies Act and by FRS 15 *Tangible fixed assets*, provided that the revaluations are kept up to date.

# KEY TERMS

**User groups** – people who use published financial information.

**Entity** – any organisation that is required to publish financial statements.

**Accounting policies** – the specific accounting standards or the accounting principles adopted by an entity. These should be the most appropriate policies for that entity.

**Accounting standards** – authoritative statements of how transactions and events are reported in published financial statements. In the UK, these standards are published by the Accounting Standards Board. Accounting standards should comply with the general rules set out in a conceptual framework.

**Conceptual framework** – acts like an accounting constitution. It set out the objectives of financial reporting, defines the content of financial statements, and outlines the qualities that financial information must possess in order to be useful and reliable.

**Statement of Principles** – the conceptual framework published by the Accounting Standards Board.

**Accounting concepts** – FRS 18 defines two accounting concepts, accruals and going concern. These form the basis of all other accounting standards. Accounting concepts are fundamental principles or assumptions that underpin the preparation of financial statements.

**Accounting principles** – these include going concern, consistency, prudence, accruals and separate valuation. Financial statements should be prepared in accordance with these principles.

**Assets** – rights or other access to future economic benefits controlled by an entity as a result of past transactions or events.

**Liabilities** – the obligations of an entity to transfer economic benefits as a result of past transactions or events.

**Ownership interest** – the residual amount found by deducting all of the entity's liabilities from all of the entity's assets.

# SELF TEST QUESTIONS

*Paragraph*

| | | |
|---|---|---|
| 1 | Who are the main users of financial statements? | 1 |
| 2 | What are the main requirements of management from financial information? | 1.2 |
| 3 | What would be potential shareholders' interests in the financial statements? | 1.3 |
| 4 | What is the name of the accounting standards issued by the Accounting Standards Board? | 2.5 |
| 5 | What is a conceptual framework? | 3 |
| 6 | What is meant by the relevance of information? | 4.5 |
| 7 | What is meant by information being reliable? | 4.5 |
| 8 | Describe the factors in financial statements which make information relevant. | 4.5 |
| 9 | Describe the factors in financial statements which make information reliable. | 4.5 |

10 How does the Statement of Principles define:

- assets

- liabilities

- ownership interest? 4.6

| | | |
|---|---|---|
| 11 | Name the two accounting concepts and the five accounting principles. | 6.1 |
| 12 | Does FRS 18 require disclosure of accounting concepts? | 6.2 |
| 13 | What is the going concern concept? | 6.4 |
| 14 | What is another name for the accruals concept? | 6.5 |

## ADDITIONAL QUESTION

### DEFINITIONS

Define the following accounting concepts and give, for each, one an example of its application:

(a) accruals

(b) consistency (see note below)

(c) prudence.

**Note:** Your answer to (b) should include a brief explanation of the circumstances in which the consistency concept should *not* be applied.

*For a suggested answer, see the 'Answers' section at the end of the book.*

# Chapter 2

# LIMITED COMPANIES

**This chapter describes the legal and financial structure of limited companies.**

## CONTENTS

1    Types of limited company

2    The legal records of a limited company

3    Company finance

4    Stewardship

5    Accounting systems and business organisations

## LEARNING OUTCOMES

At the end of this chapter you should be able to:

- explain the need for, and objectives of, financial statements

- discuss how the accounting systems of an organisation are affected by its roles, organisational structure, its administrative systems and procedures and the nature of its business transactions

- explain the legal framework and obligations of directors

- distinguish between issued and authorised share capital and between called up and paid up share capital

- distinguish between ordinary and preference shares

- distinguish between the market value and nominal value of a share

- explain why companies will be concerned with the value of their shares

- define and account for debentures.

# 1 TYPES OF LIMITED COMPANY

## 1.1 INTRODUCTION

In the UK the predominant form of business enterprise is the limited company. Most companies are limited by shares, meaning that in the event of the failure of a company, the amount the shareholders can lose is restricted to the amount paid for their shares.

It is important to appreciate that not all limited companies are large – they vary in size from the very small to the huge quoted company which operates worldwide.

## 1.2 KEY FEATURES OF A LIMITED COMPANY

### Shares and shareholders

The ownership of the company is split into **shares**. There are ordinary shares and preference shares, but for now we are only interested in the **ordinary shares** (also known as **equity shares**). Each ordinary share is entitled to a share of the net assets of the company (if and when it is wound up) and to a share of any dividends paid.

Shares are owned by shareholders. A limited company is jointly owned by its **ordinary shareholders**. The ordinary shareholders themselves are referred to as the **members** of the company. The total investment by the ordinary shareholders in the company is sometimes called **equity**.

For legal purposes shares have a **nominal value**. This can be for any amount, but is usually £1. There is no link between the nominal value of a share and its issue price or market value.

### Separate legal identity and limited liability

The company has a **separate legal identity** from its shareholders. This is very different from a partnership or a sole trader, where, in the eyes of the law, the owners and the business are one and the same.

If the company runs into financial difficulties, then the shareholders can lose their entire investment. However, they cannot be forced to make any further contributions to the business. This is a consequence of the concepts of separate legal identity and limited liability, and contrasts with the position of partners who must make good all business losses from their own personal wealth. (The one exception to this rule is when shares are issued partly paid. In these cases the shareholders can be asked to contribute the balance owing on their shares up to their nominal value. However, this situation is unusual.)

### Directors and stewardship

The members elect a **Board of Directors** to manage the company. In the election, each ordinary share has one vote, so the more shares that a member owns, then the more votes that they will have. This will be important when we come to look at Group Accounts.

The Board of Directors run the company on behalf of the shareholders, not themselves. This is known as **stewardship**.

**Legal formalities**

Because of the large number of investors involved in a limited company, and because of the problems that limited liability might pose for customers and suppliers, limited companies are more tightly regulated than sole traders or partnerships. Most of these regulations are contained in the **Companies Act 2006**.

One of the main features of this Act is the requirement for the Directors to present an **Annual Report** to their shareholders. This report contains the Statutory Accounts (financial statements).

*Note:* The **Companies Act 2006** came into force in stages during 2007 and 2008 to replace the 1985 and 1989 Acts and was examinable from the June 2008 sitting onwards. The schedules in the Companies Act 1985(89) which detailed the format of accounts were replaced in secondary legislation by Regulations issued on 19 February 2008.

There were a small number of important changes e.g. medium-sized companies need to disclose their turnover in the accounts delivered to the Registrar of Companies, etc.

## 1.3 FINANCIAL DIFFERENCES BETWEEN SOLE TRADERS AND COMPANIES

The main financial differences between companies and sole traders are in the following respects:

(a)     the form of the capital accounts

(b)     the form of loans to the company

(c)     the way in which profits are withdrawn by the proprietors

(d)     the form in which retained funds are presented.

The differences may be summarised as follows:

| Item | | Sole trader | Company |
|---|---|---|---|
| (a) | Capital introduced by proprietors | Capital account | Issued share capital |
| (b) | Loans from third parties | Loan account | Debentures |
| (c) | Profits withdrawn by proprietors | Drawings | Dividends |
| (d) | Profits retained in the business | Capital account | Reserves |

These differences will all be considered later in this chapter.

## 1.4 THE ADVANTAGES AND DISADVANTAGES OF OPERATION AS A LIMITED COMPANY RATHER THAN AS A SOLE TRADER

The advantages of operation as a limited company rather than as a sole trader are as follows:

(a)     The liability of the shareholders is limited to the capital already introduced by them. This is useful if the business venture is relatively risky, but is not such an advantage if the business is low risk. For example, a venture requiring a lot of capital investment and employing a lot of staff should be undertaken via a limited company. However, a low risk venture (such as buying residential property for letting out) does not need the benefits of limited liability.

(b)     There is a formal separation of the business from the owners of the business, which may be helpful to the running of the business.  For example, if several members of a family are the shareholders in a company but only two of the family are directors, it is clear to all concerned who is running the company.

(c)     Ownership of the business can be shared between people more easily than other forms of business organisation e.g. a partnership.

(d)     Shares in the business can be transferred relatively easily.

(e)     There may be tax advantages.

The disadvantages of operation as a limited company rather than as a sole trader are as follows:

(a)     The costs of formation of the company.  Documentation needs to be prepared to form the company, although these costs are only about £100 for a company with 'normal' type of memorandum and articles of association.

(b)     The annual running costs of the company.  Annual returns need to be completed and sent to the Registrar of Companies.  The audit fee is a further additional cost though companies obviously derive a benefit from having their accounts audited, not least from the greater reliability they acquire as a result of the audit.

(c)     Directors of a company are subject to greater legislative duties than others running an unincorporated business.

(d)     It is difficult/expensive to return capital surplus to the business's requirements to the shareholders.

(e)     Shares in the business can be transferred relatively easily.

(f)     There may be tax disadvantages.


## 1.5     PRIVATE COMPANIES AND PUBLIC COMPANIES

Whether a particular company is a private company or a public company is a matter of law.

**Definition**          A **public** company is a company which must have a minimum allotted share capital of £50,000, of which at least one quarter and the whole of any premium are paid up.  A public company has the letters plc after its name, which stand for 'public limited company'.

**Definition**          A **private** company is a company that is not a public company.  A private company has the letters Ltd after its name.


## 1.6     QUOTED AND UNQUOTED COMPANIES

Legally, only public limited companies are allowed to sell their shares to the general public, but not all of them chose to do so.  If a company wishes to sell its shares to the general public then it must satisfy the strict criteria of the **Stock Exchange** as well as any legal requirements.  Once these criteria have been met, the company is said to be quoted on the Stock Exchange.  This gives rise to the term **quoted or listed company**.

This means that the public can only buy shares in a quoted public limited company.

## ACTIVITY 1

Charlie Farley is a trained piano tuner and restorer, currently working for a music school in London.  He is considering leaving the school and setting up in business.  He has identified two possible ventures, noted below.

Piano restorer

- This will require the purchase of tools costing £1,000.

- He will also need a workshop which will cost £200 per month to rent on a short term lease.

- Most restoration jobs will require five to ten days work.

Piano manufacturer

- This will require the purchase of tools and machinery costing £25,000.

- A purpose built factory will also be needed.  He has identified one unit that would cost £1,000 per month on a three-year lease.

- He will need to hire four skilled members of staff.

- Each construction job will take about one month.

**Required:**

Advise Charlie on a suitable legal structure for each venture.

*For a suggested answer, see the 'Answers' section at the end of the book.*

## 2 THE LEGAL RECORDS OF A LIMITED COMPANY

### 2.1 REGISTERED OFFICE

A company must always have a registered office and give notice of its situation because:

- any writ or other legal process is validly served on the company by delivery to its registered office, and

- certain statutory books and other documents of the company open to inspection (by members or in some cases by third parties) are held at the registered office or other specified place.  Most books should be available for public inspection for at least two hours per day during business hours.

### 2.2 STATUTORY BOOKS

The statutory books a company must keep are registers of:

(a) **Members**

Contents – details of shareholders showing name, address, date of ownership of shares, number and type of shares held.

On a total disposal of a person's shareholding, the entry would be closed off by inserting the date he ceased to be a member.

(b) **Directors and Secretary**

Contents – personal details (including name and address, nationality, business occupation (if any), date of birth).

(c) Debenture holders

Contents – details of debenture holders showing name, address and amount of holding.

## 2.3 STATUTORY ACCOUNTS

At least once in every calendar year, the directors must lay before the members of the company in general meeting a profit and loss account and balance sheet (the statutory accounts). These must be filed with the Registrar of Companies within seven months from the end of the accounting period (for a public company) and ten months from the end of the accounting period (for a private company).

Under the Companies Act 2006 the statutory accounts must be filed with the Registrar of Companies within six months from the end of the accounting period (for a public company) and nine months from the end of the accounting period (for a private company). A private company will no longer have to hold an Annual General Meeting, but must still send a copy of the statutory accounts to every member (shareholder) of the company and every debenture holder. (Debentures are covered later in this chapter.)

The requirement to prepare financial statements for the shareholders arises from the directors' stewardship function. This is discussed further in Section 4.

## 2.4 ANNUAL RETURN

Once a year a company is required to deliver to the Registrar of Companies the annual return. This return includes:

- the address of the registered office

- the type of company and its business activities

- particulars of the directors

- a summary of the company's share capital

- a list of members showing individual shareholdings and changes which have occurred during the year.

# 3 COMPANY FINANCE

## 3.1 INTRODUCTION

The way in which the assets of a company (fixed assets, stock, debtors and cash) are financed will vary from one company to another. Part of the finance may be provided by the owners or proprietors of the company (referred to as shareholders), while part may be provided by outsiders including trade creditors, banks and other lenders of funds.

Companies will also normally be partly financed by their own accumulated profits known as reserves.

## 3.2 THE NATURE AND PURPOSE OF SHARE CAPITAL AND RESERVES

**Definition**   **Share capital** represents the capital invested in the company by its shareholders by the purchase of shares.

**Definition**   **Reserves** represent the balance of net assets belonging to the shareholders. These may include part of past issues of share capital (known as share premium), retained trading profits and revaluation gains on the revaluation of fixed assets.

The total of share capital and reserves represents the book value of the net assets of the company.

## 3.3 DISTINCTION BETWEEN NOMINAL VALUE AND MARKET VALUE OF SHARE CAPITAL

**Definition**   The **nominal value** of a share is its face value e.g. £1 ordinary shares or 50p ordinary share.

Each share has a stated nominal (or par) value. This has little practical significance except as a base line price below which further shares may not generally be issued. The nominal value is also used as a means of calculating dividends to shareholders.

**Definition**   The **market value** of a share is the price at which that share could be bought or sold.

The market value of a share is not fixed at any particular date. The market value is related to the market value of the business of the company. For example, if a business is worth £100,000 and there are 1,000 £1 shares in issue in the company, the market value of each share is £100 whereas the nominal value is £1.

If the company is listed on a stock exchange then a price will be quoted for the shares based upon recent transactions between purchasers and sellers of shares. This is also referred to as the market value of a share, but this may not be the same value that would apply if the entire business was sold and thus all the shares were sold as one transaction.

## 3.4 WHY COMPANIES ARE CONCERNED WITH THE VALUE OF THEIR SHARES

Companies are concerned with the value the stock market places on the shares for two main reasons:

(a)   Shareholders will look at a steadily rising price of the shares as evidence of sound management of the company by the directors. It would indicate additional profits being made every year.

(b)   If the company wishes to raise further finance through the issue of shares, the current market price will be used as a basis for issuing more shares. The higher the price, the less number of shares will need to be issued and the less dilution there will be of the existing shareholders' effective interest in the company.

It is important to appreciate that the market value of a share quoted on the Stock Exchange has no direct relationship to the nominal value.

## 3.5  SHARE CAPITAL

The share capital of a company may be divided into various classes. The company's internal regulations (the Articles of Association) define the respective rights attached to the various shares e.g. as regards dividend entitlement or voting at company meetings. The various classes of share capital are dealt with below. In practice it is usually only larger companies which have different classes of share capital.

## 3.6  ORDINARY SHARES

**Definition**      **Ordinary shares** are the normal shares issued by a company. The normal rights of ordinary shareholders are to vote at company meetings and to receive dividends from profits.

Ordinary shares are often referred to as equity shares. A special class of ordinary share is the redeemable ordinary share where the terms of issue specify that it is repayable by the company.

## 3.7  PREFERENCE SHARES

**Definition**      **Preference shares** are shares carrying a fixed rate of dividend, the holders of which have a prior claim to any company profits available for distribution.

The rights and advantages of the shares will be specified in the articles of association.

Special categories of preference shares include:

(i)      Participating preference shares – where shareholders are entitled to participate together to a specified extent in distributable profits and surpluses on liquidation. Again, the rights of the shareholders are set out in the articles.

(ii)     Redeemable preference shares – the terms of issue specify that they are repayable by the company.

Redeemable Preference Shares are more like debt than equity.

## 3.8  ORDINARY AND PREFERENCE SHARES COMPARED

| Aspect | Ordinary shares | Preference shares |
|---|---|---|
| Voting power | Carry a vote. | Do not carry a vote. |
| Distribution of profits (dividends) | A dividend which may vary from one year to the next after the preference shareholders have received their dividend. | A fixed dividend (fixed percentage of nominal value) in priority to ordinary dividend. |
| Liquidation of the company | Entitled to surplus assets on liquidation after liabilities and preference shares have been repaid. | Priority of repayment over ordinary shares but not usually entitled to surplus assets on liquidation. |

### 3.9 DEBENTURES OR LOAN STOCK

**Definition**    A **debenture** is a written acknowledgement of a loan to a company, given under the company's seal, which carries a fixed rate of interest.

A debenture may relate to a loan from one person. Debenture stock, on the other hand, rather like shares, may be held by a large number of individuals. The conditions and regulations are set out in a debenture trust deed.

Debentures are not part of a company's share capital – they are third party liabilities. Debenture interest is therefore a charge against profit and must be paid whether or not the company makes a profit.

Debentures are shown as liabilities in the balance sheet, just like any other loan.

## 4    STEWARDSHIP

### 4.1    THE ANNUAL REPORT

The shareholders own the company, but they do not necessarily run the company. Instead, the shareholders appoint a Board of Directors to manage the company on their behalf. This relationship is known as **stewardship**.

The directors have day-to-day control over the assets and operations of the shareholders' company. The shareholders will want to assure themselves that their company is being run profitably and honestly. Therefore the directors must prepare an account of their performance during the year and a summary of the assets and liabilities of the company at the end of the year. From this, the shareholders can see whether their company is making a profit or a loss, and whether their investment in the company is getting bigger or smaller. These form part of the annual financial statements.

Because the directors have control of the company money, there are always concerns about the amount of money that the directors are paying themselves. Therefore, the directors have to disclose the amount of pay and other benefits that they have received during the year. The other benefits might include pension contributions, perks such as motor cars, or shares issued for free or at a below market price. The amount of pay and benefits received by directors is referred to as **Directors' Remuneration** or **Directors' Emoluments**.

### 4.2    USING THE FINANCIAL STATEMENTS

Having read the directors' report, the shareholders must then decide the following:

*    whether or not to re-elect the Board of Directors

*    how much the directors should be paid

*    how much dividend should be paid

*    whether or not to approve the financial statements.

### 4.3    RE-ELECTING THE DIRECTORS AND APPROVING THEIR REMUNERATION

If the directors have performed a good job then the shareholders will want to re-elect them, and to reward them with good pay. This will encourage them to do even better in the future. If they have performed badly, then the shareholders may vote-off one or more of the directors from the board, or they may cut their pay. There have been concerns recently that when lazy or incompetent directors have been voted off, they have been given multi-million pound pay-offs. It is up to the shareholders to monitor these situations, because it is their money that is being paid out. An unusual situation arose in May 2003, when shareholders in GlaxoSmithKline voted down a proposal that would have given a £22m pay off to one director if he was dismissed.

## 4.4 DIVIDENDS

Shareholders need a return on their investment. Their return comes in the form of the dividend. Dividends on shares are similar to interest on savings.

The **preference dividend** is normally fixed, and must be paid each and every year.

The **ordinary dividend** is variable. Each year the Directors will review the amount of profit that the company has made, and the amount of cash available. On the basis of this, the directors will propose a dividend. The shareholders must then approve this dividend. They may decide that they want more, or they may decide that the proposed dividend is more than the company can afford. Either way, it is the shareholders who make the final decision.

## 4.5 APPROVING THE FINANCIAL STATEMENTS

The members (shareholders) must approve the financial statements. This means that they accept that the financial statements are an accurate record of their company's position and performance. To do this they need help from the auditors.

## 4.6 THE AUDITORS AND THE AUDIT REPORT

You may have noticed that the shareholders assess their directors' performance on the basis of financial statements prepared by the directors themselves. It will obviously be in the directors' interests to be as optimistic as possible in order to boost the company's profits, and consequently boost their own pay. This is where auditors come in.

The shareholders appoint registered auditors to audit the financial statements prepared by the directors. Normally the auditors will report that the financial statements give a **true and fair view** of the financial position and performance of the company. This means that the accounts are not misleading; it does not mean that they are 100% correct. The auditors will also audit certain disclosures, such as Directors' Remuneration. These clean audit reports are known as unqualified opinions.

If the auditors think that the financial statements do not show a true and fair view, then they will issue a qualified opinion. This should state what, in the auditor's opinion, the profit for the year really should be.

In practice, the directors have a lot of influence over the auditors. In particular, the directors can award other work to their auditors, such as management consultancy. Therefore, the financial statements must disclose:

*   the audit fee for the year; plus

*   fees paid by the company to the audit firm for any other work done during the year.

The shareholders will become suspicious if the auditors are receiving as much from their non-audit work as from their audit work. This is because the auditors will be unwilling to criticise the directors for fear of losing valuable work.

# 5 ACCOUNTING SYSTEMS AND BUSINESS ORGANISATIONS

## 5.1 INTRODUCTION – THE COMPANIES ACT

The Companies Act states that companies must maintain adequate accounting records.

These records must be sufficient to:

- show and explain the company's transactions

- show with reasonable accuracy, at any time, the financial position of the company

- enable the directors to ensure that any accounts required to be prepared comply with all the relevant requirements of the Companies Act and accounting standards.

This means that a company's accounting records must be able to:

- identify to whom goods and services have been sold (except for retail businesses)

- identify from whom goods and services were bought

- record all cash receipts and payments

- enable annual financial statements to be prepared.

The Act does not tell businesses how to achieve these requirements.

A small company (in terms of volume of transactions) would probably only need a cash book, remittance advices and files of paid and unpaid invoices. There would be no need for a computerised accounts package or even a nominal ledger. As long as these records were kept, there would be sufficient information to enable their accountants to prepare the annual financial statements.

Larger companies will obviously need much more formal accounting systems, not just to comply with the law but also to ensure that they have the information to enable them to monitor and control what is going on in their business.

## 5.2 OTHER LEGAL REQUIREMENTS

For many small businesses, the need for modern accounting systems arises when they hit the VAT threshold and have to start keeping detailed and auditable records of sales and purchases, receipts and payments.

Likewise, once employees are taken on, then there is a legal obligation to maintain records of PAYE and National Insurance contributions.

## 5.3 ORGANISATIONAL STRUCTURES

Businesses can be highly centralised or decentralised. A centralised business will have one large accounts department with very rigid and formal accounting procedures. A decentralised business will have smaller systems at its various locations that then submit returns on a weekly or monthly basis to the head office. This is more flexible than a centralised system, but it does increase the risk of errors and fraud.

The choice of a centralised or decentralised organisational structure will depend upon the nature of the business. A manufacturing business will tend to be centralised, whereas a professional organisation will be decentralised. Indeed, many national chains of accountants or estate agents are often in fact collections of virtually independent offices and businesses.

Overseas operations also tend to be fairly independent of the head office. They will usually have completely separate accounting systems to take into account their different legal and business environments.

## 5.4   CONFIDENTIALITY

Accountants in all organisations have access to commercially sensitive and personal information. It is essential that this information is kept secure and is not disclosed to unauthorised people. All professional accountants, and that includes CAT students, must treat all information that they receive in the strictest confidence.

All businesses will have commercially sensitive information such as the profitability of their products, the terms that they get from their suppliers and so on. They form a key part of the knowledge and experience that makes them successful. If the information is disclosed it could damage relations with business contacts, or give rivals an opportunity to compete.

Disclosure of payroll information can also be damaging. Not only can it be embarrassing for those concerned and give rise to disputes, but it is also a breach of the company's duty of confidentiality towards its employees.

If you work for a publicly quoted company (a plc whose shares are traded on the stock exchange) then you may have access to what is known as price sensitive information. This is information that might affect the price of the company's shares on the stock exchange. For example, if you knew that your company had just won a hugely profitable new contract, then you could buy some shares in the hope that they would go up in value when the news was publicly announced. Using price sensitive information, or passing it on to others, is known as insider dealing. It is a criminal offence.

# KEY TERMS

**Limited company** – also known as a *limited liability company*. A company jointly owned by shareholders. The shareholders enjoy limited liability.

**Limited liability** – the shareholders of a limited company are not personally liable for any losses incurred by the company.

**Share capital** – the money contributed to a company by its owners, the shareholders. Share capital does not have to be repaid.

**Directors** – the people appointed by the shareholders to manage a company.

**Stewardship** – the idea that directors are managing a company for the benefit of the shareholders rather than for themselves.

**Ordinary shares** – the basic sort of share capital. Ordinary shares will claim a share of the profits and net assets of a company, after all other claims have been met. Ordinary shareholders elect the Board of Directors.

**Preference shares** – all preference shares are different, but typically these shares will receive a fixed dividend and a fixed share of the net assets of the company. Preference shareholders do not normally have any voting rights.

**Auditors** – an independent group of professional accountants, appointed by the shareholders, who ensure that the annual accounts prepared by the directors show a true and fair view.

# SELF TEST QUESTIONS

*Paragraph*

| | | |
|---|---|---|
| 1 | Who are the managers of a company? | 1.2 |
| 2 | Who are the owners of a company? | 1.2 |
| 3 | What are the key factors that distinguish a company from a sole trader? | 1.3 |
| 4 | What is the difference between a private and a public company? | 1.5 |
| 5 | What is the relationship between the nominal value and the market value of a company's shares? | 3.3 |
| 6 | What are preference shares? | 3.7 |
| 7 | What are debentures? | 3.9 |
| 8 | What is meant by the term 'stewardship'? | 4.1 |
| 9 | What sort of accounting records are required by the Companies Act? | 5.1 |
| 10 | What offence will you have committed if you use or pass on price sensitive information? | 5.4 |

## ADDITIONAL QUESTION

### LIMITED COMPANIES COMPARISONS

A client of your firm has been trading successfully as a sole trader in the UK for a number of years. However, her business has grown so much that she now thinks it is time to consider converting the business into a limited company.

You are to meet your client tomorrow to discuss her plans.

**Required:**

Prepare some brief notes for the meeting that explain:

(a) the main advantages and disadvantages of operating as a limited company rather than as a sole trader

(b) the main types of share capital and their characteristics.

*For a suggested answer, see the 'Answers' section at the end of the book.*

# Chapter 3

# SHARE CAPITAL, DIVIDENDS AND TAXATION

This chapter takes a closer look at share capital, taxation and dividends, including how to adjust for these items from the trial balance.

---

## CONTENTS

1   Ordinary shares

2   Ordinary dividends

3   Preference shares and dividends

4   Accounting for reserves

5   Debentures and other loans

6   Taxation

---

## LEARNING OUTCOMES

At the end of this chapter you should be able to:

- define and account for current tax

- draft appropriate disclosure of current taxation in the published statements

- distinguish between issued and authorised share capital and between called up and paid up share capital

- distinguish between ordinary and preference shares

- account for a share issue

- explain the share premium account

- define and account for a bonus issue and a rights issue

- outline the advantages and disadvantages of a rights issue and a bonus issue

- distinguish between the market value and nominal value of a share

---

- explain why companies will be concerned with the value of their shares

- define and account for debentures

- explain the advantages and disadvantages of raising finance by issuing debentures rather than issuing ordinary or preference shares.

# 1 ORDINARY SHARES

## 1.1 ORDINARY SHARES AND EQUITY

Every limited company must have ordinary shares in issue. These shares are known as the **equity** of the business. These shares represent the ownership interest in the business. Each ordinary share normally has one vote, and these votes appoint the Board of Directors. The shares themselves will be owned by **shareholders**. The ordinary shareholders as a body are known as the **members** of the company.

They are the last claimants to be repaid when a company is dissolved. They will receive all of the residual assets of the company after all of the liabilities have been settled. This means that they will receive all of the profits made by the company. It also means that if the company's liabilities exceed its assets then they will receive nothing. However, it must be remembered that the shareholders will not normally be required to make good any losses.

This section looks at how to record the initial issue of ordinary shares by a company. Once shares have been issued the shareholders may buy and sell their shares as they please. These later sales will not affect the books of the company. (In the same way that selling your car on the second hand market has no effect on the dealer that you bought your car from.)

## 1.2 AUTHORISED AND ISSUED SHARE CAPITAL; CALLED UP AND PAID UP SHARE CAPITAL

The **authorised share capital** is the maximum number of shares that a company may issue. This prevents the directors from issuing extra shares to themselves or their friends.

The Companies Act 1985 required every company to have an authorised share capital. The Companies Act 2006 has abolished authorised share capital for new companies. Existing companies will continue to have a maximum number of shares that can be issued.

The **issued share capital** is the actual number of shares in issue at any point in time. It is the issued share capital which appears on a company's balance sheet.

Usually, all of the shares in issue will have been paid for in full. However, when shares are first issued they are often paid for in instalments. This gives rise to the difference between called up and paid up share capital.

The **called up** share capital is the total nominal value payable by the share holder.

**Paid up** share capital is the amount of nominal value paid at the current date.

In the ICB syllabus all shares will be issued and paid for in full at the same time. There will be no partly paid shares.

### 1.3 ISSUE OF SHARES AT NOMINAL VALUE

When shares are issued at their nominal value they are said to have been issued at par. The double entry for issuing shares at their nominal value is:

|  |  | Debit | Credit |
|---|---|---|---|
| Debit | Cash | X | |
| Credit | Share Capital Account | | X |

with the issue proceeds.

#### Example

A company issues 200,000 50p ordinary shares at par. Write up the ledger accounts.

#### Solution

**Cash book**

|  | £ |  | £ |
|---|---|---|---|
| Ordinary share capital | 100,000 | | |

**Ordinary share capital account**

|  | £ |  | £ |
|---|---|---|---|
| | | Cash | 100,000 |

### 1.4 ISSUE OF SHARES AT A PREMIUM

Companies often issue their shares for more than their nominal value. The difference between the proceeds of issue and the nominal value is called the **share premium**, and it is credited to a separate account.

The double entry for issuing shares at a premium is:

|  |  | Debit | Credit |
|---|---|---|---|
| Debit | Cash | X | |
| Credit | Share Capital Account | | X |
| Credit | Share Premium Account | | X |

Although shares can be issued at a premium, the Companies Act prohibits the issue of shares at a discount – in other words at a value less than their nominal value.

#### Example

Axe Ltd has just been incorporated. Its initial share issue was for 200,000 ordinary shares of 50 pence each at an issue price of 75p.

#### Required:

(a) Write up the ledger accounts.

(b) Show how these shares will be presented in the balance sheet.

#### Solution

**Cash book**

|  | £ |  | £ |
|---|---|---|---|
| Ordinary share capital | 100,000 | | |
| Share premium | 50,000 | | |

### Ordinary share capital account

|  | £ |  | £ |
|---|---|---|---|
|  |  | Cash | 100,000 |

### Share premium account

|  | £ |  | £ |
|---|---|---|---|
|  |  | Cash | 50,000 |

### Axe Ltd – Balance sheet extracts

|  |  | £ |
|---|---|---|
|  |  | £ |
| Net assets | (Cash) | 150,000 |
|  |  |  |
| Capital and reserves |  |  |
| Called up share capital | 200,000 Ordinary Shares of 50 pence each | 100,000 |
| Share premium account |  | 50,000 |
| P&L reserve |  | – |
|  |  | 150,000 |

## ACTIVITY 1

Bradawl Ltd has been trading profitably for many years.  Its balance sheet immediately before the share issue in this activity is noted below.  Bradawl Ltd has just issued a further 500,000 ordinary shares of 25 pence each.  The issue price for each share was 60 pence.

### Bradawl Ltd – Balance sheet extracts

|  |  | £ |
|---|---|---|
| Net assets (cash) |  | 456,789 |
|  |  |  |
| Capital and reserves |  |  |
| Called up share capital | 900,000 ordinary shares of 25 pence each | 225,000 |
| Share premium account |  | 75,000 |
| P&L reserve |  | 156,789 |
|  |  | 456,789 |

**Required:**

(a)    Write up the ledger accounts.

(b)    Show how these shares will be presented in the balance sheet.

**Guidance**

(1)    The existing share capital and premium will be the brought forward balances in the T accounts.

(2)    The net assets in the balance sheet will be increased by the cash proceeds.

(3)    The balance sheet will show the carry down values for the share capital and share premium.

*For a suggested answer, see the 'Answers' section at the end of the book.*

## 1.5 USES OF THE SHARE PREMIUM ACCOUNT

The share premium account is a non-distributable reserve. It cannot be used to pay a dividend. The share premium account can be used to cover the cost of new share issues, and can also be turned into share capital via a bonus issue.

## 1.6 ISSUES AT FULL MARKET PRICE AND RIGHTS ISSUES

The simplest form of share issue is when new shares are issued at their full market price. The share issue is open to anyone who can afford the asking price. This type of share issue is most common when a company's shares are first issued.

It is normal practice for any subsequent issue of shares to be a *rights issue*. In a rights issue, existing shareholders have the right to purchase enough shares to maintain their original percentage shareholding. The issuing company offers new shares to existing shareholders at slightly below the market price. This encourages the existing shareholders to take up their rights entitlement and promotes shareholder loyalty.

**Example of a rights issue**

Wright plc has 800,000 £1 ordinary shares in issue. They were originally issued at a premium of 40 pence each. The current market price of these shares is £3.50.

Wright plc has announced a *1 for 4* rights issue at £3 per share.

**Tasks**

(1)    Prepare the ledger accounts to record this transaction.

(2)    Prepare the share capital and share premium section of the balance sheet before and after the rights issue.

(3)    Mr Bright owned 32,000 shares in Wright plc before the rights issue. How many shares will he own after the issue? What will his share of the voting right in Wright plc be before and after the rights issue? Assume that he takes up his full entitlement of shares.

**Solution**

(1)    Prepare the ledger accounts to record this transaction.

### Ordinary shares

|  |  |  |  |
|---|---|---|---|
|  |  | Opening balance | 800,000 |
|  |  | New issue (a) | 200,000 |
| Closing balance | 1,000,000 |  |  |
|  | 1,000,000 |  | 1,000,000 |

### Share premium

|  |  |  |  |
|---|---|---|---|
|  |  | Opening balance (b) | 320,000 |
|  |  | New issue (c) | 400,000 |
| Closing balance | 720,000 |  |  |
|  | 720,000 |  | 720,000 |

**Cash**

| Proceeds of new issue | | |
|---|---|---|
| Capital | 200,000 | |
| Premium | 400,000 | |

(a) One new share will be issued for every four shares already in issue. There are 800,000 shares in issue and so 200,000 shares will be issued, bringing the total share capital to £1m.

(b) 800,000 shares @ 40 pence = £320,000.

(c) The new shares are issued at £3 each, which is a premium of £2 per share. 200,000 shares at £2 per share gives a premium on issue of £400,000. The new balance on the share premium account is £720,000.

(2) Capital and reserves

| | Before £ | After £ |
|---|---|---|
| £1 ordinary shares | 800,000 | 1,000,000 |
| Share premium | 320,000 | 720,000 |
| | 1,120,000 | 1,720,000 |

(3) Mr Bright's shares and voting rights.

Before the rights issue Mr Bright owned 32,000 shares out of a total of 800,000 shares. This gave him 4% of the voting rights of the business.

The 1 for 4 rights issue gives him another 8,000 shares and increases his share holding to 40,000. He now owns 40,000 shares out of 1,000,000 shares, which is still 4%. Mr Bright's voting rights have been preserved.

## 1.7 BONUS ISSUES

Bonus issues are also known as *capitalisation issues* and *scrip issues*.

In a bonus issue, a part of the company's existing reserves are reclassified as share capital. New shares will be issued fully paid, and these will be distributed to the existing shareholders in proportion to their existing shareholdings.

There are a number of uses for a bonus issue.

(1) Increasing the number of shares in issue will make it easier to divide the shares between a larger number of shareholders. This is useful when a company wants to bring in new shareholders.

(2) Increasing the value of the company's share capital will strengthen the balance sheet. This is useful if a company has grown rapidly, and the share capital is out of proportion to the net assets of the business.

(3) The market price of each share will fall. This makes the shares more affordable, and encourages more people to buy shares. This is the most common reason for publicly quoted plc's to make a bonus issue.

**Example of a bonus issue**

Bowness Ltd is a successful private company owned and managed by its three founding shareholders. The founders wish to distribute shares to their children and to their employees, but at present there are only 50 shares in issue. They also wish to bring their share capital more into line with the net assets of the business. The balance sheet of Bowness Ltd immediately before the bonus issue is as follows:

|  | £ |
|---|---|
| Ordinary shares of £1 each | 50 |
| Revaluation reserve | 380,000 |
| Revenue reserves | 570,000 |
| | |
| Shareholders' funds and net assets | 950,050 |

The terms of the bonus issue are that 10,000 new £1 ordinary shares will be issued fully paid in respect of each share already in issue. The bonus issue will be financed firstly from the revaluation reserve and then from revenue reserves.

**Required:**

(a) Prepare the ledger accounts to record this transaction.

(b) Prepare the capital and reserves section of the balance sheet after the rights issue.

**Solution**

(1) Ledger accounts

**Ordinary shares**

|  |  |  |  |  |  |
|---|---|---|---|---|---|
|  |  |  | Opening balance |  | 50 |
|  |  |  | New issue | (a) | 500,000 |
| Closing balance |  | 500,050 |  |  |  |
|  |  | 500,050 |  |  | 500,050 |

**Revaluation reserve**

|  |  |  |  |  |
|---|---|---|---|---|
|  |  |  | Opening balance | 380,000 |
| Capitalisation | (b) | 380,000 |  |  |
|  |  | 380,000 |  | 380,000 |

**Revenue reserves**

|  |  |  |  |
|---|---|---|---|
|  |  | Opening balance | 570,000 |
| Capitalisation | 120,000 |  |  |
| Closing balance | 450,000 |  |  |
|  | 570,000 |  | 570,000 |

(a) 500,000 new shares will be issued. This is 10,000 new shares for each of the 50 existing shares.

(b) The first £380,000 will be paid-up from the revaluation reserve, and the balance of £120,000 will be paid-up by reducing the balance on the revenue reserves.

(2)    The balance sheet immediately after the bonus issue will be as follows:

|  |  | £ |
|---|---|---|
| Ordinary shares of £1 each | *50 + 500,000* | 500,050 |
| Revaluation reserve | *380,000 – 380,000* | - |
| Revenue reserves | *570,000 – 120,000* | 450,000 |
| Shareholders' funds and net assets |  | 950,050 |

The net assets of the business are unchanged.

It will now be easier for the founders to redistribute some of the 500,050 shares in issue than it was to share out the original 50 shares.

---

## ACTIVITY 2

---

(a)    A plc has 200,000 50 pence ordinary shares in issue and makes a bonus issue of 50,000 50 pence ordinary shares.  Its only available reserve is the profit and loss account balance of £230,000.

(b)    B plc has 200,000 50 pence ordinary shares in issue and makes a rights issue of 50,000 50 pence shares at a price of 80 pence each and the issue is fully taken up.

Write up the ledger accounts for each transaction.

---

*For a suggested answer, see the 'Answers' section at the end of the book.*

## 1.8    ADVANTAGES AND DISADVANTAGES OF ISSUES AT FULL MARKET PRICE, RIGHTS ISSUES AND BONUS ISSUES

An issue at full market price, open to all investors, will raise the most money. However, it may result in rival businesses building up an influential or controlling interest in the company.  This may be a disadvantage to the existing shareholders in the long run.  The costs of a new issue at full market price can be high, making these issues fairly risky.

A rights issue may not raise as much money as a full market price issue, but the process is cheaper and the existing shareholders are normally keen to purchase shares in a rights issue.  (The shareholders will either keep the new shares to preserve their voting rights or sell them straight away at a profit.)

A bonus issue does not raise any cash at all.  The main purpose of a bonus issue is to increase the marketability of the shares.

## 1.9    MARKET VALUE

The shares of a quoted public limited company (plc) may be traded on the stock exchange.  These shares will be bought and sold at their market price, which will fluctuate daily.  The company whose shares are being bought and sold will not be affected by these transactions.  The company only receives any cash from its shares when they are initially issued, not when they are traded between investors.

However, the directors of public companies cannot ignore their company's share price. The following problems may be caused by a low share price:

- A low share price may anger share holders. The shareholders may then refuse to re-elect their board of directors, or they may sell their shares to a rival company. Either way, the directors may lose their jobs.

- Some directors receive part of their remuneration in shares. If the price of their shares falls, then the value of their pay also falls (and vice versa).

- Public companies use new share issues to raise finance. The higher their share price, then the more money they can raise from the same number of shares.

## 2 ORDINARY DIVIDENDS

The ordinary dividend is paid on the ordinary shares. The amount of ordinary (or equity) dividend paid will depend upon two things:

- sufficient distributable profits to cover the dividend; and

- sufficient cash to pay the dividends.

Distributable profits are defined by law. Basically, they are the cumulative retained profits (less any losses and previous dividends). Because these profits are based on the cumulative position, a company can make a loss in one year and still pay a dividend (provided that the company has been profitable in the past).

The dividend will be proposed by the Board of Directors, but it must then be approved by the shareholders after they have read the annual report. Shareholder approval is normally a formality.

The dividend can be described as an amount per share or as a total amount (which would then have to be shared out between the shares in issue).

Typically, a large company pays two dividends; an interim dividend during the year and a final dividend which would be proposed at the year end and then paid a few months later.

Equity (ordinary) dividends are normally reported in the financial statements when they are paid. The total dividend for the year, including the proposed final dividend, is disclosed in the notes to the financial statements.

**Example**

Noted below is the summary trial balance of Chisel Ltd for the year-ending 30 June 20X7.

|  | £ | £ |
|---|---|---|
| Turnover |  | 3,293,000 |
| Operating expenses | 1,737,000 |  |
| Interim dividend | 300,000 |  |
| Sundry fixed assets | 1,104,000 |  |
| Sundry current assets | 835,000 |  |
| Sundry current liabilities |  | 243,000 |
| 150,000 Ordinary Shares of 50 pence each |  | 75,000 |
| Share premium |  | 175,000 |
| P&L Reserve |  | 190,000 |
|  | 3,976,000 | 3,976,000 |

**Notes**

(1)   The corporation tax charge for the year has been estimated at £545,000.

(2)   An interim dividend of £2 per share was paid.  The Directors have proposed a final dividend of £3 per share.

**Required:**

Prepare extracts from Chisel Ltd's profit and loss account and balance sheet for the year-ending 30 June 20X7 incorporating the corporation tax and final dividend.

### Chisel Ltd: Profit and loss account

|  | £ |
|---|---|
| Turnover | 3,293,000 |
| Operating expenses | (1,737,000) |
| Profit before tax | 1,556,000 |
| Taxation | (545,000) |
| Profit for the year | 1,011,000 |

### Chisel Ltd: Balance sheet

|  | £ | £ |
|---|---|---|
| Fixed assets |  | 1,104,000 |
| Current assets | 835,000 |  |
| Creditors due within one year   **Note 2** | (788,000) |  |
| Net current assets |  | 47,000 |
| Net Assets |  | 1,151,000 |
| 150,000 ordinary shares of 50 pence each |  | 75,000 |
| Share premium |  | 175,000 |
| P&L Reserve (190,000 + 1,011,000 – 300,000) |  | 901,000 |
|  |  | 1,151,000 |

**Note 1        Dividends**

|  |  |  |  | £ |
|---|---|---|---|---|
| Interim paid | 150,000 shares @ | £2 | per share | 300,000 |
| Final proposed | 150,000 shares @ | £3 | per share | 450,000 |
|  |  |  |  | 750,000 |

**Note 2        Creditors due within one year**

|  | £ |
|---|---|
| Sundry current liabilities | 243,000 |
| Provision for corporation tax | 545,000 |
|  | 788,000 |

# 3 PREFERENCE SHARES AND DIVIDENDS

## 3.1 CHARACTERISTICS

Although every company must have ordinary shares, preference shares are an optional extra. Indeed, companies having preference shares are in the minority. Also, although the rights of ordinary shares are defined by law and apply to all ordinary shares, the rights of preference shares are varied, and are set out in their own issue documents. However, there are some typical characteristics of preference shares. These are set out below.

### Votes

Preference shares do not normally participate in the election of the Board of Directors.

### Dividends

Preference shares usually have a **fixed dividend**. This is often expressed as a percentage of the nominal value of the shares.

The preference dividend can only be paid if there are distributable profits. In any year the preference dividend must be **paid before the ordinary shareholders** receive their dividend.

**Cumulative** preference shares take this a stage further. Sometimes there will not be enough profits or cash to pay any dividends at all. In future years, the arrears of cumulative preference dividend must be settled before any dividend is paid to the ordinary shareholders.

### Repayment of capital

When a company is wound up, the preference shareholders are **paid off before the ordinary shareholders.** (The ordinary shareholders receive whatever is left over.) However, although the preference shareholders are paid before the ordinary shareholders, they are still paid off after every other creditor.

**Redeemable** preference shares have the right to be repaid, just like a loan or debenture. (Accounting for redemption is not on the syllabus.)

**Convertible** preference shares may be converted into ordinary shares, normally on generous terms. (Accounting for conversion is not on the syllabus.)

### Example

A *12% £1 redeemable preference share (20Y9)* will receive a dividend of 12 pence per annum until it is redeemed in 20Y9.

## 3.2 PRESENTATION IN THE BALANCE SHEET

Typically, preference shares have the same characteristics as liabilities. For example, they have a fixed rate of interest and a fixed date of repayment. Therefore they are classified as liabilities in the balance sheet

**Example**

The following balances have been summarised from Layout Ltd's trial balance:

|  | £ | £ |
|---|---|---|
| Sundry fixed assets | 764,000 | |
| Sundry net current assets | 536,000 | |
| 15% Debentures redeemable in 20Y5 | | 450,000 |
| 12% Preferences share redeemable in 20Y2 | | 300,000 |
| Ordinary shares | | 100,000 |
| Share premium | | 175,000 |
| Reserves | | 275,000 |
| | 1,300,000 | 1,300,000 |

**Required:** Draw up the Balance sheet

**Solution**

### Layout Ltd: Balance sheet

|  | £ |
|---|---|
| Sundry fixed assets | 764,000 |
| Sundry net current assets | 536,000 |
| | 1,300,000 |
| 15% Debentures redeemable in 20Y5 | (450,000) |
| **12% Preference shares redeemable in 20Y2** | **(300,000)** |
| Net assets | 550,000 |
| | |
| Capital and reserves | |
| Ordinary shares | 100,000 |
| Share premium | 175,000 |
| Reserves | 275,000 |
| | 550,000 |

## 3.3 PRESENTATION OF THE DIVIDEND

The preference dividend is treated as a finance cost and is reported in the profit and loss account as part of interest payable.

# 4 ACCOUNTING FOR RESERVES

## 4.1 REVENUE RESERVES

The most common reserve is the revenue reserve. (This is also called retained profits, accumulated profits, P&L Account or P&L reserve.) These are the distributable reserves of the company out of which dividends will be paid. They represent the increase in shareholders' wealth generated through trade.

These days, most companies will just have one, single revenue reserve. However, in the past it was quite common for companies to set up different categories of revenue reserve. These would be created by transfers from retained profits.

Although these reserves look distinct on the face of the balance sheet, there are no funds allocated specifically to the different reserves. The only effect they have is to encourage the directors to retain funds within the business rather than pay them out in dividends.

## 4.2  CAPITAL RESERVES

In certain circumstances the law requires a capital reserve to be set up. The three most common are:

(a)  share premium account (already covered in this chapter)

(b)  capital redemption reserve (not within the syllabus)

(c)  revaluation reserve (covered in a later chapter).

These reserves are sometimes referred to as **statutory reserves** or **non-distributable reserves**. The latter name relates to the fact that these reserves cannot be used to pay a dividend.

## 4.3  MOVEMENT ON RESERVES

Transfers to and from reserves can be shown at the foot of the profit and loss account. However, it is easier to understand what is going on if the movements on reserves are tabulated in a note.

### Example

The summary trial balance of Mallet Ltd for the year-ending 31 December 20X6 is noted below:

|  | £ | £ |
|---|---|---|
| Net assets | 1,175,000 |  |
| Profit after tax |  | 567,000 |
| Dividends paid | 167,000 |  |
| Ordinary shares of £1 each |  | 100,000 |
| Share premium account |  | 50,000 |
| General reserve |  | 350,000 |
| Retained profits |  | 275,000 |
|  | 1,342,000 | 1,342,000 |

### Notes

This trial balance does not show the issue of 200,000 ordinary shares at a premium of 75 pence per share. This issue took place on 31 December 20X6.

The directors propose to transfer £200,000 from retained profits to the general reserve.

### Required:

Prepare a statement showing the movement on share capital and reserves during the year.

### Solution

**Movements on share capital and reserves**

|  | Share capital £ | Share premium £ | General reserve £ | Retained profits £ | Total £ |
|---|---|---|---|---|---|
| Opening balances | 100,000 | 50,000 | 350,000 | 275,000 | 775,000 |
| Share issue | 200,000 | 150,000 | – | – | 350,000 |
| Retained profit for the year | – | – | – | 400,000 | 400,000 |
| Transfer | – | – | 200,000 | (200,000) | – |
| Closing balances | 300,000 | 200,000 | 550,000 | 475,000 | 1,525,000 |

## ACTIVITY 3

ZZ Ltd's summarised balance sheet at 31 December 20X7 showed:

|  | £ |
|---|---|
| Net assets | 280,000 |

|  | |
|---|---|
| Capital and reserves | |
| Called up share capital | |
| - 50p ordinary shares | 75,000 |
| - £1 8% preference shares | 60,000 |
| Share premium account | 25,000 |
| Plant replacement reserve | 30,000 |
| Profit and loss account | 90,000 |

The operating profit for the year to 31 December 20X8 has been computed as £180,000.

The following additional information is available:

(a)     Corporation tax is estimated at £70,000.

(b)     An interim dividend of 2p has been paid on the ordinary shares, and one half of the dividend on the preference shares.

(c)     It is proposed to pay the remaining dividend on the preference shares and a final dividend of 5p on the ordinary shares.

(d)     £20,000 is to be transferred to the plant replacement reserve.

**Required:**

(a)     Construct the profit and loss account for the year.

(b)     Show the balance sheet at the end of the year to the extent that information is available.

*For a suggested answer, see the 'Answers' section at the end of the book.*

# 5 DEBENTURES AND OTHER LOANS

## 5.1 DEBENTURES

Debentures are long-term loans. A typical debenture will be for a period of 15 years or more. It will be secured on the fixed assets of the company and it will pay a fixed rate of interest. The interest must be paid, even if the company is making a loss. If the interest is not paid then the debenture holders can appoint a receiver to sell off the company's assets in order to pay off the outstanding interest and capital. This makes debentures a safe investment for the lenders, which in turn means that they will be prepared to accept a relatively low rate of interest. A low interest rate will obviously benefit the borrower who issued the debentures.

Debentures may be long-term loans, but they will eventually be repaid. This means that they are recognised as liabilities in the balance sheet. They will be classified as *Creditors, amounts due after more than one year* until they are within a year of repayment.

## 5.2 LOANS AND SHARES COMPARED

A company can raise finance by issuing shares or by raising loans. There are advantages and disadvantages of both forms of finance, and so most large companies will have a mix of both. Ordinary shares and loans are compared below.

### Repayment

A loan will eventually have to be repaid. This means that a company will have to generate enough cash over the life of a loan in order to pay it back at the end. If a company cannot repay its loan then the company is insolvent.

Ordinary shares do not have to be repaid. From the company's point of view, this makes shares a lower risk option compared with loans.

### Servicing of finance

Loan interest must be paid as it falls due. If a company defaults on its interest payments then the lender can normally demand repayment of the loan as well as any outstanding interest.

On the other hand, an ordinary dividend is discretionary. Although most companies pay a regular dividend, there is always the option to suspend dividend payments if profits are low or if the company wishes to spend the cash on, say, fixed assets rather than dividends. This also reduces the risks of share finance in comparison with loans.

### Cost of finance

We have seen that, from the company's point of view, shares are lower risk than loans. This means that from the investor's point of view shares must be a higher risk than loans. When a company becomes insolvent, the shareholders normally lose their entire investment, whereas lenders will normally recover all or part of the money owed to them.

This in turn means that shareholders demand a higher return on their investment than lenders do. This means that companies often find it cheaper to borrow than to raise new share capital. There is also a tax advantage from borrowing; interest is allowed as a charge against profits, whereas dividends are an appropriation of profits after tax has been charged and deducted.

**Summary**

Companies have to balance the advantages of low risk (but high cost) share capital against the advantages of low cost (but high risk) loans. The balance between capital and loans is called the *debt equity ratio*. It is studied in the chapter on ratio analysis.

# 6 TAXATION

## 6.1 INTRODUCTION

The accounting treatment for corporation tax is set out in FRS 16 *Current Taxes* and in the Companies Act. A brief overview of deferred tax is also needed. Calculating corporation tax or deferred tax is not on the syllabus.

## 6.2 PROVISION FOR CORPORATION TAX

Corporation tax for many companies is payable nine months after the year-end. When the accounts are published, the final assessment has not normally been agreed. Therefore the balance sheet liability and P&L charge are based on an estimated provision for Corporation Tax. Because tax rates may vary, the tax rate used for the provision must be disclosed. Obviously this provision will never be exactly correct, and sometimes it might be deliberately underestimated.

The notes to the P&L tax charge shows the charge for this year's provision and any correction to last year's provision. The tax rates used when making this year's provision should also be disclosed. This enables the reader to estimate the reliability of the Directors' tax estimates.

**Example**

Extracts from Crowbar Ltd's trial balance for the year-ending 31 December 20X6 are noted below:

|  | Debit £ | Credit £ |
|---|---|---|
| Profits for 20X6 |  | 435,000 |
| Under provision for corporation tax in 20X5 | 23,000 |  |

The Directors estimate that the corporation tax charge for 20X6 will be £130,000.

**Task**

Show how these balances will be presented in the profit and loss account and balance sheet.

**Crowbar Ltd: Profit and loss account**

|  | £ |
|---|---|
| Profit before tax | 435,000 |
| Taxation   Note 1 | (153,000) |
| Profit after tax | 282,000 |

**Note 1    Tax charge**

|  | £ |
|---|---|
| Corporation tax charge on the profits for the year at XX % | 130,000 |
| Under provision for corporation tax in prior years | 23,000 |
|  | 153,000 |

**Crowbar Ltd: Balance sheet**

|  | £ |
|---|---|
| *Included within creditors due within 12 months* |  |
| Corporation tax | 130,000 |

The tax balance in the trial balance normally relates to the previous year. In this example the tax left over from last year was a debit, an under-provision. This debit has to be charged this year to make up for last year's under provision.

If the balance were a credit it would show that last year's provision was too high, too prudent. This over provision would be released the following year, reducing the tax charge.

## ACTIVITY 4

A company has operating profits before tax of £200,000 and the estimated corporation tax charge for the current year is £56,000. In the previous year the estimated corporation tax charge was £49,000 and the eventual corporation tax payment was £47,000. In the current year the directors have paid an interim dividend of £5,000 and are proposing a final dividend of £17,000.

**Required:**

Show the figures that would appear in the profit and loss account and the notes that would be required for corporation tax and dividends.

*For a suggested answer, see the 'Answers' section at the end of the book.*

### 6.3    SUMMARY OF THE P&L TAX CHARGE

There will normally be three components to the profit and loss account tax charge. These components must be disclosed in a note to the financial statements. The proforma note below illustrates this.

|  |  | £ |
|---|---|---|
| Corporation tax charge for the year | This will be given to you in the notes to the question. | X |
| (Over) under provision for taxation in the previous year. | This will be shown in the trial balance. An over provision will be a credit and an under provision will be a debit. | (X) |
| Increase (decrease) in deferred tax | The opening provision will be in the trial balance. The closing provision will be given to you in the notes to the question. | X |
| Tax charge in the profit and loss account |  | XX |

## 6.4    VALUE ADDED TAX (VAT)

Value added tax is levied on all sales made by VAT registered traders. The VAT on sales is called **output VAT**. A VAT registered trader can also reclaim any VAT on its purchases. The VAT on purchases is known as **input VAT**. The trader must then pay over the net amount (output VAT less input VAT) to HM Revenue and Customs. This is normally done on a monthly or quarterly basis.

The trader is basically acting as an unpaid tax collector. The VAT collected from customers is not income for the business, and the VAT recoverable on purchases is not an expense. Therefore all items of income and expenditure are shown net of VAT in the financial statements of a VAT registered business. Fixed Assets and stocks will also be shown net of VAT. However, debtors and creditors will be shown gross, and there will normally be a balance of VAT owing to HM Revenue and Customs.

### Example

Barrel Ltd is a VAT registered business. During March 20X9 it made net sales of £10,000 (plus VAT of £2,000) and net purchases and expenses of £7,000 (plus £1,400 VAT).

At the end of the month there was no stock. All sales and purchases were on credit, and there had been no receipts or payments during the month.

### Required:

Prepare the profit and loss account and balance sheet for Barrel Ltd for the month of March 20X9.

### Solution

**Barrel Ltd: Profit and loss account for March 20X9**

|  |  | £ |
|---|---|---|
| Sales | *(net of VAT)* | 10,000 |
| Purchases and expenses | *(net of VAT)* | (7,000) |
| Profit |  | 3,000 |

**Balance sheet as at 31 March 20X9**

|  |  |  | £ |
|---|---|---|---|
| Current Assets | Trade debtors | *(gross of VAT)* | 12,000 |
| Creditors | Trade creditors | *(gross of VAT)* | 8,400 |
|  | Amount owing to HMRC | *(£2,000 less £1,400)* | 600 |

Exam questions often tend to ignore VAT.

## 6.5    VALUE ADDED TAX FOR NON-VAT REGISTERED TRADERS

If a trader is not registered for VAT then there will be no VAT levied on sales, but the trader will not be able to reclaim any of the input VAT on purchases. All purchases, expenses, fixed assets, stocks and creditors will be shown gross of VAT. There will be no VAT on sales and no balance of VAT owed to or from HM Revenue and Customs.

## KEY TERMS

**Ordinary shares** – represent the ownership interest of a company. They are the last shares to be repaid. Ordinary shares are usually the only shares with voting rights.

**Members** – the owners of the ordinary shares.

**Authorised share capital** – the authorised share capital is the maximum number of shares that a company may issue.

**Issued share capital** – the actual number of shares in issue at any point in time.

**Share premium** – the difference between the proceeds of issue and the nominal value is called the share premium.

**Rights issue** – in a rights issue existing shareholders have the right to purchase enough shares to maintain their original percentage shareholding.

**Bonus issue** – in a bonus issue a part of the company's existing reserves are reclassified as share capital. Bonus issues are also known as *capitalisation issues* and *scrip issues*.

**Revenue reserve** – this is also called retained profits, accumulated profits, P&L account or P&L reserve. These are the distributable reserves of the company out of which dividends will be paid.

**Corporation tax** – the tax levied on the profits made by a limited company.

## SELF TEST QUESTIONS

|   |   | *Paragraph* |
|---|---|---|
| 1 | What are the ordinary shareholders also called? | 1.1 |
| 2 | What is the difference between authorised and issued share capital? | 1.2 |
| 3 | What is the difference between the nominal value of a share and the share proceeds? | 1.4 |
| 4 | What are the differences between preference shares and ordinary shares? | 3.1 |
| 5 | How might an over provision for corporation tax arise and how and when will it be corrected? | 6.2 |
| 7 | Will a VAT registered company include VAT in its turnover and cost of sales? | |

## ADDITIONAL QUESTION

### RESERVES

(a)     The term 'reserves' is frequently found in company balance sheets.

**Required:**

(i)     Explain the meaning of 'reserves' in this context.

(ii)    Give two examples of reserves and explain how each of your examples comes into existence.

(b)     A company's issued share capital may be increased by a bonus (capitalisation) issue or by a rights issue.

**Required:**

Define 'bonus issue' and 'rights issue' and explain the fundamental difference between these two types of share issue.

*For a suggested answer, see the 'Answers' section at the end of the book.*

# Chapter 4

# FIXED ASSETS

This chapter explains the difference between capital and revenue expenditure. It also sets out the rules for calculating the cost, depreciation, amortisation and (where appropriate) valuation of tangible and intangible fixed assets.

---

## CONTENTS

---

## LEARNING OUTCOMES

At the end of this chapter you should be able to:

•    distinguish between capital and revenue expenditure

•    explain, calculate and demonstrate the inclusion of the profit or loss on disposal in the profit and loss account

•    account for the revaluation of fixed assets and for gains and losses on the disposal of revalued assets

•    account for depreciation – definition, reasons and methods, including straight line, reducing balance and sum of digits

•    account for changes in the useful economic life or residual value of assets

•    explain how fixed asset balances and movements are disclosed in the financial statements

---

- define and calculate goodwill and distinguish between purchased and internally generated goodwill

- explain and apply the accounting treatment for both types of goodwill

- explain and apply the requirements of accounting standards for research and development.

# 1 ASSETS AND EXPENSES

## 1.1 CAPITAL AND REVENUE EXPENDITURE

Expenditure can either be charged to the profit and loss account as an expense or capitalised as an asset in the balance sheet. Expenditure charged to the profit and loss account is known as revenue expenditure. Expenditure capitalised in the balance sheet is known as capital expenditure.

For an item to be capitalised as an asset it must meet the definition and recognition criteria for an asset. If it does not meet these criteria then it must be charged to the profit and loss account as an expense.

**Definition**      An **asset** is an item arising from a past transaction or event that will bring economic benefits to the business in the future.

An asset will be recognised in the balance sheet if its cost (or value) can be measured with reasonable certainty.

Assets themselves are further classified between current assets and fixed assets, and tangible assets and intangible assets.

## 1.2 CURRENT ASSETS AND FIXED ASSETS

**Current assets**

**Definition**      A **current asset** is an asset which will be converted into money soon within the normal course of the business's trading cycle. Normally, it will be converted into cash within the next 12 months.

There are three items that have been looked at so far which fall into this sub-category:

- Stock                 will be sold in the near future.

- Debtors               will be collected in the near future.

- Cash and bank         is already money.

**Fixed assets**

**Definition**      A **fixed asset** is an asset purchased not for resale, but for use within the business in the generation of profits over more than one accounting period.

**Definition**      **Capital expenditure** is expenditure on fixed assets.

Usually, the classification of an item will depend on the management's intentions. For example, if a furniture removal company buys a van, then it is probably going to be used in the business over many years for transporting furniture. Therefore it is a fixed asset.

If a motor dealership purchases a van then it is probably intending to sell it on to a customer, so the van will be the current asset of stock. (Of course, from time to time the dealership will have to purchase a van for its own use – say for parts delivery – and these vans would then be fixed assets.)

## 1.3 TANGIBLE AND INTANGIBLE FIXED ASSETS

**Definition** **Tangible fixed assets** are assets that can be physically touched.

Examples of tangible fixed assets are:

- property

- vehicles

- machines

- tools

- office equipment.

**Definition** **Intangible fixed assets** are assets that cannot be physically touched. These assets may not exist in a physical sense, but, money has been spent on them and hopefully they will generate profits in the future.

Examples of intangible fixed assets are:

- goodwill

- development costs.

Goodwill arises when a business is bought. The amount paid for the business is often more than the market value of the physical assets within that business. The difference is known as goodwill. Goodwill represents reputation, the quality of the staff, customer contacts, and many, many other factors. In this paper you will meet goodwill in the context of partnership accounts and group accounts.

Development costs arise when money is spent on developing new products. These new products will hopefully create profitable sales in the future.

Tangible and intangible assets will be discussed in more detail in the following chapters.

## 1.4 FRS 15 *TANGIBLE FIXED ASSETS*

FRS 15 sets out the accounting treatment for:

- establishing the initial cost of tangible fixed assets and how to account for subsequent expenditure

- depreciation

- revaluation.

These are looked at in detail over the following sections.

## 2 INITIAL COST AND SUBSEQUENT EXPENDITURE

### 2.1 INITIAL COST

All fixed assets must initially be recognised at cost. The cost of a fixed asset is its purchase price (after deducting any trade discounts and rebates) and any costs directly attributable to bringing it into working condition for its intended use.

The initial cost specifically excludes administration costs, general overheads, abnormal costs and any costs incurred after the asset is ready for use.

**Example**

Head Ltd incurred the following costs when installing a new machine at their factory:

|  | £ |
|---|---|
| Purchase price | 234,500 |
| Transport costs from the supplier to the factory. | 12,746 |
| Construction of plinth to stand the machine on: |  |
| materials | 9,283 |
| own labour (from job cards) | 4,751 |
| administrative overheads | 1,500 |
| Repair to machine. The damage was caused when the machine was being set on its plinth. | 19,456 |
| Rebate received from the supplier | (2,345) |
| Commissioning work done up to the date the machine was ready for use. | 12,846 |
| Further work done after the machine was ready for use | 7,263 |
| Total | 300,000 |

**Required:**

What will be the initial capital cost of this fixed asset?

**Solution**

|  | Total | Capitalise | Charge to P&L |
|---|---|---|---|
|  | £ | £ | £ |
| Purchase price | 234,500 | 234,500 |  |
| Transport costs | 12,746 | 12,746 |  |
| Construction of plinth: |  |  |  |
| materials | 9,283 | 9,283 |  |
| own labour | 4,751 | 4,751 |  |
| overheads | 1,500 |  | 1,500 |
| Repair to machine | 19,456 |  | 19,456 |
| Rebate | (2,345) | (2,345) |  |
| Commissioning before the machine was ready for use. | 12,846 | 12,846 |  |
| Work done after the machine was ready for use | 7,263 |  | 7,263 |
| Total | 300,000 | 271,781 | 28,219 |

## 2.2 SUBSEQUENT EXPENDITURE

Subsequent expenditure can only be capitalised if it enhances the economic benefits of an asset. The old rule of thumb that improvements can be capitalised but repairs must be expensed still holds true.

Economic performance can be enhanced by improving the quality of a product or process, extending **an asset's life, or by improving efficiency.**

## 2.3 SEPARATE COMPONENTS

Certain large assets do not fit easily into these rules. For example, aeroplanes have quite a long life, but their engines and avionics will be replaced a number of times throughout the plane's useful life. To charge the huge costs of these events to the P & L account as repairs and maintenance would distort the reported profits.

The solution to this problem is to treat the engines and avionics as separate components of the aeroplane, with their own costs. useful lives and depreciation. When the components are replaced the event will be treated as a normal disposal, and the new component purchased will be capitalised. Although this technique was first applied to machines, etc by FRS 15, it is in fact an old idea. Land and buildings have been treated as separate components for years.

### Example

During 20X8 Star Airlines Ltd purchased a Douglas DC 3 for £500,000. The cost included £100,000 for the engines (with a remaining life of ten years) and £30,000 for avionics (with a remaining life of two years). The rest of the aeroplane has a remaining life of 25 years.

At the end of 20X9 the avionics were scrapped and new equipment costing £125,000 was bought. This should last for ten years. During 20X9 repairs to the airframe and engines totalled £25,000.

### Required:

(a)     Prepare the fixed asset schedules for Star Airlines Ltd for 20X8 and 20X9.

(b)     Summarise the P&L charges for 20X8 and 20X9 in respect of this aeroplane.

### Solution

**Fixed asset schedule for 20X8**

|  |  | Airframe £ | Engines £ | Avionics £ | Total £ |
|---|---|---|---|---|---|
| Cost |  |  |  |  |  |
| Opening and closing | (a) | 370,000 | 100,000 | 30,000 | 500,000 |
| Depreciation |  |  |  |  |  |
| Charge and closing balance | (b) | 14,800 | 10,000 | 15,000 | 39,800 |
| Closing Net Book Value |  | 355,200 | 90,000 | 15,000 | 460,200 |

**Fixed asset schedule for 20X9**

|  | Airframe £ | Engines £ | Avionics £ | Total £ |
|---|---|---|---|---|
| Cost |  |  |  |  |
| Opening balance | 370,000 | 100,000 | 30,000 | 500,000 |
| Additions | – | – | 125,000 | 125,000 |
| Disposals | – | – | (30,000) | (30,000) |
| Closing balance | 370,000 | 100,000 | 125,000 | 595,000 |

Depreciation

|  |  |  |  |  |
|---|---|---|---|---|
| Opening balance | 14,800 | 10,000 | 15,000 | 39,800 |
| Charge for the year | 14,800 | 10,000 | 12,500 | 37,300 |
| Disposals | – | – | (15,000) | (15,000) |
| Closing balance | 29,600 | 20,000 | 12,500 | 62,100 |
| Closing Net Book Value | 340,400 | 80,000 | 112,500 | 532,900 |

(a)    The cost of the airframe is the remaining cost of the aeroplane after separating out the other components.

(b)    Each component is depreciated over its own useful life.

(c)    The old avionics are retired.

(d)    The new component is capitalised and depreciated over its useful life.

**Summary of P&L charges**

|  | 20X8 £ | 20X9 £ |
|---|---|---|
| Depreciation | 39,800 | 37,300 |
| Loss on disposal | – | 15,000 |
| Repairs | – | 25,000 |
|  | 39,800 | 77,300 |

## ACTIVITY 1

QG Jones plc owns and operates a chain of department stores in London.  It has just built a new store costing £140m.  The property is on a leasehold site with 90 years lease remaining.  The building itself cost £80m and has been engineered to last for 150 years, but changes in retail habits will probably mean that the building will be obsolete within fifty years.  The £80m cost of the building excludes the frontage.  The frontage is very modernistic and cost £15m.  It will probably go out of fashion within 10 years and need replacing.  The balance of the cost relates to the land.

**Required:**

What will the annual depreciation charge be on this store?

*For a suggested answer, see the 'Answers' section at the end of the book.*

# 3    DEPRECIATION

The mechanics of depreciation have been covered many times during your studies. This section concentrates on some key provisions of FRS 15 and the Companies Act.

## 3.1    WHAT IS DEPRECIATION?

The depreciation charge in the profit and loss account represents the cost of using a fixed asset.  If a fixed asset costs £1m and will be used for four years, then the cost of using that asset in each year is £250,000.

**Definition**    **Depreciation** is the measure of the cost of the economic benefits of the fixed asset that have been consumed during the period.

Consumption includes:

- the wearing out

- using up; or

- other reduction in the useful economic life of a tangible fixed asset.

This can arise from:

- use

- the effluxion of time; or

- obsolescence caused by changes in technology or demand.

(Taken from the official definition in FRS 15. Examples are given in 3.3 below.)

It is important to remember that depreciation does not represent the fall in value of an asset. Fixed assets are held for use, not for resale, and so their market values are not relevant. The 'net book value' left in the balance sheet after depreciation has been charged does not represent market values. As a separate exercise fixed assets may be revalued to reflect changes in their market values. This is covered at the end of this chapter.

## 3.2 DEPRECATION AND ACCRUALS

Depreciation is based on the accruals concept. Costs are matched to the benefits that they help to create. Because a fixed asset will help to generate profits over a number of periods, then its cost is capitalised and spread over those periods.

## 3.3 WHICH FIXED ASSETS SHOULD BE DEPRECIATED?

All fixed assets with a finite life must be depreciated. Because nothing lasts forever, all fixed assets should be depreciated. The only exception to this rule is freehold land. Land lasts forever, and so it should not be depreciated, unless it is being used as a mine or quarry in which case the land will eventually be consumed.

The following table summarises the situation.

| Freehold land | Don't depreciate | Land does not normally wear out. It has an infinite life. |
| --- | --- | --- |
| Freehold land used for quarrying | Depreciate | The economic value of the land will lie in the minerals being extracted. Once the minerals in the quarry have been used up then its useful life will be over. |
| Leasehold land | Depreciate | The lease will be for a fixed period. The lease will be consumed due to the effluxion of time. |
| Freehold building | Depreciate | Buildings may last for a long time, but they do not last forever. Commercial premises often have a shorter life than, say, houses because they may be replaced after a few years with bigger or better premises. |
| Machinery, vehicles, computers, etc | Depreciate | Machines will obviously get worn out as they are used. They may also suffer from obsolescence. Either the product they are making will be discontinued (market obsolescence), or a new machine will be invented that can do the same job more efficiently (technological obsolescence). |

## 3.4 DEPRECIABLE AMOUNT AND USEFUL ECONOMIC LIFE

The *depreciable amount* of a fixed asset is written off over its *useful economic life*.

| | |
|---|---|
| **Definition** | The **depreciable amount** is the cost of a tangible fixed asset (or, where an asset is revalued, the revalued amount) less its *residual value*. |
| **Definition** | The **residual value** of an asset is the net realisable value of an asset at the end of its useful economic life. Residual values are based on prices prevailing at the date of the acquisition (or revaluation) of the asset and do not take account of expected future price rises. |
| **Definition** | The **useful economic life** of a tangible fixed asset is the period over which the entity expects to derive economic benefit from that asset. |

### Example

An asset costs £100,000 and has an expected useful life of ten years. The purchaser intends to use the asset for six years at which point the expected residual value will be £40,000 (at current prices). If inflation is taken into account the residual value is expected to be £55,000. What is the depreciable amount?

The depreciable amount is £(100,000 – 40,000) £60,000 spread over six years. Which method of depreciation is used to allocate the charge is left for the purchaser to decide.

## 3.5 ALLOWABLE DEPRECIATION METHODS

An appropriate method should be selected and then applied consistently. The standard does not favour any method over another. Current practice is to use the straight line method unless another method is more appropriate. For example, if a machine wears out after a certain number of hours of use, then a machine hours method may be appropriate. If an asset is more productive in earlier years than later years, then a reducing balance or a sum of the digits method may be appropriate. The straight line and reducing balance methods are on the Level II Syllabus and so they are not covered in detail here. However, Activity 2 below will help to refresh your memory of these methods.

---

## ACTIVITY 2

---

**Straight line method**

Calculate the annual depreciation charge from the following information:

| | |
|---|---|
| Original cost of asset | £4,200 |
| Estimated useful life | 4 years |
| Estimated scrap value | £200 |

**Reducing balance or decreasing charge method**

An asset cost £1,000. Its estimated useful life was four years with a scrap value at the end of four years of approximately £60.

Calculate the depreciation charge for each of the four years on a reducing balance basis at a rate of 50%.

---

*For a suggested answer, see the 'Answers' section at the end of the book.*

---

### 3.6  THE MACHINE HOURS DEPRECIATION METHOD

The machine hours method charges depreciation over the expected operational life of an asset.  For example, if an aircraft component cost £150,000 and could be used for 10,000 flying hours before it needed replacing, then depreciation would be charged at £15 per flying hour.  If the plane flew for 2,300 hours in the year then the annual charge would be £34,500.

### ACTIVITY 3

The useful life of a machine is estimated to be 60,000 hours of use with a nil scrap value at the end of its life.  The cost of the machine is £1,800.  The expected usage of this machine is 12,000 hours in Year 1 and 9,000 hours in Year 2.  What is the depreciation charge for these two years?

*For a suggested answer, see the 'Answers' section at the end of the book.*

### 3.7  THE SUM OF THE DIGITS DEPRECIATION METHOD

The sum of the digits method is useful for an asset that will be used more heavily in the earlier years of its life than in the later years.  The sum of the digits will weight the depreciation charge towards the earlier years when the machine is used more and (in theory) should earn more revenue.

#### Example

Trendy Ltd is an internet service provider.  It has just spent £3m on new hardware that should last for four years.  The hardware will rapidly become obsolete, and so the economic benefits of the hardware will be concentrated in the earlier years of the asset's life.  Therefore the hardware will be depreciated over four years using the sum of the digits method.

The sum of the digits for four years is ten    (4 + 3 + 2 + 1)

The charge in the first year will be £1.2m    (£3m × 4/10 = £1.2m)

The charge in the second year will be £0.9m    (£3m × 3/10 = £0.9m)

The charge in the third and fourth years will be £0.6m and £0.3m respectively.

### ACTIVITY 4

Groovy Ltd pays £72,000 for a machine with a five-year useful life.  The machine is depreciated using the sum of the digits method.

Calculate the depreciation charge in each of the five years of the machine's life.

*For a suggested answer, see the 'Answers' section at the end of the book.*

## 4  DISPOSALS

### 4.1  INTRODUCTION

When a fixed asset is sold or scrapped the cost and accumulated depreciation must be removed from the accounting records.  Any proceeds of disposal are matched against the net book value of the asset sold in order to calculate the profit or loss on disposal.

## 4.2   EXAMPLE

Discard Ltd sells a fixed asset for £24,000.  The asset cost £143,000 and the cumulative depreciation was £75,000.

**Step 1**   The cost and accumulated depreciation are cleared out of the fixed asset ledger accounts and into the *Disposals Account*.  The journal entry and the disposal account are noted below:

| **Journal** | | Debit £ | Credit £ |
|---|---|---|---|
| Debit | Fixed asset disposals account | 143,000 | |
| Credit | Fixed assets at cost | | 143,000 |
| | | | |
| Debit | Accumulated depreciation | 75,000 | |
| Credit | Fixed asset disposals account | | 75,000 |

**Fixed assets disposal account**

| | £ | | £ |
|---|---|---|---|
| Fixed assets at cost | 143,000 | Accumulated depreciation | 75,000 |

**Step 2**   Match the proceeds of disposal to the net book value of the asset being disposed of. The journal entry and the disposal account are noted below:

| **Journal** | | Debit £ | Credit £ |
|---|---|---|---|
| Debit | Cash book | 24,000 | |
| Credit | Fixed asset disposals account | | 24,000 |

**Fixed assets disposal account**

| | £ | | £ |
|---|---|---|---|
| Fixed assets at cost | 143,000 | Accumulated depreciation | 75,000 |
| | | Proceeds of disposal | 24,000 |

**Step 3**   Balance off the disposal account.  The double entry for the balancing figure will be the profit or loss on disposal.  The disposal account and the journal entry are noted below:

**Fixed assets disposal account**

| | £ | | £ |
|---|---|---|---|
| Fixed assets at cost | 143,000 | Accumulated depreciation | 75,000 |
| | | Proceeds of disposal | 24,000 |
| | 143,000 | | 99,000 |
| | | Loss on disposal | 44,000 |
| | 143,000 | | 143,000 |

| **Journal** | | Debit £ | Credit £ |
|---|---|---|---|
| Debit | Profit and loss account:  Loss on disposal | 44,000 | |
| Credit | Fixed asset disposals account | | 44,000 |

If the balancing figure is on the debit side of the Disposal Account, then the proceeds are greater than the net book value of the asset and a profit has been made.

If the balancing figure is on the credit side of the Disposal Account then a loss has been made.

## ACTIVITY 5

On 1 January 20X1 Zenith Ltd bought an asset costing £39,000. It was expected to have a five-year life and a residual value of £4,000. The asset was sold for £12,300 during 2004. Zenith has a 31 December year-end and charges a full year's depreciation in the year of acquisition and none in the year of disposal.

**Required:**

(a)    Prepare the T accounts to record the disposal of this asset.

(b)    Draft the journal to record this transaction.

*For a suggested answer, see the 'Answers' section at the end of the book.*

## 4.3    DISPOSALS AND PART-EXCHANGE

Sometimes when a new fixed asset is purchased, the fixed asset that it is replacing is given in part-exchange. This is particularly common with motor vehicles. The new asset will have a list price which, instead of being satisfied in full by a cash payment will be satisfied partly by cash and partly in the form of the old asset. In this way the purchase of the new asset and the disposal of the old asset are linked.

In terms of the disposal of the old asset, the same principles apply as before. However, the proceeds of disposal of the old asset are the part-exchange value (see definition below) given against the cost of the new asset.

For the new fixed asset, the main thing to remember is that the figure recorded in the fixed asset cost account is the full list price of the asset, comprising cash and the part exchange value.

**Example**

A car has a list price of £8,000. An older car is offered in part-exchange and as a result the business only pays £6,000 for the new car.

The part-exchange value is calculated as:

|  | £ |
|---|---|
| List price | 8,000 |
| Less: part-exchange value | (2,000) |
| Cash paid | 6,000 |

The steps in accounting for a disposal of a fixed asset with a part exchange are as follows:

**Step 1**    Set up the Disposal of fixed assets T account.

**Step 2** Remove the cost of the old fixed asset from its nominal ledger account

Dr Disposal of fixed asset account

Cr Fixed asset cost account

**Step 3** Remove the accumulated depreciation on the old fixed asset from its nominal ledger account

Dr Accumulated depreciation

Cr Disposal of fixed asset account

**Step 4** Bring down the balance on the disposal of fixed asset account

(**Note:** The above steps are identical to the basic disposal of a fixed asset.)

Account for the disposal proceeds of the old asset, which is linked with the purchase of the new asset:

|  |  |  | £ | £ |
|---|---|---|---|---|
| Debit | B/S | Fixed assets at cost | 8,000 | |
| Credit | P&L | Disposal of fixed assets | | 2,000 |
| Credit | B/S | Cash at bank | | 6,000 |

This double entry deals neatly with both the purchase of the new asset at its full cost of £8,000 and the disposal of the old asset.

**Step 5** Balance up the disposal account and work out the profit or loss

This is the same final step as in the basic disposal.

## 4.4 EXAMPLE

Hammer Ltd is to buy a new motor van, which has a list price of £9,000. The new van is to replace a van which cost £7,500 four years ago, and has accumulated depreciation of £6,000 on it.

Hammer Ltd will pay the motor van dealer £7,000 for the new van and therefore the part exchange value is (£9,000 – £7,000) £2,000.

**Step 1** Set up a T account called 'disposal of fixed assets'

**Step 2** Remove the cost of the fixed asset from its nominal ledger account

### Van account  (B/S)

| | £ | | £ |
|---|---|---|---|
| Balance b/d | 7,500 | Disposal a/c | 7,500 |

### Disposal of fixed assets account  (P&L)

| | £ | | £ |
|---|---|---|---|
| Van at cost | 7,500 | | |

**Step 3** Remove the accumulated depreciation on the fixed asset from its nominal ledger account

### Disposal of fixed assets account  (P&L)

| | £ | | £ |
|---|---|---|---|
| Van at cost | 7,500 | Provision for deprecation | 6,000 |

### Van provision for depreciation account   (B/S)

| | £ | | £ |
|---|---|---|---|
| Disposal a/c | 6,000 | Balance b/d | 6,000 |

**Step 4**     Bring down the balance on the disposal of fixed assets account

### Disposal of fixed assets account   (P&L)

| | £ | | £ |
|---|---|---|---|
| Van at cost | 7,500 | Provision for deprecation | 6,000 |
| | | Balance c/d | 1,500 |
| | 7,500 | | 7,500 |
| Balance b/f | 1,500 | | |

**Step 5**     Account for the disposal proceeds of the old asset, and the purchase of the new asset

### Disposal of fixed assets account   (P&L)

| | £ | | £ |
|---|---|---|---|
| Van at cost | 7,500 | Provision for deprecation | 6,000 |
| | | Balance c/d | 1,500 |
| | 7,500 | | 7,500 |
| Balance b/f | 1,500 | | |
| | | Proceeds:  Part-exchange | 2,000 |

### Cash at bank account   (B/S)

| | £ | | £ |
|---|---|---|---|
| | | Cost of fixed asset | 7,000 |

### Fixed asset cost account   (B/S)

| | £ | | £ |
|---|---|---|---|
| Balance b/d | 7,500 | Disposal a/c | 7,500 |
| Cost of fixed asset:  Part-exchange | 2,000 | | |
| Cost of fixed asset:  Cash | 7,000 | Balance c/d | 9,000 |
| | 16,500 | | 16,500 |
| **Balance b/f** | 9,000 | | |

**Step 6**     Balance the disposal account and work out the profit or loss

### Disposal of fixed assets account   (P&L)

| | £ | | £ |
|---|---|---|---|
| Van at cost | 7,500 | Provision for deprecation | 6,000 |
| | | Balance c/d | 1,500 |
| | 7,500 | | 7,500 |
| Balance b/f | 1,500 | Proceeds:  Part-exchange | 2,000 |
| Profit on disposal | 500 | | 2,000 |
| | 2,000 | | |

## ACTIVITY 6

In 20X3 Armand Ltd bought an elevator for £45,000. It was to have a twenty year life and a £5,000 residual value. In 20X9 Armand decided to upgrade their elevator for a new one with a list price of £99,000. This will have a useful life of 30 years and a residual value of £9,000. The supplier will give Armand a £20,000 trade in allowance on their old elevator.

Charge a full year's depreciation in the year of acquisition and none in the year of disposal.

**Required:**

Prepare the following accounts for the year ending 31 December 20X9:

Elevators at cost, provision for depreciation on elevators and disposals account.

*For a suggested answer, see the 'Answers' section at the end of the book.*

# 5 REVALUATION

## 5.1 PURPOSE

The net book value of assets with long lives will soon become unrealistic in comparison with their market value. This also means that the depreciation charge in the profit and loss account no longer reflects the cost of using those assets. The solution to these problems is to revalue these assets and to charge depreciation on the revalued amount.

## 5.2 REVALUATION RULES IN FRS 15 AND THE COMPANIES ACT

There is no requirement to revalue fixed assets. If a company chooses to revalue assets then it must revalue all assets in a particular class, but it need not revalue all of its fixed assets. For example, the most common approach is to revalue all freehold properties and to leave all other assets at historic cost.

Once assets have been revalued then the revaluations must be kept up to date. Full valuations must be held every five years at least, with additional revaluations whenever there are material changes in value.

## 5.3 VALUATION METHODS

The main valuation method is the **existing use** basis. This means that a warehouse will be valued on the assumption that it will be used as a warehouse. There may be alternative uses for the premises (such as housing) and these may give different values, but these values are not relevant.

Properties *surplus to requirements* should be valued on an **open market** basis. For example if the warehouse above were surplus to requirements then it could be sold off to a property developer at its market value. This value is therefore the most relevant for surplus properties.

## 5.4 REVALUATION GAINS AND LOSSES

**Revaluation gains** are taken directly to the Revaluation Reserve. They are reported in the Statement of Total Recognised Gains and Losses, not in the P&L account, as they are not realised. The Revaluation Reserve represents unrealised gains. They cannot be used to pay a dividend.

**Revaluation losses** are dealt with in a number of ways, depending on the circumstances. These are as follows:

If a property has been revalued upwards in the past, then any revaluation losses are taken directly to the Revaluation Reserve, until the revaluation reserve for that asset is exhausted. Any further losses must be taken to the profit and loss Account.

If a fall in value has been caused by damage, then this should always be taken to the profit and loss account.

## 5.5 DEPRECIATION ON REVALUED ASSETS

The depreciation charge on revalued assets is calculated as follows:

$$\frac{\text{Revalued amount less revised residue value}}{\text{Remaining useful life of the asset}}$$

## 5.6 BOOKKEEPING ENTRIES

(1) The cost/valuation of the asset is increased to its new value.

|  |  | Debit | Credit |
|---|---|---|---|
| Debit | Fixed assets at cost / valuation | X | |
| Credit | Revaluation reserve | | X |

*with the difference between the historic cost and the revalued amount*

(2) The accumulated depreciation is transferred to the revaluation reserve.

|  |  | Debit | Credit |
|---|---|---|---|
| Debit | Accumulated depreciation | X | |
| Credit | Revaluation reserve | | X |

*with the difference between the historic cost and the revalued amount*

(3) The revaluation reserve is balanced off. It will be included as part of capital and reserves in the balance sheet

(4) Depreciation will now be charged on the revalued amount.

**Example**

A company's building is currently included in the balance sheet at its original cost as follows:

|  | £ |
|---|---|
| Cost | 200,000 |
| Depreciation | 40,000 |
| Net book value | 160,000 |

It is being depreciated over its useful economic life of 50 years and it has already been owned for 10 years.

It is now to be revalued to its current existing use value of £450,000.

Write up the accounting entries for this revaluation and explain how the building will be depreciated from now on.

**Solution**

**Step 1**        Bring the fixed asset – cost account up to the revalued amount.

### Fixed asset – cost

| | £ | | £ |
|---|---|---|---|
| Balance b/d | 200,000 | Balance c/d | 450,000 |
| Revaluation reserve | 250,000 | | |
| | 450,000 | | 450,000 |

**Step 2**        Remove the accumulated depreciation already charged on the asset.

### Fixed asset – accumulated depreciation

| | £ | | £ |
|---|---|---|---|
| Revaluation reserve | 40,000 | Balance b/d | 40,000 |

**Step 3**        Write up the revaluation reserve account.

### Revaluation reserve

| | £ | | £ |
|---|---|---|---|
| Balance c/d | 290,000 | Fixed asset – cost | 250,000 |
| | | Fixed asset – accumulated depreciation | 40,000 |
| | 290,000 | | 290,000 |

The balance on the revaluation reserve is the amount required to take the building from its current carrying value of £160,000 to its revalued figure of £450,000 (£290,000).

The depreciation charge for the building for each year will now be based upon the carrying value on the balance sheet, £450,000, and the remaining useful life, 40 years.

$$\text{Annual depreciation charge} = \frac{£450,000}{40 \text{ years}}$$

£11,250 per annum

## ACTIVITY 7

Ten years ago Increment Ltd paid £300,000 for a building. It had an expected useful life of 50 years, and 10 years' depreciation has now been charged on it. The directors wish to revalue the property to its current existing use value of £720,000. There has been no change to its expected useful life, and there will be no residual value.

**Required:**

(a) Prepare the T accounts to record this revaluation.

(b) Calculate the revalued depreciation charge.

*For a suggested answer, see the 'Answers' section at the end of the book.*

# 6 INTANGIBLE FIXED ASSETS

Fixed assets are assets that are held for use rather than for resale. Intangible fixed assets are fixed assets without physical substance. They include patents, licences, franchises, development costs and goodwill.

Patents, licences, franchises and so on are normally purchased. They will be capitalised at cost and amortised over the life of the asset. Amortisation is the name for the depreciation charge on an intangible asset. It is calculated in the same way as for a tangible asset. The maximum life of the asset is normally set out in the terms of the purchase agreement; for example you might purchase a four year patent. However, circumstances might cause this life to be reduced; for example you might have the marketing rights to a footballer who changes club and country, and thereby reduces the value of his marketing rights.

Research and development costs, and goodwill, are not quite so straightforward. The accounting treatments for these items are explained in the following sections.

# 7 SSAP 13 *ACCOUNTING FOR RESEARCH AND DEVELOPMENT*

## 7.1 DEFINITIONS

The term **research and development** can be used to cover a wide range of activity. The following definitions are simplified versions of those in SSAP 13:

- **Research**, whether **pure** or **applied**, is work undertaken to gain new scientific or technical knowledge. There may, or may not, be a commercial use for this knowledge.

- **Development** is the use of existing scientific or technical knowledge to produce new or improved materials, devices, products, services or processes.

For example, the work undertaken inventing the technology for CD ROM computer games would be classified as research. The work undertaken today to write a new computer game using the existing technology would be classified as development.

## 7.2 THE ACCOUNTING PROBLEM

The costs of research and development today can run into hundreds of millions. However, it may be many years before the new technology or product is commercially viable. Following the accruals concept, the cost of research and development should be capitalised when incurred, and them amortised when the products are eventually marketed. This would then match the costs with the benefits.

However, prudence would say that the eventual profits are so uncertain and so far away that it would be better to write off all research and development expenditure when it is incurred.

## 7.3 THE ACCOUNTING SOLUTION

SSAP 13 finds a compromise between accruals and prudence.

*All research expenditure must be charged to the P&L account as it is incurred.* This is because there is such a long time gap between research commencing and a profitable product being launched. In fact in many high tech industries (such as the pharmaceutical industry) the vast majority of research projects will never produce a viable product.

*Development expenditure **may** be capitalised.* Theoretically this is the correct thing to do, because this will match the costs to the hoped for benefits. However, in practice very few companies capitalise their development expenditure. There are strict rules restricting the situations when development expenditure can be capitalised, and what costs can be capitalised. These are looked at in the next sections.

*The annual charge for research and development must be disclosed.*

## 7.4 CRITERIA FOR CAPITALISATION

*Development expenditure can only be capitalised if the project meets all of the following criteria:*

(1) The project is clearly defined.

(2) The costs are separately identifiable.

(3) The project is technically feasible.

(4) The project is commercially viable.

(5) The expected revenues will exceed all costs to date plus any future costs.

(6) The company has the financial resources needed to complete the project.

## 7.5 DEVELOPMENT COSTS

If a project meets the criteria for capitalisation than all costs allocated to that specific project may be (but are not required to) be capitalised. These costs will include materials, wages and salaries, depreciation of scientific equipment and facilities, a proportion of overheads and any other direct costs.

## 7.6 AMORTISATION

Capitalised development expenditure can be carried forward until the product being developed is ready for commercial production. At this point it must be amortised over the expected commercial life of the product. The amortisation method used must match the costs of the project with the benefits from selling or using the product. This could be over a set number of years or it may be tied into the level of production or sales.

### Example

Improve plc has deferred development expenditure of £600,000 relating to the development of New Miracle Brand X. It is expected that the demand for the product will stay at a high level for the next three years. Annual sales of 400,000, 300,000 and 200,000 units respectively are expected over this period. Brand X sells for £10.

### Required:

How might this expenditure be amortised?

**Solution**

There are two possibilities for writing off the development expenditure:

(a)     in equal instalments over the three year period i.e. £200,000 pa; or

(b)     in relation to total sales expected (900,000 units):

Year 1     $\dfrac{400,000}{900,000} \times £600,000 = $     £266,667

Year 2     $\dfrac{300,000}{900,000} \times £600,000 = $     £200,000

Year 3     $\dfrac{200,000}{900,000} \times £600,000 = $     £133,333

# 8     FRS 10 *ACCOUNTING FOR GOODWILL*

## 8.1     INTRODUCTION

Goodwill is rare in company financial statements, but is very common in group situations. The mechanics of calculating and amortising goodwill in group situations will be covered in the chapters on group accounts. This chapter outlines the requirements of FRS 10 in respect of goodwill.

## 8.2     THE NATURE OF GOODWILL

Any successful and profitable business will have goodwill of its own. This goodwill will arise because of the quality of the business's products and staff, its reputation, its technical know-how, the loyalty of its customers and the reliability of its suppliers. In short, anything that makes a company successful is part of its goodwill.

The goodwill that a business generates through its own efforts is known as **inherent goodwill**. Inherent goodwill is **never capitalised** in corporate financial statements. It has no cost and it is impossible to value.

When one company purchases another company part of the price paid will represent the value of the goodwill in the company being acquired. This is known as **purchased goodwill**. The cost of this purchased goodwill can be calculated accurately and reliably, and this purchased goodwill **must be capitalised**.

## 8.3     CALCULATING THE COST OF PURCHASED GOODWILL

Purchased goodwill is the difference between the fair value of the consideration given and the fair value of the net assets acquired. For example. if X plc paid £1m for Y Ltd, and Y Ltd had a fair value of £800,000, then purchased goodwill of £200,000 would be recognised.

It must be remembered that goodwill is a balancing figure. The two parties agree a price for the shares being bought; the fair value of the net assets acquired is then calculated; the goodwill is the difference between the two. This does mean that the goodwill will be affected by the bargaining skills of the two parties, and/or the state of the stock market as a whole.

## 8.4　CAPITALISATION AND AMORTISATION

All purchased goodwill must be capitalised.

FRS 10 assumes that goodwill will be amortised over a period not exceeding 20 years. In practice, the nature of goodwill means that the amortisation period will be less than this. With the pace of change in business being so fast, it is unlikely that goodwill will remain intact for as long as 20 years.

FRS 10 does allow a longer period to be used, but this is only allowed if the reasons for doing so are disclosed and the balance of goodwill is reviewed regularly for impairment.

FRS 10 also allows goodwill to be held in the balance sheet indefinitely, without any amortisation. This is only allowed if the balance of goodwill is reviewed for impairment annually. It also requires the true and fair view override to be invoked because all fixed assets with a finite life should be depreciated or amortised. In practice, very few companies adopt this non-amortisation policy.

## 8.5　IMPAIRMENT

Goodwill is more susceptible to impairment than most assets. Reputations and customers are easily lost. For example, within the space of a few months, as the result of the Enron accounting scandal, the good name of Arthur Andersen disappeared altogether. It is therefore important to review goodwill regularly to ensure that the profits generated by the related businesses are sufficient to recover the net book value of the goodwill in the balance sheet.

## 8.6　PRESENTATION

The movements in the carrying value of goodwill should be disclosed by note, along with details of the amortisation policy.

## 8.7　NEGATIVE GOODWILL

Negative goodwill arises when the price paid for a business is less than the fair value of the net assets acquired. This is rare, and only usually happens if there has been a forced sale of a business.

Negative goodwill is capitalised as a negative fixed asset. It is deducted from the total of positive goodwill. The negative goodwill is then released to the profit and loss account as income over the periods expected to benefit from its use.

## 8.8　EXAMPLE OF CAPITALISATION, AMORTISATION, AND PRESENTATION.

On 1 January 20X1 Able plc purchased Baker, an unincorporated business, for £5m. The net assets of Baker were £4,460,000. Goodwill is to be amortised over six years on a straight line basis.

**Required:**

(a)　Calculate the cost of goodwill in 20X1.

(b)　Calculate the expected annual amortisation charge.

Present the results in the form of the goodwill disclosure note for 20X1 and 20X2.

Solution

| Able plc | | Extracts from the balance sheet – goodwill | | |
|---|---|---|---|---|
| | | 20X1 | 20X2 | |
| | | £000 | £000 | |
| Opening balance | | – | 450 | |
| Acquisitions | (a) | 540 | – | |
| Amortisation | (b) | (90) | (90) | |
| Closing balance | | 450 | 360 | |

Goodwill is capitalised and amortised over six years.

| | | | £ |
|---|---|---|---|
| (a) | Calculation of the cost and amortisation | | |
| | Fair value of the consideration | | 5,000,000 |
| | Less: Fair value of the net assets acquired | | (4,460,000) |
| | **Goodwill at cost** | | 540,000 |
| (b) | Annual amortisation charge over six years | | 90,000 |

## ACTIVITY 8

On 1 January 20X1 Charlie plc purchased Dude, an unincorporated business, for £9m. The net assets of Dude were £6m. Dude's business is old fashioned and well established, and so a 25-year amortisation period is considered to be appropriate.

**Required:**

(a) Calculate the cost of goodwill in 20X1.

(b) Calculate the expected annual amortisation charge.

Present the results in the form of the goodwill disclosure note for 20X1 and 20X2.

*For a suggested answer, see the 'Answers' section at the end of the book.*

## KEY TERMS

**Current assets** – an asset which will be converted into cash within the next 12 months.

**Fixed assets** – an asset purchased not for resale, but for use within the business in the generation of profits over more than one accounting period.

**Capital expenditure** – expenditure on fixed assets.

**Tangible fixed assets** – assets that can be physically touched.

**Intangible fixed asset** – assets that cannot be physically touched.

**Depreciation** – the measure of the cost of the economic benefits of the fixed asset that have been consumed during the period.

**Amortisation** – depreciation charge on an intangible asset.

**Useful economic life** – the period over which the entity expects to derive economic benefit from that asset.

**Development** – the use of existing scientific or technical knowledge to produce new or improved materials, devices, products, services or processes.

**Purchased goodwill** – the difference between the fair value of the consideration given and the fair value of the net assets acquired.

# SELF TEST QUESTIONS

|    |                                                                                          | *Paragraph* |
|----|------------------------------------------------------------------------------------------|-------------|
| 1  | What is a tangible fixed asset?                                                          | 1.3         |
| 2  | When can subsequent expenditure on a fixed asset be capitalised?                        | 2.2, & 2.3  |
| 3  | What is the purpose of depreciation?                                                    | 3.1         |
| 4  | How are revaluation gains dealt with?                                                   | 5.4         |
| 5  | How should research costs be accounted for?                                             | 7.3         |
| 6  | What are the two alternative ways in which development costs can be accounted for?       | 7.3         |
| 7  | What criteria must be met before development expenditure can be capitalised?            | 7.4         |
| 8  | What is the difference between inherent and purchased goodwill?                         | 8.2         |
| 9  | What is the accounting treatment for inherent goodwill?                                 | 8.2         |
| 10 | What is the accounting treatment for purchased goodwill?                                | 8.2         |
| 11 | Under what conditions can purchased goodwill be amortised for a period in excess of 20 years? | 8.4    |
| 12 | How might negative goodwill arise?                                                      | 8.7         |

## ADDITIONAL QUESTION

**ARBALEST**

The summarised balance sheet of Arbalest Limited at 30 September 20X6 was as follows:

|  | Cost | Aggregate depreciation | Net book value |
|---|---|---|---|
|  | £000 | £000 | £000 |
| Fixed assets |  |  |  |
| Land | 2,000 | nil | 2,000 |
| Buildings | 1,500 | 450 | 1,050 |
| Plant and machinery | 2,800 | 1,000 | 1,800 |
|  | 6,300 | 1,450 | 4,850 |
| Current assets |  | 3,180 |  |
| Less: Current liabilities |  | 2,070 | 1,110 |
|  |  |  | 5,960 |
| Capital and reserves |  |  |  |
| Called-up share capital |  |  |  |
| 3,000,000 ordinary shares of 50p each |  |  | 1,500 |
| Share premium account |  |  | 400 |
| Profit and loss account |  |  | 4,060 |
|  |  |  | 5,960 |

During the year ended 30 September 20X7 the company had the following transactions:

(1)     1 November 20X6:

A rights issue of one share for every three held at a price of £1.50 per share. All the rights issue shares were taken up.

(2)     1 December 20X6:

Sale for £70,000 of plant and machinery which had cost £1,000,000 and had a book value of £200,000.

(3)     1 March 20X7:

A bonus (capitalisation) issue of one share for every one held at that date using the share premium account as far as possible for the purpose.

(4)     1 June 20X7:

Purchased a new factory block for £3,000,000 (including land £600,000).

(5)     1 July 20X7:

Purchased plant and machinery for £1,800,000.

(6)    30 September 20X7:

The company decided to revalue the freehold land held at 30 September 20X6 from £2,000,000 to £2,500,000.

The company depreciation policies are:

| Land | no depreciation |
|---|---|
| Buildings | 2% per annum on cost, straight-line basis |
| Plant and machinery | 10% per annum on cost, straight-line basis |

Proportionate depreciation is provided in the year of purchase of an asset, with none in the year of disposal. The retained profit for the year was £370,000.

**Required:**

Prepare the notes required for the company's balance sheet for publication at 30 September 20X7 detailing:

(a)    movements on reserves

(b)    movements on fixed assets.

Ledger accounts for the transactions are not required.

*For a suggested answer, see the 'Answers' section at the end of the book.*

# Chapter 5

# STOCKS

This chapter revises the accounting treatment of stocks.

## CONTENTS

1    Stocks

2    Stock valuation methods

## LEARNING OUTCOMES

At the end of this chapter you should be able to:

• calculate the cost and net realisable value of stocks.

## 1    STOCKS

### 1.1    THE REASON FOR RECOGNISING STOCK IN THE BALANCE SHEET

Profit is calculated by matching costs with revenues.  Revenues are normally claimed when a sale is made, and all related costs and expenses are then matched to that revenue.  As stock is bought, it is charged to the P&L as purchases.  There is nearly always a time lag between purchasing stock and selling it, and so at the year-end there will be unsold stock on hand.  This unsold stock must be carried forward in the balance sheet so that it can be matched with next year's revenues.  This is applying the accruals concept.

### 1.2    VALUING STOCK IN THE BALANCE SHEET

Stocks are valued at the lower of cost and net realisable value.  This is an application of the prudence concept.  Most items will be valued at cost, which excludes any future profits.  However, if any losses are foreseen then they will be recognised immediately. Valuation is a two stage process; firstly the cost is calculated and then this is compared with its net realisable value.

## 1.3   THE COST OF STOCK

SSAP 9 states that the cost of stock includes all costs that have been incurred in the normal course of business in bringing the product or service to its present condition and location.  (This rule is similar to that for calculating the cost of a tangible fixed asset.)

These costs will include the costs of purchase and the costs of conversion.

(a)   **Costs of purchase**: material costs, import duties, freight.

(b)   **Costs of conversion**: this includes direct costs and production overheads.

### Example

Head Ltd incurred the following costs in respect of some stock:

|  | £ |
| --- | --- |
| Invoice price of raw materials | 123,456 |
| Transport costs from the supplier to the factory | 5,283 |
| Repair to damaged materials | 15,389 |
| Own labour (from job cards) | 18,627 |
| Production overheads | 12,634 |
| Administration and marketing overheads | 24,611 |
| Total | 200,000 |

### Task

What will be the cost of this stock?

### Solution

|  | Total | Stock |  |
| --- | --- | --- | --- |
|  | £ | £ |  |
| Invoice price | 123,456 | 123,456 | Purchase cost |
| Transport costs | 5,283 | 5,283 | Purchase cost |
| Repair | 15,389 |  |  |
| Own labour | 18,627 | 18,627 | Conversion cost |
| Production overheads | 12,634 | 12,634 | Conversion cost |
| Administration and marketing | 24,611 |  |  |
| Total | 200,000 | 160,000 |  |

The repair costs are not in the normal course of business (unless there is a steady amount of wastage in the production process). The stock will be valued at £160,000.

## 1.4   METHODS OF CALCULATING THE COST OF PURCHASE

There are different ways in which the cost of stock can be calculated.  FIFO (first in first out) is by far the most common and the most accurate. This, and other methods are discussed in section 2.

## 1.5   NET REALISABLE VALUE

Having calculated the cost of stock, it is then compared with its net realisable value.  This is done on a line-by-line basis (or by categories) in accordance with the principle of separate valuation.  The expected profit on one item cannot be offset against the expected loss on another item.

STOCKS : **CHAPTER 5**

**Definition**    **Net realisable value** is the estimated proceeds of sale less any further costs to completion and all costs to be incurred in distributing, marketing and selling.

## Example – Net realisable value

A product sells for £2,000. The costs incurred so far total £987 and the costs to complete the product are estimated at £126. Marketing costs will be about £47. The manufacturer delivers the products to the customer for free, and this normally costs £66. The administrative costs of sale (invoicing and so on) amount to £58.

## Required:

Calculate the cost, net realisable value and balance sheet value for this item of stock.

## Solution

| | | |
|---|---|---|
| Cost | £987 | |
| Net realisable value | £1,703 | £(2,000 – 126 – 47 – 66 – 58) |
| Balance sheet value | £987 | |

## Example – Cost and net realisable value

Charles Smart runs a sweet shop. His annual stock count in December revealed a few seasonal items of stock which would have to be reduced in price in the new year. These were as follows:

| Range | Number of boxes | Cost | Normal retail price | Expected selling price |
|---|---|---|---|---|
| Venus | 35 | £5.30 | £8 | £4 |
| Earth | 54 | £5.70 | £9 | £6 |
| Saturn | 85 | £7.80 | £11 | £8 |
| Pluto | 47 | £9.90 | £14 | £8 |
| Jupiter | 72 | £6.50 | £10 | £8 |

## Task

Calculate the balance sheet value of his closing stock. (Assume that selling costs are immaterial.)

## Solution

| Range | Number of boxes | Cost | Expected selling price | Lower of cost & NRV | Valuation £ |
|---|---|---|---|---|---|
| Venus | 35 | £5.30 | £4 | £4 | 140.00 |
| Earth | 54 | £5.70 | £6 | £5.70 | 307.80 |
| Saturn | 85 | £7.80 | £8 | £7.80 | 663.00 |
| Pluto | 47 | £9.90 | £8 | £8 | 376.00 |
| Jupiter | 72 | £6.50 | £8 | £6.50 | 468.00 |
| | | | | | 1,954.80 |

The balance sheet value of these stock items is £1,954.80.

## ACTIVITY 1

The following information relates to five dissimilar stock items:

| Range | Cost | NRV |
|---|---|---|
| | £ | £ |
| Alpha | 480 | 510 |
| Beta | 220 | 200 |
| Gamma | 170 | 220 |
| Delta | 150 | 200 |
| Epsilon | 600 | 450 |
| | 1,620 | 1,580 |

**Required:**

What will be the total balance sheet value of this stock?

*For a suggested answer, see the 'Answers' section at the end of the book.*

## 1.6   DISCLOSURE REQUIREMENTS – SSAP 9

Stocks and work-in-progress should be sub-classified in the notes to the financial statements in an appropriate manner.

The accounting policies used to value stock should be disclosed.

The following would be a typical example:

| Note X   Stocks | £ |
|---|---|
| Raw materials | 19,273 |
| Work-in-progress | 4,927 |
| Finished goods | 43,568 |
| | 67,768 |

Stocks are valued at the lower of cost and net realisable value.

Cost is calculated on a First in First out basis.

# 2   STOCK VALUATION METHODS

There are several allowable ways of valuing stocks.  These include:

(a)   identified, actual or unit cost

(b)   average cost

(c)   first-in-first-out (FIFO).

Some countries use the *last-in-first-out* (LIFO) method, but this is not allowed in the UK.

### 2.1 IDENTIFIED, ACTUAL OR UNIT COST

Unsold or unused stocks are linked with their purchase. This method is limited to large or valuable items where individual units can be easily identified with their cost of acquisition e.g. diamonds. This method, therefore, has limited usefulness in practice, but is acceptable under SSAP 9.

### 2.2 AVERAGE COST

Where raw materials or goods go, for example, into a bin, e.g. grain, it may be impossible or impracticable to identify particular items. All units going into and out of the store are pooled and an average price determined. This average price should be calculated as a weighted average (this is preferable to a simple average).

**Example**

| 200 units | Purchased | Day 1 at £15 per unit |
| 100 units | Purchased | Day 2 at £21 per unit |
| 200 units | Sold | Day 3 at £25 per unit |

Calculate the gross profit earned on Day 3 and the valuation of stock remaining at the end of Day 3, using the weighted average method.

**Solution**

Weighted average price at end of Day 2 $= \dfrac{(200 \times £15) + (100 \times £21)}{300}$

$\qquad\qquad\qquad\qquad\qquad = £17$ per unit

**Calculation of gross profit**

|  |  | £ |
|---|---|---|
| Proceeds of sale | 200 × £25 = | 5,000 |
| Less: Cost of goods sold | 200 × £17 = | 3,400 |
| Gross profit |  | 1,600 |

**Calculation of stock in the balance sheet**

|  |  | £ |
|---|---|---|
| 100 units stated at | 100 × £17 = | 1,700 |

*Note:* Calculations based on a simple average would give a different gross profit of £1,400.

The aim of the weighted average method is to even out price fluctuations. It is complex to operate, but acceptable under SSAP 9.

### 2.3 FIRST-IN-FIRST-OUT (FIFO)

This is the most common method in practice. This method assumes that goods are sold or used in production in the order in which they are brought into stock. The first items sold will be the earliest purchases.

**Example**

Using the figures from the previous activity calculate the gross profit on Day 3 and the value of stock at the end of Day 3 using FIFO.

**Solution**

The assumption here is that the 200 units sold on Day 3 were the 200 units acquired on Day 1.

**Calculation of gross profit**

|  |  | £ |
|---|---|---|
| Proceeds of sale | $200 \times £25 =$ | 5,000 |
| Less: Cost of goods sold | $200 \times £15 =$ | 3,000 |
| Gross profit | | 2,000 |

**Calculation of stock in the balance sheet**

|  |  | £ |
|---|---|---|
| 100 units stated at | $100 \times £21 =$ | 2,100 |

One of the features of FIFO is that stock in the balance sheet tends to be stated at the most recent values, whereas cost of goods sold is based on the more historical values. In a period of inflation FIFO tends to overstate gross profit because current revenues are matched with historical costs.

# KEY TERMS

**Cost of stock** – SSAP 9 states that the cost of stock includes all costs that have been incurred in the normal course of business in bringing the product or service to its present condition and location

**Net realisable value** – the estimated proceeds of sale less any further costs to completion and all costs to be incurred in distributing, marketing and selling.

**FIFO** – (First in First Out) – the most common method of estimating the cost of stock. This method assumes that goods are sold or used in production in the order in which they are brought into stock. The first items sold will be the earliest purchases.

# SELF TEST QUESTIONS

*Paragraph*

| | | |
|---|---|---|
| 1 | Which two accounting concepts are most relevant to the accounting treatment of stocks? | 1.1 & 1.2 |
| 2 | What is the SSAP 9 definition of the cost of stocks? | 1.3 |
| 3 | What is the net realisable value of stocks? | 1.5 |
| 4 | What is the assumption behind a FIFO cost valuation for stocks? | 2.3 |
| 5 | What effect does the FIFO method of stock valuation have on reported profits? | 2.3 |

## EXAM-STYLE QUESTION

### SAMPI

Sampi is a manufacturer of garden furniture. The company has consistently used FIFO (first in, first out) in valuing stock, but it is interested to know the effect on its stock valuation of using weighted average cost instead of FIFO.

At 28 February 20X8 the company had a stock of 4,000 standard plastic tables, and had computed its value on each of the three bases as:

| Basis | Unit cost £ | Total value £ |
|---|---|---|
| FIFO | 16 | 64,000 |
| Weighted average | 13 | 52,000 |

During March 20X8 the movements on the stock of tables were as follows:

**Received from factory**

| Date | Number of units | Production cost per unit £ |
|---|---|---|
| 8 March | 3,800 | 15 |
| 22 March | 6,000 | 18 |

**Sales**

| Date | Number of units |
|---|---|
| 12 March | 5,000 |
| 18 March | 2,000 |
| 24 March | 3,000 |
| 28 March | 2,000 |

**Required:**

Compute what the value of the stock at 31 March 20X8 would be using:

(a)   FIFO

(b)   Weighted average cost.

In arriving at the total stock values you should make calculations to three decimal places (where necessary) and deal with each stock movement in date order.

*For a suggested answer, see the 'Answers' section at the end of the book.*

# Chapter 6

# ACCRUALS AND PREPAYMENTS

The accruals concept requires that expenses are included in the profit and loss account in the period in which they are incurred.

Therefore adjustments are required at the accounting period end for any expenses incurred but not yet paid or invoiced and any expenses paid for but not yet used. These adjustments result in accruals and prepayments.

Similar adjustments are required to ensure that the income shown in the profit and loss account is that which is due in the accounting period, rather than that which has been received or invoiced.

This chapter explains how the required adjustments are calculated and how they are accounted for.

## CONTENTS

## LEARNING OUTCOMES

At the end of this chapter, you should be able to:

- describe the nature and purpose of accruals

- describe the nature and purpose of prepayments

- calculate accruals

- calculate prepayments

- account for accruals

- account for prepayments

- report accruals in the final accounts

- report prepayments in the final accounts.

# 1    THE ACCRUALS CONCEPT

**Definition**  The **accruals concept** states that income and expenses should be matched together and dealt with in the profit and loss account for the period to which they relate regardless of the period in which the cash was actually received or paid.

As a result the following are recognised in the balance sheet:

- creditors (for purchases made on credit)

- debtors (for sales made on credit)

- accruals (for expenses incurred but not yet paid)

- prepayments (for expenses paid in advance)

Calculating the adjustments for accruals and prepayments can form the whole of an exam question or, more commonly, form a part of a larger question.

## ACTIVITY 1

Calculate or estimate how much should be charged for each of the following expenses in the profit and loss account for the year ended 31 December 20X1:

(a)    Rent – charged at £5,000 per quarter, paid quarterly in advance.

(b)    Electricity – paid in the year £1,000; invoice received in January 20X2 for £300, covering the period 1 October to 31 December 20X1.

(c)    Telephone – £820 paid for calls up to 30 November; the bill for the following quarter received in February 20X2 was for £240.

(d)    Insurance – paid annually in advance, on 1 April each year.  The bill for the year ended 31 March 20X1 was for £3,000; the following year's bill was £4,200.

*For a suggested answer, see the 'Answers' section at the end of the book.*

# 2 ACCRUED EXPENSES

## 2.1 THE NATURE AND PURPOSE OF ACCRUALS

**Definition**   An **accrual** is an item of expense that has been incurred during the accounting period but has not been paid at the period end.

In order to ensure that all expenses incurred in a period have been included in the profit and loss account the accountant must ensure that the expense accounts include not only those items that have been paid for during the period but also any outstanding amounts. In some instances, an invoice will have been received for any such outstanding amounts by the time the accounts are prepared and therefore the accrual can be accurately calculated. Otherwise, the accrual will need to be estimated from previous years and earlier invoices.

## 2.2 EXAMPLE WITH NO OPENING ACCRUAL

John Simnel's business has an accounting year end of 31 December 20X1. He rents factory space at a rental cost of £5,000 per quarter, payable in arrears. During the year to 31 December 20X1 his cash payments of rent have been as follows:

|  | £ |
|---|---|
| 31 March (for quarter to 31 March 20X1) | 5,000 |
| 29 June (for quarter to 30 June 20X1) | 5,000 |
| 2 October (for quarter to 30 September 20X1) | 5,000 |

The final payment due on 31 December 20X1 for the quarter to that date was not paid until 4 January 20X2.

Write up the ledger accounts for factory rent for the year ended 31 December 20X1.

## 2.3 SOLUTION

It should be quite clear that the rental expense for John Simnel's business for the year to 31 December 20X1 is £20,000 (4 × £5,000) even though the final payment for the year was not made until after the year end. It should also be noted that at 31 December 20X1 John Simnel's business owes the landlord £5,000 of rental for the period from 1 October to 31 December 20X1.

**Step 1**   Bring down any opening balance on the account. In this example there is no opening balance. The significance of this step will become apparent in the next example.

**Step 2**   Record the cash payments in the factory rent account.

### Factory rent

| 20X1 |  | £ | 20X1 |  | £ |
|---|---|---|---|---|---|
| 31 Mar | Cash at bank | 5,000 |  |  |  |
| 29 June | Cash at bank | 5,000 |  |  |  |
| 2 Oct | Cash at bank | 5,000 |  |  |  |

**Step 3**   The charge to the profit and loss account that is required at 31 December 20X1 is £20,000 and this is entered into the account on the credit side (the debit is the expense in the profit and loss account).

**Factory rent**

| 20X1 | | £ | 20X1 | | £ |
|---|---|---|---|---|---|
| 31 Mar | Cash at bank | 5,000 | 31 Dec | P&L a/c | 20,000 |
| 29 June | Cash at bank | 5,000 | | | |
| 2 Oct | Cash at bank | 5,000 | | | |

**Step 4**    In order for the account to balance, a further debit entry of £5,000 is required.

- This will be the balance carried down on the account, the accrual.

- This gives a brought down credit balance representing the amount owed to the landlord for the final quarter's rent.

**Factory rent**

| 20X1 | | £ | 20X1 | | £ |
|---|---|---|---|---|---|
| 31 Mar | Cash at bank | 5,000 | 31 Dec | P&L a/c | 20,000 |
| 29 June | Cash at bank | 5,000 | | | |
| 2 Oct | Cash at bank | 5,000 | | | |
| 31 Dec | Bal c/d | 5,000 | | | |
| | | ——— | | | ——— |
| | | 20,000 | | | 20,000 |
| | | ——— | | | ——— |
| | | | 20X2 | | |
| | | | 1 Jan | Bal b/d | 5,000 |

- By this method the correct expense has been charged to the profit and loss account under the accruals concept, £20,000, and the amount of £5,000 owed to the landlord has been recognised as a credit balance on the account.

- This credit balance would be listed in the balance sheet under the heading of current liabilities and described as an accrual.

Note that Steps 3 and 4 above may be performed in reverse order depending on personal preference and sometimes, the information given.

## 2.4   EXAMPLE WITH AN OPENING ACCRUAL

During the year to 31 December 20X2 John Simnel's rental charge remained the same and his payments were as follows:

| | £ |
|---|---|
| 4 January (for quarter to 31 December 20X1) | 5,000 |
| 28 March (for quarter to 31 March 20X2) | 5,000 |
| 28 June (for quarter to 30 June 20X2) | 5,000 |
| 4 October (for quarter to 30 September 20X2) | 5,000 |
| 23 December (for quarter to 31 December 20X2) | 5,000 |

Write up the ledger account for factory rent for the year ended 31 December 20X2.

## 2.5 SOLUTION

**Step 1**   Bring down the opening balance on the account, in this case an opening accrual of £5,000.

**Factory rent**

| 20X2 | | £ | 20X2 | | £ |
|---|---|---|---|---|---|
| | | | 1 Jan | Bal b/d | 5,000 |

**Step 2**   Record the cash payments made in the year.

**Factory rent**

| 20X2 | | £ | 20X2 | | £ |
|---|---|---|---|---|---|
| 4 Jan | Cash at bank | 5,000 | 1 Jan | Bal b/d | 5,000 |
| 28 Mar | Cash at bank | 5,000 | | | |
| 28 June | Cash at bank | 5,000 | | | |
| 4 Oct | Cash at bank | 5,000 | | | |
| 23 Dec | Cash at bank | 5,000 | | | |

**Step 3**   Calculate the closing accrual. There is no accrued expense to be carried forward this year since the amount due for the final quarter of the year was paid before the year end.

**Step 4**   Balance the account. The balancing figure is the factory rent expense of £20,000 (4 × £5,000) which is transferred to the profit and loss account.

**Factory rent**

| 20X2 | | £ | 20X2 | | £ |
|---|---|---|---|---|---|
| 4 Jan | Cash at bank | 5,000 | Jan | Bal b/d | 5,000 |
| 28 Mar | Cash at bank | 5,000 | 31 Dec | P&L a/c (bal fig) | 20,000 |
| 28 June | Cash at bank | 5,000 | | | |
| 4 Oct | Cash at bank | 5,000 | | | |
| 23 Dec | Cash at bank | 5,000 | | | |
| | | 25,000 | | | 25,000 |

Note that Steps 3 and 4 were performed in reverse order in comparison with the previous example.

## ACTIVITY 2

John Ball is a sole trader with a 30 June year-end. His purchase ledger for the year-ending 30 June 20X8 includes all Invoices dated up to and including 30 June 20X8. Any invoice received after that, was posted to the July (or subsequent) purchase ledger. Estimate the closing accruals for the following items:

(a)   An electricity bill for £900 for the three months to 31 August 20X8.

(b)   Water bill for £780 for the quarter to 31 July 20X8.

(c)     Sewerage bill for £642 for the quarter to 31 May 20X8.  When the annual accounts were being prepared no further bills had been received, although John Ball had continued to use the service.

(d)     John Ball also uses gas supplied through a gas main.  The meter reading on the last invoice received before the year-end was 23645 units; on 30 June the meter read 24098 units.  Gas costs 10 pence per unit.

*For a suggested answer, see the 'Answers' section at the end of the book.*

## ACTIVITY 3

James Bell has a December year-end.  Prepare the T accounts for the following expense headings and calculate the annual profit and loss account charge.

(a)     Electricity. Invoices totalling £697 were received and posted to the ledgers during the year. The opening accrual was £172 and the closing accrual is £238.

(b)     Rates. Invoices totalling £756 were received and posted to the ledgers during the year. The opening accrual was £365 and the closing accrual is £28.

*For a suggested answer, see the 'Answers' section at the end of the book*

## 2.6   JOURNAL TO RECORD AN ACCRUAL

The correct journal to record a period end accrual is:

Debit    Expense account (P&L)

Credit   Accrual (B/S)

# 3   PREPAID EXPENSES

## 3.1   THE NATURE AND PURPOSE OF PREPAYMENTS

**Definition**   A **prepayment** is an item of expense that has been paid during the current accounting period but will not be incurred until the next accounting period.

As well as ensuring that all of the expenses incurred in the period appear in the profit and loss account the accountant must also ensure that no items of expense that relate to future periods, but have already been paid for, are shown as expenses of the current period.

## 3.2   EXAMPLE WITH NO OPENING PREPAYMENT

John Simnel pays insurance on the factory that he rents and this is paid in advance. His payments during 20X1 for this insurance were as follows:

|  | £ |
|---|---|
| 1 January (for three months to 31 March 20X1) | 800 |
| 28 March (for six months to 30 September 20X1) | 1,800 |
| 2 October (for six months to 31 March 20X2) | 1,800 |

Calculate the insurance expense for the year ended 31 December 20X1 and write up the insurance ledger account.

## 3.3  SOLUTION

The insurance expense for the year to 31 December 20X1 can be calculated as follows:

|  | £ |
|---|---|
| 1 January to 31 March 20X1 | 800 |
| 1 April to 30 September 20X1 | 1,800 |
| 1 October to 31 December 20X1 ($\frac{3}{6} \times 1,800$) | 900 |
|  | 3,500 |

The remaining £900 that was paid on 2 October which is not to be charged to the profit and loss account for the year to 31 December 20X1 is a prepaid expense. It is an amount that has been paid in advance to the insurance company and as such it has the characteristics of a debtor, the insurance company effectively owing the £900 back to John Simnel at 31 December 20X1.

The ledger account will be written up as follows:

**Step 1**   Bring down any opening balance on the expense account. In this example the balance is £nil.

**Step 2**   Enter the cash payments into the Factory insurance account.

### Factory insurance

| 20X1 |  | £ | 20X1 |  | £ |
|---|---|---|---|---|---|
| 1 Jan | Cash at bank | 800 |  |  |  |
| 28 Mar | Cash at bank | 1,800 |  |  |  |
| 2 Oct | Cash at bank | 1,800 |  |  |  |

**Step 3**   The charge to the profit and loss account calculated above as £3,500 is then entered in the account.

**Step 4**   In order for the account to balance a further credit entry of £900 is required.

- This is the prepayment that is to be carried down and will appear as a brought down debit balance or debtor.

### Factory insurance

| 20X1 |  | £ | 20X1 |  | £ |
|---|---|---|---|---|---|
| 1 Jan | Cash at bank | 800 | 31 Dec P&L a/c | | 3,500 |
| 28 Mar | Cash at bank | 1,800 | 31 Dec Bal c/d | | 900 |
| 2 Oct | Cash at bank | 1,800 |  |  |  |
|  |  | 4,400 |  |  | 4,400 |
| 20X2 |  |  |  |  |  |
| 1 Jan | Bal b/d | 900 |  |  |  |

- This has given the correct charge to the profit and loss account of £3,500 for the year to 31 December 20X1 and has recognised that there is a debtor or prepayment of £900 at 31 December 20X1.

- The £900 balance will appear in the balance sheet in current assets under the heading of prepayments. Prepayments appear just below debtors, or may be included with debtors and described as debtors and prepayments.

## 3.4    EXAMPLE WITH OPENING PREPAYMENT

In writing up expense accounts, care must be taken to remember to include any opening balances on the account which were accruals or prepayments at the end of the previous year. For example, John Simnel pays his annual rates bill of £4,000 in two equal instalments of £2,000 each on 1 April and 1 October each year.

Write up the rates account for the year ended 31 December 20X1.

## 3.5    SOLUTION

His rates account for the year to 31 December 20X1 would look like this:

**Rates**

| 20X1 | | £ | 20X1 | | £ |
|------|------|------|------|------|------|
| 1 Jan | Bal b/d ($\frac{3}{6} \times 2,000$) | 1,000 | | | |
| 1 April | Cash | 2,000 | 31 Dec | P&L a/c (bal fig) | 4,000 |
| 1 Oct | Cash | 2,000 | 31 Dec | Bal c/d ($\frac{3}{6} \times 2,000$) | 1,000 |
| | | ───── | | | ───── |
| | | 5,000 | | | 5,000 |
| | | ───── | | | ───── |

Note that at 1 January 20X1 there is an opening debit balance on the account of £1,000. This is the three months rates from 1 January 20X1 to 31 March 20X1 that had been paid for on 1 October 20X0. You were not specifically told this opening balance but would be expected to work it out from the information given.

The treatment of a prepaid expense is to credit the expense account with the amount of the prepayment, thereby reducing the expense to be charged to the profit and loss account, and to carry the balance forward as a debtor, a prepayment, in the balance sheet.

## ACTIVITY 4

John Ball is a sole trader with a 30 June year-end. His purchase ledger includes all invoices dated up to and including 30 June 20X8. Estimate the closing prepayments for the following items:

(a)    An insurance invoice for £2,136 paid in January 20X8 for the year to 28 February 20X9.

(b)    £7,800 rent for the quarter to 31 July 20X8 paid in April 20X8.

*For a suggested answer, see the 'Answers' section at the end of the book.*

## ACTIVITY 5

James Bell has a December year-end. Prepare the T-accounts for the following expense headings and calculate the annual profit and loss account charge.

(a)   Insurance. Invoices totalling £7,295 were received and posted to the ledgers during the year. The opening prepayment was £3,672 and the closing prepayment is £4,107.

(b)   Rent. Invoices totalling £19,540 were received and posted to the ledgers during the year. The opening prepayment was £3,908 and the closing prepayment is £2,798.

*For a suggested answer, see the 'Answers' section at the end of the book.*

### 3.6   JOURNAL TO RECORD A PREPAYMENT

The correct journal to record a year end prepayment is:

Debit   Prepayment (B/S)

Credit   Expense account (P&L)

# 4   EXPENSES WITH PREPAID AND ACCRUED ELEMENTS

### 4.1   INTRODUCTION

Some expenses may have both brought down and carried down accruals and prepayments. An example is a telephone bill which comprises two elements: a charge for the rental of the telephones and lines paid in advance, and a further charge for calls made, paid in arrears.

### 4.2   EXAMPLE

The details of John Simnel's telephone bills for 20X1 are as follows:

|  | £ |
|---|---|
| Quarterly rental payable in advance on 1 February, 1 May, 1 August and 1 November each year | 60 |
| Calls paid in arrears for previous three months |  |
| 1 February 20X1 | 120 |
| 1 May 20X1 | 99 |
| 1 August 20X1 | 144 |
| 1 November 20X1 | 122 |
| 1 February 20X2 | 132 |

**You are required** to write up his telephone account for the year to 31 December 20X1.

## 4.3 SOLUTION

**Step 1**    Calculate and enter the opening balances for accruals or prepayments at the beginning of the year in the telephone account.

- The opening debit balance represents the prepayment of the rental at 31 December 20X0. On 1 November 20X0 a payment of £60 would have been made to cover the period from 1 November 20X0 to 31 January 20X1. The amount of the 20X1 expense paid in 20X0 is therefore $\frac{1}{3} \times £60 = £20$.

- The opening credit balance represents the calls made in November and December 20X0 that were not paid for until 1 February 20X1. This can be approximated as $\frac{2}{3} \times £120 = £80$.

**Telephone**

| 20X1 | | £ | 20X1 | | £ |
|---|---|---|---|---|---|
| 1 Jan | Bal b/d | 20 | 1 Jan | Bal b/d | 80 |

**Step 2**    Enter the cash payments made during the year.

**Telephone**

| 20X1 | | £ | 20X1 | | £ |
|---|---|---|---|---|---|
| 1 Jan | Bal b/d | 20 | 1 Jan | Bal b/d | 80 |
| 1 Feb | Cash – rental | 60 | | | |
| 1 Feb | Cash – calls | 120 | | | |
| 1 May | Cash – rental | 60 | | | |
| 1 May | Cash – calls | 99 | | | |
| 1 Aug | Cash – rental | 60 | | | |
| 1 Aug | Cash – calls | 144 | | | |
| 1 Nov | Cash – rental | 60 | | | |
| 1 Nov | Cash – calls | 122 | | | |

**Step 3**    Calculate and enter the closing accruals and prepayments.

- There is a closing prepayment of telephone rental. £60 was paid on 1 November 20X1 for the following three months' rental. This covers November and December 20X1 as well as January 20X2. The prepayment is the amount that relates to January 20X2 = $\frac{1}{3} \times £60 = £20$.

- The accrued expense at 31 December 20X1 is for November and December's calls that will not be paid for until 1 February 20X2. These can be estimated as $\frac{2}{3} \times £132 = £88$.

**Step 4**    Enter the profit and loss account charge as the balancing figure in the account.

**Telephone**

| 20X1 | | £ | 20X1 | | £ |
|---|---|---|---|---|---|
| 1 Jan | Bal b/d | 20 | 1 Jan | Bal b/d | 80 |
| 1 Feb | Cash – rental | 60 | 31 Dec | P&L a/c (bal fig) | 733 |
| 1 Feb | Cash – calls | 120 | 31 Dec | Bal c/d (prepayment) | 20 |
| 1 May | Cash – rental | 60 | | | |
| 1 May | Cash – calls | 99 | | | |
| 1 Aug | Cash – rental | 60 | | | |
| 1 Aug | Cash – calls | 144 | | | |
| 1 Nov | Cash – rental | 60 | | | |
| 1 Nov | Cash – calls | 122 | | | |
| 31 Dec | Bal c/d (accrual) | 88 | | | |
| | | ——— | | | ——— |
| | | 833 | | | 833 |
| | | ——— | | | ——— |
| 20X2 | | | 20X2 | | |
| 1 Jan | Bal b/d (prepayment) | 20 | 1 Jan | Bal b/d (accrual) | 88 |

The profit and loss account expense that was included in the account as a balancing figure could be proved although this is not generally necessary in actual questions.

| | £ |
|---|---|
| Rental charge for 1 January to 31 December 20X1 ($4 \times 60$) | 240 |
| Calls: | |
| 1 January to 31 January 20X1 ($\frac{1}{3} \times 120$) | 40 |
| 1 February to 30 April 20X1 | 99 |
| 1 May to 31 July 20X1 | 144 |
| 1 August to 31 October 20X1 | 122 |
| 1 November to 31 December 20X1 ($\frac{2}{3} \times 132$) | 88 |
| | ——— |
| | 733 |
| | ——— |

Where there are opening and closing accruals and/or prepayments, the easiest way to get the right figure for the profit and loss charge is to calculate it as the balancing figure on the account after entering all accruals/prepayments and cash paid in the year.

# 5 MISCELLANEOUS INCOME

## 5.1 INTRODUCTION

In addition to accrued and prepaid expenses, some organisations also have sources of miscellaneous income which may also be received in advance or arrears. The key to understanding the entries in income accounts is that, in comparison with expense accounts, they are the opposite way round.

## 5.2 EXAMPLE

John Simnel sublets part of his factory space for a quarterly rental in advance of £900. The payments are due on 1 March, 1 June, 1 September and 1 December each year and are always paid on time.

Write up his rental receivable account for the year ended 31 December 20X1.

## 5.3 SOLUTION

The rent receivable account for the year to 31 December 20X1 will show both an opening and a closing balance of rental paid in advance of ($\frac{2}{3} \times £900$) = £600.

Income received in advance results in a liability. In this case John Simnel 'owes' two months of factory space, worth £600. The opening and closing balances will therefore be credit balances brought down.

The cash received in the year will be credit entries in the rent receivable account (debit in the cash account).

The income which will be transferred to the profit and loss account from the rent receivable account will be £3,600 (4 × £900).

### Rental receivable

| 20X1 | | £ | 20X1 | | £ |
|---|---|---|---|---|---|
| | | | 1 Jan | Bal b/d | 600 |
| | | | 1 Mar | Cash at bank | 900 |
| | | | 1 June | Cash at bank | 900 |
| 31 Dec | P&L a/c | 3,600 | 1 Sept | Cash at bank | 900 |
| 31 Dec | Bal c/d | 600 | 1 Dec | Cash at bank | 900 |
| | | ——— | | | ——— |
| | | 4,200 | | | 4,200 |
| | | ——— | | | ——— |
| | | | 20X2 | | |
| | | | 1 Jan | Bal b/d | 600 |

The £600 credit balance brought down at 31 December 20X1 would be shown in the balance sheet as a creditor and described as **income received in advance** or **deferred income**.

It is probably best not to think in terms of accruals and prepayments when dealing with income. Think instead of whether the business is owed money at the end of the year (in which case the balance will be brought down on the debit side as an asset) or whether it has received some income in advance i.e. it effectively 'owes' it to the payer (in which case the balance would be brought down on the credit side as a liability.

## ACTIVITY 6

Jane Bolt is preparing her accounts for the year-ending 31 December 20X6. She has two sources of miscellaneous income; franchising and rents. Prepare the T accounts for these items and calculate the annual income to be claimed in the profit and loss account.

(a)   Franchising. £56,364 of franchise income was received during the year. £14,726 related to income earned in 20X5, and she estimates that there is a further £28,645 receivable in respect of 20X6. (This was all received in January and February 20X7.)

(b)   Rent. Invoices totalling £74,936 were issued and posted to the ledgers during the year. £23,985 of these invoices relates to periods in 20X7. In 20X5 £17,625 of invoices were issued in respect of rent periods in 20X6.

*For a suggested answer, see the 'Answers' section at the end of the book.*

# 6 PREPAYMENTS AND ACCRUALS IN THE FINANCIAL STATEMENTS

## 6.1 THE BALANCE SHEET

A balance on an income or expense account represents a prepayment or an accrual and will be shown in the balance sheet with all other account balances. They appear under the headings current assets and current liabilities as they tend to be short term in nature. The extract from a balance sheet, below, shows their usual positions.

|  | £ | £ |
|---|---|---|
| Current assets |  |  |
| Stock |  | x |
| Debtors |  | x |
| **Prepayments** |  | x |
| Cash at bank |  | x |
| Cash in hand |  | x |
|  |  | x |
| Current liabilities |  |  |
| Creditors | x |  |
| **Accruals and deferred income** | x |  |
|  |  | (x) |
| Net current assets |  | x |

## 6.2 THE PROFIT AND LOSS ACCOUNT

Accruals or prepayments are included within the normal expense charges in the profit and loss account. An accrual has the effect of increasing the charge for an expense and a prepayment will reduce the charge. Similarly, income received in advance (or deferred income) will decrease the income credited to the profit and loss account and income due (or in arrears) will increase the amount credited.

# CONCLUSION

At the end of each accounting period, adjustments must be made to ensure that the expense **incurred** in the period is charged to the profit and loss account.

- Expenses incurred but not paid for are accruals. They are charged (debited) to the profit and loss account (increasing the relevant expense) and appear as a liability (a credit) on the balance sheet.

- Expenses paid for but not yet incurred are prepayments. They are credited to the profit and loss account, reducing expenses, and appear as an asset (a debit) on the balance sheet.

Similarly, adjustments must be made to ensure that the income **due** in the period is credited to the profit and loss account:

- Income received in advance is removed (debited) from the profit and loss account and appears as a liability (a credit) on the balance sheet.

- Income earned but not yet received or invoiced is credited to the profit and loss account, increasing income, and appears as an asset (a debit) on the balance sheet. This is known as accrued income.

# KEY TERMS

**Accruals concept** – income and expenses should be matched together and dealt with in the profit and loss account for the period to which they relate regardless of the period in which the cash was actually received or paid.

**Accrual** – an item of expense that has been incurred during the accounting period but has not been paid at the period end. Increases expenses in the profit and loss account and is shown as a liability on the balance sheet.

**Prepayment** – an item of expense that has been paid during the current accounting period but will not be incurred until the next accounting period. Decreases expenses in the profit and loss account and is shown as an asset on the balance sheet.

**Accrued income** – income that has been earned but not yet received at the accounting period end. Increases income in the profit and loss account and is shown as an asset in the balance sheet.

**Deferred income** – income that has been received in advance of a service being provided. Decreases income in the profit and loss account and is shown as a liability in the balance sheet.

# SELF TEST QUESTIONS

*Paragraph*

1    Why is it important to include the expense incurred in the period in the
     profit and loss account, rather than the cash paid or the bills received?                1

2    What is an accrual?                                                                      2.1

3    What do we call an expense that has been paid in advance of the period
     to which it relates?                                                                     3.1

4    Explain how a single expense can have an accrued element and a
     prepaid element.                                                                         4.1

5    Is rental income received in advance brought down as a debit or a credit
     balance at the period end?                                                               5.3

6    How are accruals and prepayments shown in the balance sheet?                             6.1

7    What effect will an accrual have on the amount of an expense included in
     the profit and loss account?                                                             6.2

# ADDITIONAL QUESTIONS

1    Alan has an accounting year that ends on 30 June. He has paid rent of £4,500 for the
     six months to 31 August. What accrual or prepayment is required when preparing
     accounts for the year ended 30 June?

     **A**    Accrual of £1,500

     **B**    Accrual of £3,000

     **C**    Prepayment of £1,500

     **D**    Prepayment of £3,000

2    Gina has an accounting year that ends on 31 March. She estimates that as at 31
     March, her sales staff have earned sales commission of £4,000 which has not yet
     been recorded in the accounts. How should the accrual or prepayment be accounted
     for when preparing the profit and loss account for the year to 31 March?

     **A**    Debit Accrual £4,000, Credit Commissions £4,000

     **B**    Debit Prepayment £4,000, Credit Commissions £4,000

     **C**    Debit Commissions £4,000, Credit Prepayment £4,000

     **D**    Debit Commissions £4,000, Credit Accrual £4,000

*For suggested answers, see the 'Answers' section at the end of the book.*

## PRACTICE QUESTION

### RATES AND RENTALS

(a)   A trader paid the following business rates bills during 20X7 and 20X8.

| Date of invoice | Amount £ | Relating to |
| --- | --- | --- |
| 8 March 20X7 | 160 | 3 months to 31 March 20X7 |
| 8 April 20X7 | 920 | 12 months to 31 March 20X8 |
| 10 April 20X8 | 1,260 | 12 months to 31 March 20X9 |

**Required:**

Write up the rates account for the year ended 31 December 20X7.

(b)   A farmer rents out a car park and field to a local organisation who wish to hold a car boot sale in January 20X4.  They pay £250 in advance, on 3 December 20X3.  How would this transaction be treated in the 20X3 accounts of the farmer?  Briefly explain the effect in the 20X4 accounts.

*For a suggested answer, see the 'Answers' section at the end of the book.*

# Chapter 7

# THE EXTENDED TRIAL BALANCE

In your earlier studies, a trial balance, extracted from the nominal ledger was used to draft a simple profit and loss account and balance sheet.

In practice, adjustments, such as depreciation, accruals and prepayments, irrecoverable debts, closing stock, and provisions need to be made before the financial statements are produced.

These can be incorporated into an extended trial balance (ETB). This is a worksheet which takes an initial trial balance, makes all the year end adjustments and then produces a draft balance sheet and profit and loss account.

## CONTENTS

## LEARNING OUTCOMES

At the end of this chapter, you should be able to:

- record the correction of errors on the ETB

- record post-trial balance adjustments on the ETB

- extend and complete the ETB.

# 1 THE EXTENDED TRIAL BALANCE

## 1.1 INTRODUCTION

**Definition**  **Extended trial balance** – a worksheet which takes a trial balance, makes year-end adjustments and can then be used to produce a draft balance sheet and profit and loss account.

## 1.2 WHAT AN EXTENDED TRIAL BALANCE LOOKS LIKE

An extended trial balance (ETB) can be seen below, with an explanation of the layout:

### Extended trial balance at 31 December 20X2

| Account | Balances per ledger (trial balance) | | Ref | Adjustments | | Accrued | Prepaid | Profit and loss | | Balance sheet | |
|---|---|---|---|---|---|---|---|---|---|---|---|
| | Dr £ | Cr £ | | Dr £ | Cr £ | £ | £ | Dr £ | Cr £ | Dr £ | Cr £ |
| ..................... | | | | | | | | | | | |
| ..................... | | | | | | | | | | | |
| Accrued/prepaid | | | | | | | | | | | |
| Totals | | | | | | | | | | | |
| Profit for year | | | | | | | | | | | |

(a)  **Account** – the first column is used to list all the nominal ledger accounts.

(b)  **Trial balance** – the next section containing two columns is used to list the balances on all the nominal ledger accounts.  The balance on an account is put into either the debit column or the credit column as appropriate.

(c)  **Ref and adjustments** – these sections are used to record any period-end adjustments to the trial balance made via journals.  The journal references are put into the 'ref' column to enable the figures in the adjustment section to be traced back to source documentation. (Note that the 'ref' column will be omitted from future examples.)  Proper double entry is needed for each adjustment using the debit and credit columns.

(d)  **Accrued and prepaid** – these record the accruals and prepayments needed to adjust the transactions already recorded in the ledger accounts and on the trial balance.  The individual P&L account entries are recorded in these columns, and the posting to the balance sheet is done in total.

(e)  **Profit and loss** – account balances that belong in the profit and loss account will be carried across to one of these columns.

(f)  **Balance sheet** – account balances that belong in the balance sheet will be carried across to one of these columns.

It is of vital importance that the debit column total and credit column total of the trial balance and adjustments sections balance before completing the P&L and balance sheet columns.

## ACTIVITY 1

Take a piece of A4 paper, turn it sideways and prepare a proforma extended trial balance from memory. Do not put in any account names yet.

*For a suggested answer, see the 'Answers' section at the end of the book.*

### 1.3 FROM TRIAL BALANCE TO EXTENDED TRIAL BALANCE

The starting point for any extended trial balance is the trial balance. A trial balance is extracted from the nominal ledger in the normal way. If the double entry has been correct, then the trial balance will balance and can be inserted directly into the extended trial balance. (If the double entry has broken down somewhere, then the trial balance will not balance and a suspense account will be needed. This was covered in your earlier studies).

## ACTIVITY 2

The following balances have been extracted from the books of XYZ.

|  | Dr £ | Cr £ |
|---|---|---|
| Capital account | | 12,000 |
| Opening stock | 15,000 | |
| Sales | | 100,000 |
| Purchases | 40,000 | |
| Rent and rates | 10,000 | |
| Drawings | 12,000 | |
| Electricity | 2,000 | |
| Motor van cost | 8,000 | |
| Motor van accumulated depreciation | | 4,000 |
| Bank balance | 4,500 | |
| Trade debtors (sales ledger control account) | 20,000 | |
| Trade creditors (purchase ledger control account) | | 21,000 |
| Sundry expenses | 500 | |
| Wages and salaries | 25,000 | |
|  | 137,000 | 137,000 |

Set up an extended trial balance for XYZ, using the proforma you created in Activity 1.

*For a suggested answer, see the 'Answers' section at the end of the book.*

## 2 PERIOD END ADJUSTMENTS

**Definition** **Period end adjustments** are accounting adjustments to the trial balance required for the preparation of the period end financial accounts. They include:

- accruals and prepayments (Section 3)

- closing stock (Section 4)

- irrecoverable debts written off (earlier studies)

- movements on the allowance for debtors (earlier studies)

- depreciation (earlier studies)

- disposals of fixed assets (chapter 4)

- correction of errors (earlier studies)

- the creation of provisions.(earlier studies)

All the period end adjustments likely to arise have already been covered in previous chapters or earlier studies. The purpose of this section is to demonstrate how those adjustments are shown on the extended trial balance.

In most cases, the required journal entry, is entered into the adjustments columns, with the debit and credit entries being against the appropriate nominal ledger account.

Where the required account is not already showing in the trial balance, e.g. depreciation expense, this is added underneath all other nominal ledger accounts as an extra row.

---

### ACTIVITY 3

---

Using the example extended trial balance in Activity 2, produce the journals and make the following adjustments to the trial balance:

(a)    a depreciation charge for the year of £500;

(b)    an irrecoverable debt write off amounting to £1,000; and

(c)    correction for drawings of £200 incorrectly included in sundry expenses.

---

*For a suggested answer, see the 'Answers' section at the end of the book.*

## 3 ACCRUALS AND PREPAYMENTS

### 3.1 INTRODUCTION

Although they are also period end adjustments, accruals and prepayments are often shown as separate adjustments with their own columns in the extended trial balance, as seen in our proforma. Their treatment warrants separate attention only because it is slightly different in the extended trial balance compared with the ledger accounts. If anything, it is more straightforward.

### 3.2 HOW TO ENTER ACCRUALS INTO THE EXTENDED TRIAL BALANCE

When an expense accrual is calculated, it is entered in the expense ledger account by carrying down a balance. The balance c/d (above the total) has the effect of increasing the expense taken to the profit and loss account. The credit balance b/d (below the total) is the accrual shown in the balance sheet.

The double entry achieved by this process is:

Debit          Profit and loss expense account

Credit         Accrual in the balance sheet

In the extended trial balance the individual accruals are entered once in the 'accrued' column, against the relevant expense account.

When 'extending' the trial balance (TB) figures into the final financial statements columns, this entry is used twice, to achieve the above double entry:

(a)    First, it is added to the existing expense account balance in the TB to increase the charge to the profit and loss account.

(b)    Secondly, it is added into the total at the bottom of the 'accrued' column, which will represent total accruals for the period, and which will be shown as a liability in the balance sheet columns.

## ACTIVITY 4

Continuing with the example in Activity 3, the following accruals are needed at the year end:

| | |
|---|---|
| Electricity | £150 |
| Sundry expenses | £50 |

Show how these would be entered into the accrued column in your extended trial balance. Do not yet extend the trial balance into the financial statements columns.

*For a suggested answer, see the 'Answers' section at the end of the book.*

### 3.3 HOW TO ENTER PREPAYMENTS INTO THE EXTENDED TRIAL BALANCE

A prepayment on an expense account comprises a debit balance b/d which is the prepayment shown in the balance sheet and a credit entry for the balance c/d (above the total) which has the effect of reducing the expense taken to the profit and loss account. Again, this may be represented by a double entry:

Debit        Prepayment in the balance sheet

Credit       Profit and loss account expense

In the ETB, the prepayments are listed individually in the 'prepaid' column against the relevant expense account.

Again, when 'extending' the trial balance (TB) figures into the final financial statements columns, this entry is used twice, to achieve the above double entry:

- First, it is deducted from the existing expense account balance in the TB to reduce the charge to the profit and loss; and

- Secondly, it is added into the total at the bottom of the 'prepaid' column, which will represent total prepayments for the period, and which will appear as an asset in the balance sheet columns.

### ACTIVITY 5

Carrying on the last activity, a prepayment of rent of £800 is required. Show how this would be entered into the prepaid column in the ETB.

*For a suggested answer, see the 'Answers' section at the end of the book.*

## 4 STOCK AND THE EXTENDED TRIAL BALANCE

### 4.1 INTRODUCTION

In the chapter on stock it was shown that the period end adjustment to account for closing stock is:

Debit        Stock account (balance sheet)

Credit       Stock account (profit and loss account)

An entry is also required to transfer last year's closing stock, now forming this year's opening stock, to the profit and loss account:

Debit        Stock account (profit and loss account)

Credit       Stock account (balance sheet)

This section considers both entries in the ETB.

### 4.2 ENTERING CLOSING STOCK INTO THE EXTENDED TRIAL BALANCE

A new line is needed for *closing* stock. The closing stock value will then be entered twice, once in each of the debit and credit adjustment columns, against this line.

These two figures will be used as follows:

(a) debit – recorded as an asset in the balance sheet columns

(b) credit – record in the profit and loss to decrease the cost of sales expense.

---

### ACTIVITY 6

---

XYZ's closing stock was valued at £17,000. Show how this is recorded in the adjustments column of the ETB.

*For a suggested answer, see the 'Answers' section at the end of the book.*

### 4.3 OPENING STOCK AND THE EXTENDED TRIAL BALANCE

For extended trial balance purposes, the opening stock is cleared directly to the profit and loss columns when the trial balance is extended later. No adjustment is necessary at this stage.

## 5 COMPLETING THE EXTENDED TRIAL BALANCE

### 5.1 INTRODUCTION

The final step in preparing an extended trial balance is to complete the profit and loss and balance sheet columns.

### 5.2 EXTENDING THE ACCOUNT BALANCES ACROSS THE TRIAL BALANCE

Each account balance should be carried across, taking account of any entries in the adjustments columns, to the profit and loss / balance sheet columns.

This process requires:

(a) knowledge of which accounts go into the profit and loss account and which accounts go into the balance sheet

(b) careful addition (casting).

### 5.3 TOTAL ACCRUALS AND PREPAYMENTS

In cross-casting the individual expense lines, the effect of accruals and prepayments on the profit and loss charge is accounted for. The totals now need to be shown as liabilities and assets in the balance sheet columns.

To do this:

1      Subtotal the accrued and prepaid columns.

2      Show the total of the accrued column in the balance sheet credit column in a new row 'accruals'.

3      Show the total of the prepaid column in the balance sheet debit column in a new row 'prepayments'.

Work through the following activity carefully to ensure you understand where the figures in the last four columns came from and why they are in these columns.

## ACTIVITY 7

Starting with the trial balance and adjustments in Activity 6, extend each account into the appropriate financial statement columns, showing how accruals and prepayments are carried to the balance sheet columns.

*For a suggested answer, see the 'Answers' section at the end of the book.*

## 5.4   FINDING THE PROFIT OR LOSS FOR THE PERIOD

Having completed the profit and loss and balance sheet columns, the final step of the extended trial balance is to find the profit or loss for the period.

The steps for doing this are as follows:

**Step 1**     Add up the credit column of the profit and loss section.

**Step 2**     Add up the debit column of the profit and loss section.

**Step 3**     Take the total debit away from the total credit.

              If there are more credits than debits, a profit has been made, whereas an excess of debits over credits means a loss has been incurred.

**Step 4**     Insert the figure to make the two balances equal in the 'profit for year' box (under the totals row).

**Step 5**     If a profit has been made (more credits) a balancing figure will be required in the debit column. A loss (more debits) would go as a balancing figure on the credit side.

**Step 6**     Cast the two balance sheet columns (including total accruals and prepayments).

**Step 7**     Insert the same profit (or loss) figure as a balancing figure in the balance sheet. However, this time the profit figure goes as a balancing figure on the credit side whereas a loss would have to sit on the debit side.

Do not worry unduly about which side the profit figure or loss figure goes on. If the double entry has been maintained it will be obvious where the resultant figure lives.

## ACTIVITY 8

Complete the ETB from Activity 8 by calculating the profit or loss, using the result to balance the profit and loss and balance sheet columns.

*For a suggested answer, see the 'Answers' section at the end of the book.*

## CONCLUSION

The extended trial balance is a summary of every transaction that has taken place during the year (as extracted from the nominal ledger) and every period end adjustment required to prepare the financial statements.

It is produced as a first step in preparing the financial statements.

By making sure that the ETB columns balance, mistakes can be identified and corrected before the financial statements are prepared.

## KEY TERMS

**Extended trial balance** – a worksheet which takes a trial balance, makes all the year end adjustments and produces a draft balance sheet and profit and loss account.

**Period end adjustments** – adjustments made after the initial trial balance is extracted, but before the financial statements are prepared. Includes depreciation, accruals and prepayments.

## SELF TEST QUESTIONS

|  |  | *Paragraph* |
|---|---|---|
| 1 | What is an extended trial balance? | 1.1 |
| 2 | What are the six main headings on the extended trial balance? | 1.2 |
| 3 | Give four examples of period end adjustments that can be made on the extended trial balance. | 2 |
| 4 | How is a double entry in respect of an accrual achieved if only a single entry is made on the extended trial balance? | 3.2 |
| 5 | How is closing stock adjusted for on the extended trial balance? | 4.2 |
| 6 | How would you deduce the profit or loss for the period from the extended trial balance? | 5.4 |

## PRACTICE QUESTION

### ELMDALE

The trial balance of Elmdale at 31.12.X8 is as follows:

|  | Dr £ | Cr £ |
|---|---|---|
| Capital account |  | 7,802 |
| Stock | 2,700 |  |
| Sales |  | 21,417 |
| Purchases | 9,856 |  |
| Rates | 1,490 |  |
| Drawings | 4,206 |  |
| Electricity | 379 |  |
| Freehold shop | 7,605 |  |
| Freehold shop depreciation |  | 500 |
| Debtors | 2,742 |  |
| Allowance for debtors |  | 300 |
| Creditors |  | 3,617 |
| Cash at bank |  | 1,212 |
| Cash in hand | 66 |  |
| Sundry expenses | 2,100 |  |
| Wages and salaries | 3,704 |  |
|  | 34,848 | 34,848 |

In addition, Elmdale provides the following information:

(a)  Closing stock has been valued for accounts purposes at £3,060.

(b)  Rates includes a payment of £1,260 made on 10.4.X8 in respect of the year to 31.3.X9.

(c)  An electricity bill amounting to £132 in respect of the quarter to 28.2.X9 was paid on 7.3.X9.

(d)  The depreciation charge for the year is £190.

(e)  Irrecoverable debts of £200 are to be written off and an allowance of 5% of the remaining debtors is required.

Prepare a trading and profit and loss account for the year ended 31 December 20X8 and a balance sheet at that date, using an extended trial balance worksheet.

A blank worksheet is provided overleaf.

*For a suggested answer, see the 'Answers' section at the end of the book.*

| | Trial balance | | Adjustments | | Accrued | Prepaid | Profit and loss | | Balance sheet | |
|---|---|---|---|---|---|---|---|---|---|---|
| | Dr £ | Cr £ | Dr £ | Cr £ | £ | £ | Dr £ | Cr £ | Dr £ | Cr £ |
| Capital account | | | | | | | | | | |
| Stock | | | | | | | | | | |
| Sales | | | | | | | | | | |
| Purchases | | | | | | | | | | |
| Rates | | | | | | | | | | |
| Drawings | | | | | | | | | | |
| Electricity | | | | | | | | | | |
| Freehold shop | | | | | | | | | | |
| Shop depreciation | | | | | | | | | | |
| Debtors | | | | | | | | | | |
| Allowance for debtors | | | | | | | | | | |
| Creditors | | | | | | | | | | |
| Cash at bank | | | | | | | | | | |
| Cash in hand | | | | | | | | | | |
| Sundry expenses | | | | | | | | | | |
| Wages & salaries | | | | | | | | | | |
| Depreciation | | | | | | | | | | |
| Irrecoverable debts | | | | | | | | | | |
| Stock | | | | | | | | | | |
| Accruals/prepayments | | | | | | | | | | |
| Profit/loss for the year | | | | | | | | | | |
| | | | | | | | | | | |
| | | | | | | | | | | |

*For a suggested answer, see the 'Answers' section at the end of the book.*

# Chapter 8

# SOLE TRADER ACCOUNTS

In the previous chapter the extended trial balance was produced.

In this chapter financial statements in the accepted format for a sole trader are produced, with or without the use of an ETB.

After the final accounts have been prepared, the ledger accounts for the old year need to be closed off, and the opening balances for the new year brought forward. This process is covered at the end of this chapter.

## CONTENTS

1    Technique for producing a set of final accounts from a trial balance

2    Preparing an extended trial balance and accounts

3    Closing the books at the year end

## LEARNING OUTCOMES

At the end of this chapter, you should be able to:

- close off ledger accounts for preparation of final accounts

- prepare the final accounts (trading account, profit and loss account and balance sheet) for a sole trader

- record the profit or loss for the period and drawings in the capital account

- prepare the opening trial balance for the next accounting period.

## 1    TECHNIQUE FOR PRODUCING A SET OF FINAL ACCOUNTS FROM A TRIAL BALANCE

Not all organisations prepare an extended trial balance; some prepare accounts directly from an adjusted initial trial balance. This often happens in exam questions.

In exam questions, moving from a trial balance to the balance sheet and profit and loss account generally involves three steps, as follows:

**Step 1**     Working out the double entries for the adjustments.

**Step 2**     Working out the effect of these entries on the balances in the trial balance.

**Step 3**     Slotting the adjusted balances into the balance sheet and profit and loss account.

The following example illustrates how this is achieved.

**Example**

The trial balance of Jason and Co at 31 May 20X6 is as follows:

|  | £ | £ |
|---|---:|---:|
| Capital | | 15,258 |
| Drawings | 5,970 | |
| Purchases | 73,010 | |
| Returns inwards | 1,076 | |
| Returns outwards | | 3,720 |
| Discounts | 1,870 | 965 |
| Credit sales | | 96,520 |
| Cash sales | | 30,296 |
| Customs duty | 11,760 | |
| Carriage inwards | 2,930 | |
| Carriage outwards | 1,762 | |
| Salesman's commission | 711 | |
| Salesman's salary | 3,970 | |
| Office salaries | 7,207 | |
| Bank charges | 980 | |
| Loan interest | 450 | |
| Light and heat | 2,653 | |
| Sundry expenses | 2,100 | |
| Rent and rates | 7,315 | |
| Printing and postage | 2,103 | |
| Advertising | 1,044 | |
| Bad debts | 1,791 | |
| Allowance for debtors | | 437 |
| Stock | 7,650 | |
| Debtors | 10,760 | |
| Creditors | | 7,411 |
| Cash at bank | 2,534 | |
| Cash in hand | 75 | |
| New delivery van (less trade-in) | 2,200 | |
| Motor expenses | 986 | |
| Furniture and equipment: | | |
|     Cost | 8,000 | |
|     Depreciation at 1 June 20X5 | | 2,400 |
| Old delivery van: | | |
|     Cost | 2,100 | |
|     Depreciation at 1 June 20X5 | | 1,000 |
| Loan account at 9% (repayable in five years) | | 5,000 |
| | 163,007 | 163,007 |

You ascertain the following information:

(a) Closing stock has been valued for accounts purposes at £8,490.

(b) The motor van was sold on 1 June 20X5 and traded in against the cost of a new van. The trade-in price was £1,000 and the cost of the new van was £3,200.

(c) Depreciation on the straight line basis is to be charged at the following annual rates:

| | |
|---|---|
| Motor vans | 20% |
| Furniture and equipment | 10% |

(d) 5% of the closing debtors total is estimated to be doubtful.

**Required:**

1 Prepare ledger accounts to record the transactions listed in (a) to (d) above.

2 Prepare a trading and profit and loss account for the year ended 31 May 20X6 and a balance sheet as at 31 May 20X6.

**Solution**

**Step 1** Work through the adjustments.

T-accounts have been asked for: these will help you to work out the double entries and find the new balances on accounts.

(a) **Closing stock**

**Stock account (trading)**

| | £ | | £ |
|---|---|---|---|
| Transfer from balance sheet | 7,650 | Trading a/c (opening stock) | 7,650 |
| Trading a/c (closing stock) | 8,490 | Accounting adjustment | 8,490 |
| | ——— | | ——— |
| | 16,140 | | 16,140 |
| | ——— | | ——— |

**Stock account (balance sheet)**

| | £ | | £ |
|---|---|---|---|
| Per trial balance | 7,650 | Transfer to stock (trading) | 7,650 |
| Accounting adjustment | 8,490 | Balance c/d | 8,490 |
| | ——— | | ——— |
| | 16,140 | | 16,140 |
| | ——— | | ——— |
| Balance b/d (closing stock) | 8,490 | | |

(b)    **Van disposal**

### Van cost account

|                                    | £     |                   | £     |
|------------------------------------|-------|-------------------|-------|
| Old van per trial balance          | 2,100 | Disposal account  | 2,100 |
| New van – cash paid (per           |       | Balance c/d       | 3,200 |
|   trial balance)                   | 2,200 |                   |       |
| Part exchange value (disposal      |       |                   |       |
|   proceeds)                        | 1,000 |                   |       |
|                                    | ───── |                   | ───── |
|                                    | 5,300 |                   | 5,300 |
|                                    | ───── |                   | ───── |
| Balance b/d                        | 3,200 |                   |       |

### Van accumulated depreciation account

|                    | £     |                           | £     |
|--------------------|-------|---------------------------|-------|
| Disposal account   | 1,000 | Old van per trial balance | 1,000 |

### Old van disposal account

|                   | £     |                                    | £     |
|-------------------|-------|------------------------------------|-------|
| Van cost account  | 2,100 | Accumulated depreciation           | 1,000 |
|                   |       | Part exchange value                | 1,000 |
|                   |       | Loss on disposal (bal fig) P&L a/c | 100   |
|                   | ───── |                                    | ───── |
|                   | 2,100 |                                    | 2,100 |
|                   | ───── |                                    | ───── |

Note that the part exchange value is given in the question as £1,000.

(c)    **Depreciation**

Calculation

| | |
|---|---|
| Motor van (3,200 × 20%) | £640 |
| Furniture and equipment (8,000 × 10%) | £800 |

**Double entry**

### Van accumulated depreciation account

|                   | £     |                           | £     |
|-------------------|-------|---------------------------|-------|
| Disposal account  | 1,000 | Old van per trial balance | 1,000 |
| Balance c/d       | 640   | Depreciation expense a/c  |       |
|                   |       | (P&L)                     | 640   |
|                   | ───── |                           | ───── |
|                   | 1,640 |                           | 1,640 |
|                   | ───── |                           | ───── |
|                   |       | Balance b/d               | 640   |

### Furniture and equipment accumulated depreciation account

| | £ | | £ |
|---|---|---|---|
| Balance c/d | 3,200 | Per trial balance b/d | 2,400 |
| | | Depreciation expense a/c | |
| | | (P&L) | 800 |
| | ——— | | ——— |
| | 3,200 | | 3,200 |
| | ——— | | ——— |
| | | Balance b/d | 3,200 |

### Depreciation expense account

| | £ | | £ |
|---|---|---|---|
| Van | 640 | P&L account | 1,440 |
| Furniture & equipment | 800 | | |
| | ——— | | ——— |
| | 1,440 | | 1,440 |
| | ——— | | ——— |

(d)  **Debtors allowance**

**Calculation of allowance**

| | | | |
|---|---|---|---|
| Closing debtors per trial balance | = | £10,760 | |
| 5% of debtors (£10,760) | = | £538 | |
| Increase in allowance required | = | (538 – 437) | £101 |

**Double entry**

### Allowance for debtors account

| | £ | | £ |
|---|---|---|---|
| Required bal c/d | 538 | Per trial balance | 437 |
| (see working above) | | P&L a/c (bal fig) | 101 |
| | ——— | | ——— |
| | 538 | | 538 |
| | ——— | | ——— |
| | | Balance b/d | 538 |

### Irrecoverable debt expense account

| | £ | | £ |
|---|---|---|---|
| Per trial balance | 1,791 | P&L a/c | 1,892 |
| Allowance for debtors | 101 | | |
| | ——— | | ——— |
| | 1,892 | | 1,892 |
| | ——— | | ——— |

**Step 2**     Produce the adjusted trial balance from the original trial balance and your journals and workings.  It is important to keep neat workings to support your figures.

## Adjusted trial balance

| | £ | £ |
|---|---:|---:|
| Capital | | 15,258 |
| Drawings | 5,970 | |
| Purchases | 73,010 | |
| Returns inwards | 1,076 | |
| Returns outwards | | 3,720 |
| Discounts | 1,870 | 965 |
| Credit sales | | 96,520 |
| Cash sales | | 30,296 |
| Customs duty | 11,760 | |
| Carriage inwards | 2,930 | |
| Carriage outwards | 1,762 | |
| Salesman's commission | 711 | |
| Salesman's salary | 3,970 | |
| Office salaries | 7,207 | |
| Bank charges | 980 | |
| Loan interest | 450 | |
| Light and heat | 2,653 | |
| Sundry expenses | 2,100 | |
| Rent and rates | 7,315 | |
| Printing and postage | 2,103 | |
| Advertising | 1,044 | |
| Irrecoverable debts (1,791 + 101) | 1,892 | |
| Allowance for debtors (437 + 101) | | 538 |
| Stock (balance sheet) | 8,490 | |
| Debtors | 10,760 | |
| Creditors | | 7,411 |
| Cash at bank | 2,534 | |
| Cash in hand | 75 | |
| Motor expenses | 986 | |
| Furniture and equipment: | | |
|     Cost | 8,000 | |
|     Depreciation at 1 June 20X5 | | 3,200 |
| Delivery van: | | |
|     Cost | 3,200 | |
|     Depreciation at 1 June 20X5 | | 640 |
| Loan account at 9% (repayable in five years) | | 5,000 |
| Stock (P&L) | 7,650 | 8,490 |
| Depreciation expense: | | |
|     Van | 640 | |
|     Equipment | 800 | |
| Loss on sale of van | 100 | |
| | 172,038 | 172,038 |

**Step 3**        Prepare the profit and loss account and balance sheet.

(a)

**Trading and profit and loss account for the year ended 31 May 20X6**

|  | £ | £ | £ |
|---|---|---|---|
| Sales: |  |  |  |
| Credit |  |  | 96,520 |
| Cash |  |  | 30,296 |
|  |  |  | 126,816 |
| Less: sales returns |  |  | (1,076) |
|  |  |  | 125,740 |
| Opening stock | 7,650 |  |  |
| Purchases | 73,010 |  |  |
| Less: purchase returns | (3,720) |  |  |
|  | 76,940 |  |  |
| Carriage inwards | 2,930 |  |  |
| Customs duty | 11,760 |  |  |
|  | 91,630 |  |  |
| Closing stock | (8,490) |  |  |
| Cost of sales |  |  | 83,140 |
| Gross profit |  |  | 42,600 |
| Discount received |  |  | 965 |
|  |  |  | 43,565 |
| Less: Expenses |  |  |  |
| Depreciation: |  |  |  |
| Van |  | 640 |  |
| Equipment |  | 800 |  |
| Loss on disposal |  | 100 |  |
| Irrecoverable debts |  | 1,892 |  |
| Light and heat |  | 2,653 |  |
| Rent and rates |  | 7,315 |  |
| Discount allowed |  | 1,870 |  |
| Carriage outwards |  | 1,762 |  |
| Salesman's commission |  | 711 |  |
| Salesman's salary |  | 3,970 |  |
| Office salaries |  | 7,207 |  |
| Bank charges |  | 980 |  |
| Loan interest |  | 450 |  |
| Sundry expenses |  | 2,100 |  |
| Printing and postage |  | 2,103 |  |
| Advertising |  | 1,044 |  |
| Motor expenses |  | 986 |  |
|  |  |  | (36,583) |
| Net profit |  |  | 6,982 |

(b)

### Balance sheet at 31 May 20X6

|  | Cost £ | Acc dep'n £ | £ |
|---|---|---|---|
| Fixed assets: |  |  |  |
| Motor van | 3,200 | 640 | 2,560 |
| Furniture and equipment | 8,000 | 3,200 | 4,800 |
|  | 11,200 | 3,840 | 7,360 |
| Current assets: |  |  |  |
| Stock |  | 8,490 |  |
| Debtors | 10,760 |  |  |
| Less: Allowance for debtors | (538) |  |  |
|  |  | 10,222 |  |
| Cash at bank |  | 2,534 |  |
| Cash in hand |  | 75 |  |
|  |  | 21,321 |  |
| Less current liabilities: |  |  |  |
| Trade creditors |  | (7,411) |  |
|  |  |  | 13,910 |
|  |  |  | 21,270 |
| Less: Long-term liability |  |  | (5,000) |
|  |  |  | 16,270 |
| Capital account: |  |  |  |
| Balance at 1 June 20X5 |  |  | 15,258 |
| Net profit for the year |  |  | 6,982 |
|  |  |  | 22,240 |
| Drawings |  |  | (5,970) |
| Balance at 31 May 20X6 |  |  | 16,270 |

### Notes on presentation

(a)  The trading account includes all expenditure incurred in bringing the goods to their present location and condition. This includes:

   (i)  purchase cost including import duty

   (ii)  carriage inwards and freight costs.

In contrast carriage outwards is treated as an expense of selling and is included with all the other expenses. Note that both carriage inwards and carriage outwards are debits (i.e. expenses).

**Definition**  **Carriage inwards** is the cost of bringing in raw materials from suppliers. Carriage outwards is the delivery charge incurred in supplying goods to customers.

'Returns' often causes difficulties. Returns inwards are the same as sales returns. Since sales are credits, sales returns are debits. For presentation purposes, sales returns are deducted from sales. In the same way purchase returns are deducted from purchases.

The discounts are shown as one line in the trial balance with both a debit and a credit balance. Remember that expenses are debit balances while items of income are credit balances. Therefore the discount allowed (given) is the debit balance and the discount received the credit balance.

In examinations the answers should precede the workings, which should clearly be labelled as such. The idea behind this is that the examiner only wishes to look at the workings if errors have been made – hopefully he will not need to.

If the workings are numbered then a reference to the working can be made in the final accounts.

# 2 PREPARING AN EXTENDED TRIAL BALANCE AND ACCOUNTS

This section follows the accounts production process from the extraction of the trial balance through to the preparation of the profit and loss account and the balance sheet. Work through the Guidance and the Solution carefully and then attempt the Activity.

## 2.1 EXAMPLE

Jill is a sole trader running a business making and selling traditional jewellery both locally and abroad. She has just finished her second year of trade, and the trial balance for this year is noted below. Her year-end is 30 June 20X8.

### Jill: Trial balance for the year ended 30 June 20X8

|  | Dr £ | Cr £ |
|---|---|---|
| Sales |  | 685,000 |
| Stock 1 July 20X7 | 43,250 |  |
| Purchases | 327,500 |  |
| Fixed assets at cost |  |  |
| Equipment | 97,600 |  |
| Motor vehicles | 43,400 |  |
| Fixed assets: Accumulated depreciation: 1 July 20X7 |  |  |
| Equipment |  | 14,280 |
| Motor vehicles |  | 13,500 |
| Rent | 71,898 |  |
| Salaries and wages | 130,000 |  |
| Carriage inwards | 3,456 |  |
| Carriage outwards | 10,000 |  |
| Postage and stationery | 11,892 |  |
| Trade debtors | 65,200 |  |
| Trade creditors |  | 28,478 |
| Insurance | 9,312 |  |
| Irrecoverable debts written off during the year | 4,825 |  |
| Petty cash | 1,190 |  |
| Sundry expenditure | 28,017 |  |
| Capital account as at 1 July 20X7 |  | 100,000 |
| Drawings | 134,601 |  |
| 10% Loan repayable in 20Y6 |  | 200,000 |
| Loan interest paid | 15,000 |  |
| Bank balance | 44,117 |  |
|  | 1,041,258 | 1,041,258 |

**Notes**

(a)     Stock was counted on 30 June 20X8 and valued at £32,900.

(b)     Equipment is depreciated at 10% per annum on a straight line basis.

(c)     Motor vehicles are depreciated at 25% pa on a reducing balance basis.

(d)     Although only £15,000 interest has been paid (as shown on the trial balance), a full year's interest at 10% should be charged in the accounts.

(e)     Insurance includes £3,504 paid on certain items covering the year to 30 November 20X8.

(f)     The rent for the year was £15,000 per quarter. However, the landlord was accidentally over paid just before the year end.

(g)     On 15 June 20X8 Jill paid a £900 electricity bill for the quarter to 30 April 20X8 and a £456 water bill for the quarter ending 31 May 20X8. These expenses are included in sundry expenditure. Jill has not paid or accounted for any electricity or water consumed since then.

**Required:**

(a)     Prepare an extended trial balance for Jill for the year ended 30 June 20X8.

(b)     Prepare a profit and loss account, balance sheet and capital account for Jill for the year ended 30 June 20X8 in a format suitable for presentation to the proprietor, bank manager and other interested parties.

Use the formats provided for you.

**Guidance**

1     Copy the balances from the trial balance given to you in the question onto the extended trial balance work sheet supplied overleaf. Make sure that you have extracted the numbers correctly. This can be done by adding up the columns and making sure that they still balance.

2     Work through the information in the **Notes** methodically, noting any adjustments required in the appropriate column of the ETB work sheet.

    (a)     *Stock was counted on 30 June 20X8 and valued at £32,900.*

        This adjustment will normally be shown in the adjustment columns of the ETB. Remember that the debit (asset) will be taken to the balance sheet and that the credit reduces cost of sales in the profit and loss account.

    (b)     *Equipment is depreciated at 10% per annum on a straight line basis.*

        Calculate the charge and then enter it onto the ETB.

        The charge will be a debit in the adjustments column and will be taken to the profit and loss account. The work sheet has already allocated a line for this charge.

The credit will increase the accumulated depreciation in the balance sheet. The TB already shows the brought forward balance. This year's credit will be entered into the adjustments column of the TB on the same line as the brought forward balance.

(c)    *Motor vehicles are depreciated at 25% pa on a reducing balance basis.*

As above. Because this is to be calculated on the reducing balance basis make sure that you work out the brought forward net book value before calculating the charge.

(d)    *Although only £15,000 interest has been paid (as recorded in the nominal ledger and on the TB), a full year's interest at 10% should be charged in the accounts.*

An accrual is probably needed here. Calculate the annual charge and compare this to what has been recorded in the trial balance. If the recorded amount is less than the full annual charge then the difference must be accrued for.

The ETB records accrued charges to the profit and loss account on a line by line basis. In this case the accrual will be entered into the accruals column on the loan interest line, increasing the charge taken to the profit and loss account.

The balance sheet entry will be dealt with later. See Guidance 4.

(e)    *Insurance includes £3,504 paid on certain items covering the year to 30 November 20X8.*

Insurance is normally paid in advance, giving rise to prepayments at the year-end.

In this case work out how much of the £3,504 mentioned relates to the period after the year-end (i.e. July through to November).

The ETB records prepayments on a line by line basis against the relevant profit and loss account charge. In this case the prepayment will be entered into the prepayments column on the insurance line, reducing the charge taken to the profit and loss account.

The balance sheet entry will be dealt with later. See Guidance 5.

(f)    *The rent for the year was £15,000 per quarter. However, the landlord was accidentally over paid just before the year end.*

This will also create a prepayment. Work out the correct annual charge and then put through a prepayment to counteract the overpayment.

(g)    *On 15 June 20X8 Jill paid a £900 electricity bill for the quarter to 30 April 20X8 and a £456 water bill for the quarter ending 31 May 20X8. These expenses are included in sundry expenditure. Jill has not paid or accounted for any electricity or water consumed since then.*

In both cases, the unpaid expense to the year end must be accrued for. The amount will have to be estimated on the basis of past consumption.

The electricity bill is £900 per quarter, and there were two months between the date of the last bill and the year-end. Therefore the business has probably consumed about £600 since the last invoice and this will have to be accrued for.

The water bill is £456 per quarter. One month elapsed between the last bill and the year-end and so an accrual of £152 will be needed (£456/3 months).

The total accrual for these two items will be £752 which will be included in sundry expenditure.

3    Add up the adjustment columns. The debit and credit columns should be equal. If they aren't make sure that you have entered the adjustments on the correct sides and for the correct amounts.

4    Add up the accruals column. The total will be taken to the credit side of the balance sheet. (The charge will be taken to the profit and loss account on a line by line basis.)

5    Add up the prepayments column. The total will be taken to the debit side of the balance sheet. (The credit entry will be taken to the profit and loss account on a line by line basis.)

6    Extend the trial balance by adding the lines across and entering the totals into the correct columns in the profit and loss and balance sheet sections of the ETB.

Remember that capital and drawings belong in the balance sheet.

7    Balance off the profit and loss columns.

(a)    If the balancing figure is on the debit side than the business has made a profit. (Sales and other credits exceed expenses.) The other half of this entry will be a credit to capital in the balance sheet.

(b)    If the balancing figure is on the credit side than the business has made a loss. (Expenses are greater than the sales and other credits.) The other half of this entry will be a debit to capital in the balance sheet.

If the profit and loss account and balance sheet columns do not balance each other out then you have made a mistake when extending the trial balance. Go back and check stage six.

You should have calculated a profit of £53,121.

8    Extract the figures from the profit and loss and balance sheet sections of the ETB and enter them into the financial statements using the formats provided.

**Extended trial balance for Jill at 30 June 20X8**

| | Trial balance | | Adjustments | | Accrued | Prepaid | Profit & loss | | Balance sheet | |
|---|---|---|---|---|---|---|---|---|---|---|
| | Dr | Cr | Dr | Cr | Dr to P&L | Cr to P&L | Dr | Cr | Dr | Cr |
| | £ | £ | £ | £ | £ | £ | £ | £ | £ | £ |
| Sales | | | | | | | | | | |
| Opening stock | | | | | | | | | | |
| Purchases | | | | | | | | | | |
| Equipment at cost | | | | | | | | | | |
| Depreciation | | | | | | | | | | |
| Vehicles at cost | | | | | | | | | | |
| Depreciation | | | | | | | | | | |
| Rent | | | | | | | | | | |
| Salaries and wages | | | | | | | | | | |
| Carriage inwards | | | | | | | | | | |
| Carriage outwards | | | | | | | | | | |
| Postage and stationery | | | | | | | | | | |
| Trade debtors | | | | | | | | | | |
| Trade creditors | | | | | | | | | | |
| Insurance | | | | | | | | | | |
| Debts written off | | | | | | | | | | |
| Petty cash | | | | | | | | | | |
| Sundry expenditure | | | | | | | | | | |
| Opening capital | | | | | | | | | | |
| Drawings | | | | | | | | | | |
| 10% Loan (20Y6) | | | | | | | | | | |
| Loan interest paid | | | | | | | | | | |
| Bank balance | | | | | | | | | | |
| | | | | | | | | | | |
| Closing stock (B/S, P&L) | | | | | | | | | | |
| Dep'n charge: Equipment | | | | | | | | | | |
| Motors | | | | | | | | | | |
| Total adjustments etc | | | | | | | | | | |
| | | | | | Cr: B/S | Dr: B/S | | | | |
| | | | | | | | | | | |
| Profit transferred to B/S | | | | | | | | | | |
| | | | | | | | | | | |

**Jill: Profit and loss account for the year ended 30 June 20X8**

|  | £ | £ |
|---|---|---|
| **Sales** | | |
| **Cost of sales** | | |
|     Opening stock | | |
|     Add: purchases | | |
|     Add: carriage inwards | | |
|     Less: closing stock | ————— | |
| | | ————— |
| **Gross profit** | | |
| *Expenses* | | |
| Rent and rates | | |
| Wages and salaries | | |
| Carriage outwards | | |
| Postage and stationery | | |
| Insurance | | |
| Irrecoverable debts | | |
| Sundry expenses | | |
| Depreciation:   Equipment | | |
|                 Motors | ————— | |
| | | ————— |
| **Operating profit** | | |
| Interest payable | | ————— |
| **Profit for the year** | | ————— |

**Jill: Balance sheet as at 30 June 20X8**

|  | Cost £ | Depreciation £ | NBV £ |
|---|---|---|---|
| **Fixed assets** | | | |
| Equipment | | | |
| Motor vehicles | | | |
| | ———— | ———— | ———— |
| | ———— | ———— | |
| **Current assets** | | | |
| Stocks | | | |
| Trade debtors | | | |
| Prepayments | | | |
| Bank and cash | | ———— | |
| | | ———— | |
| **Current liabilities** | | | |
| Trade creditors | | | |
| Accruals | | ———— | |
| | | ———— | |
| **Net current assets** | | | ———— |
| **Total assets less current liabilities** | | | |
| 10% Loan repayable 20Y6 | | | |
| **Net assets** | | | ———— |
| | | | ———— |
| **Capital** | | | |
| Opening capital | | | |
| Add: profit for the year | | | |
| Less: drawings | | | |
| **Closing capital** | | | ———— |
| | | | ———— |

## 2.2 SOLUTION

**Jill: Profit and loss account for the year ended 30 June 20X8**

|  | £ | £ |
|---|---:|---:|
| **Sales** |  | **685,000** |
| **Cost of sales** |  |  |
| Opening stock | 43,250 |  |
| Add: purchases | 327,500 |  |
| Add: carriage inwards | 3,456 |  |
| Less: closing stock | (32,900) |  |
|  |  | (341,306) |
|  |  |  |
| **Gross profit** |  | **343,694** |
| *Expenses* |  |  |
| Rent and rates | 60,000 |  |
| Wages and salaries | 130,000 |  |
| Carriage outwards | 10,000 |  |
| Postage and stationery | 11,892 |  |
| Insurance | 7,852 |  |
| Irrecoverable debts | 4,825 |  |
| Sundry expenses | 28,769 |  |
| Depreciation: Equipment | 9,760 |  |
| Motors | 7,475 |  |
|  |  | 270,573 |
|  |  |  |
| **Operating profit** |  | **73,121** |
| Interest payable |  | (20,000) |
|  |  |  |
| **Profit for the year** |  | **53,121** |

**Jill: Balance sheet as at 30 June 20X8**

|  | Cost £ | Depreciation £ | NBV £ |
|---|---|---|---|
| **Fixed assets** | | | |
| Equipment | 97,600 | 24,040 | 73,560 |
| Motor vehicles | 43,400 | 20,975 | 22,425 |
| | 141,000 | 45,015 | 95,985 |
| **Current assets** | | | |
| Stocks | | 32,900 | |
| Trade debtors | | 65,200 | |
| Prepayments | | 13,358 | |
| Bank and cash (£44,117 + £1,190) | | 45,307 | |
| | | 156,765 | |
| **Current liabilities** | | | |
| Trade creditors | | 28,478 | |
| Accruals | | 5,752 | |
| | | 34,230 | |
| **Net current assets** | | | 122,535 |
| **Total assets less current liabilities** | | | 218,520 |
| 10% Loan repayable 20Y6 | | | (200,000) |
| **Net assets** | | | £18,520 |
| **Capital** | | | |
| Opening capital | | | 100,000 |
| Add: profit for the year | | | 53,121 |
| Less: drawings | | | (134,601) |
| **Closing capital** | | | |
| | | | £18,520 |

## Jill: Extended trial balance at 30 June 20X8

| | Trial balance Dr | Trial balance Cr | Adjustments Dr | Adjustments Cr | Accruals Dr to P&L | Accruals Cr | Prepaid Cr to P&L | Prepaid Dr | Profit and loss Dr | Profit and loss Cr | Balance sheet Dr | Balance sheet Cr |
|---|---|---|---|---|---|---|---|---|---|---|---|---|
| Sales | | 685,000 | | | | | | | | 685,000 | | |
| Opening stock | 43,250 | | | | | | | | 43,250 | | | |
| Purchases | 327,500 | | | | | | | | 327,500 | | | |
| Equipment at cost | 97,600 | | | | | | | | | | 97,600 | |
| Depreciation | | 14,280 | | b 9,760 | | | | | | | | 24,040 |
| Vehicles at cost | 43,400 | | | | | | | | | | 43,400 | |
| Depreciation | | 13,500 | | c 7,475 | | | | | | | | 20,975 |
| Rent | 71,898 | | | | | | f 11,898 | | 60,000 | | | |
| Salaries and wages | 130,000 | | | | | | | | 130,000 | | | |
| Carriage inwards | 3,456 | | | | | | | | 3,456 | | | |
| Carriage outwards | 10,000 | | | | | | | | 10,000 | | | |
| Postage and stationery | 11,892 | | | | | | | | 11,892 | | | |
| Trade debtors | 65,200 | | | | | | | | | | 65,200 | |
| Trade creditors | | 28,478 | | | | | | | | | | 28,478 |
| Insurance | 9,312 | | | | | | e 1,460 | | 7,852 | | | |
| Irrecov. debts written off | 4,825 | | | | | | | | 4,825 | | | |
| Petty cash | 1,190 | | | | | | | | | | 1,190 | |
| Sundry expenditure | 28,017 | | | | g 752 | | | | 28,769 | | | |
| Opening capital | | 100,000 | | | | | | | | | | 100,000 |
| Drawings | 134,601 | | | | | | | | | | 134,601 | |
| 10% Loan (20Y6) | | 200,000 | | | | | | | | | | 200,000 |
| Loan interest paid | 15,000 | | | | d 5,000 | | | | 20,000 | | | |
| Bank balance | 44,117 | | | | | | | | | | 44,117 | |
| | 1,041,258 | 1,041,258 | | | | | | | | | | |
| Closing stock (B/S, P&L) | | | a 32,900 | a 32,900 | | | | | | 32,900 | 32,900 | |
| Dep'n charge | | | b 9,760 | | | | | | 9,760 | | | |
| Equipment | | | c 7,475 | | | | | | 7,475 | | | |
| Motors | | | | | | | | | | | | |
| Total adjustments etc | | | 50,135 | 50,135 | 5,752 | | | 13,358 | 664,779 | 717,900 | 432,366 | 379,245 |
| | | | | | Cr. B/S | | | Dr. B/S | | | | |
| | | | | | | | | | 53,121 | | | 53,121 |
| | | | | | | | | | 717,900 | 717,900 | 432,366 | 432,366 |

## ACTIVITY 1

The activity below practises all the financial accounting skills that you have learned so far.

Sally has traded successfully for a number of years and the trial balance for the year ended 30 November 20X9 is set out below:

**Sally**

**Trial balance for the year ended 30 November 20X9**

|  | Dr £ | Cr £ |
|---|---|---|
| Sales |  | 756,293 |
| Opening stock | 21,645 |  |
| Purchases | 285,365 |  |
| Equipment at cost | 157,954 |  |
| Depreciation |  | 45,487 |
| Motor vehicles at cost | 45,999 |  |
| Depreciation |  | 32,876 |
| Rent | 8,000 |  |
| Salaries and wages | 163,996 |  |
| Motor expenses | 35,947 |  |
| Certification costs | 7,354 |  |
| Training | 14,987 |  |
| Trade debtors | 2,253 |  |
| Trade creditors |  | 32,756 |
| Insurance | 14,298 |  |
| Irrecoverable debts written off | 132 |  |
| Petty cash | 5,750 |  |
| Sundry expenditure | 49,310 |  |
| Opening capital account |  | 250,000 |
| Drawings | 254,999 |  |
| 15% Loan repayable in 20Y9 |  | 100,000 |
| Loan interest paid | 3,500 |  |
| Bank balance | 145,923 |  |
|  | 1,217,412 | 1,217,412 |

**Notes**

(a)    Stock was counted on 30 November 20X9 and valued at £24,680.

(b)    Equipment is depreciated at 15% per annum on a straight line basis.

(c)    Motor vehicles are depreciated at $33\frac{1}{3}$% pa on a reducing balance basis.

(d)    Although only £3,500 interest has been paid (as shown on the trial balance), a full year's interest should be charged in the accounts.

(e)    Insurance includes £6,432 paid on certain items covering the year to 28 February 20Y0.

(f)    The rent for the year was £18,000 per quarter. However, owing to a dispute the landlord has not been paid for many months. Eventually the rent will have to be paid.

(g)    On 15 November Sally paid out £28,000 on an advertising campaign which will commence on New Year's Day. It has been included within sundry expenditure.

**Required:**

Prepare a profit and loss account, balance sheet and capital account for Sally for the year ended 30 November 20X9 in a format suitable for presentation to the proprietor, bank manager and other interested parties.

*For a suggested answer, see the 'Answers' section at the end of the book.*

# 3 CLOSING THE BOOKS AT THE YEAR END

## 3.1 WHY THE BOOKS ARE CLOSED

After the final accounts have been prepared, the books are closed. Adjustments are made so that the closing balances in the nominal ledger become the opening balances for the next period.

## 3.2 HOW TO CLOSE THE BOOKS

**Step 1**     Transfer all the balances on the individual ledger accounts for profit and loss account items to the profit and loss account (if this has not already been done).

The profit and loss account is a separate ledger account within the nominal ledger. The trading and profit and loss account that is drawn up as part of the final accounts contains exactly the same information as this ledger account.

**Step 2**     Transfer the final balance on the profit and loss account (the net profit or loss for the period) to the capital account.

**Step 3**     Transfer the balance on the drawings account to the capital account.

At the end of this process:

- The balance on the owner's capital account represents the owner's equity in the business. It is the total of: the owner's original investment, the profits made by the business, less the money the owner has drawn from the business.

- The accounts should still balance.

All the balance sheet ledger accounts continue in the following accounting period. The ledger accounts representing profit and loss amounts have been written off to the profit and loss account so that they can be started afresh in the next accounting period.

***Note:*** Any period end adjustments made on the extended trial balance must eventually be recorded in the ledger accounts, so that the correct opening balances can be brought down at the beginning of the following period. This may be done before or after the final accounts are prepared.

## 3.3 **EXAMPLE**

The ledger accounts of Swing Dancewear have been balanced off. A trial balance has been extracted and final accounts have been prepared. The ledger accounts are shown below.

### Sales account

| | £ | | £ |
|---|---|---|---|
| Transfer to P&L a/c | 21,000 | Cash at bank account | 7,000 |
| | | Debtors | 14,000 |
| | 21,000 | | 21,000 |

### Purchases account

| | £ | | £ |
|---|---|---|---|
| Cash at bank account | 5,000 | Transfer to P&L a/c | 15,000 |
| Trade creditors account | 10,000 | | |
| | 15,000 | | 15,000 |

### Sundry expenses account

| | £ | | £ |
|---|---|---|---|
| Cash at bank account | 100 | P&L a/c | 100 |
| | 100 | | 100 |

### Rent expense account

| | £ | | £ |
|---|---|---|---|
| Cash at bank account | 350 | P&L a/c | 350 |
| | 350 | | 350 |

### Rates expense account

| | £ | | £ |
|---|---|---|---|
| Cash at bank account | 600 | P&L a/c | 600 |
| | 600 | | 600 |

### Electricity expense account

| | £ | | £ |
|---|---|---|---|
| Cash at bank account | 150 | P&L a/c | 150 |
| | 150 | | 150 |

## Repairs expense account

| | £ | | £ |
|---|---|---|---|
| Cash at bank account | 100 | P&L a/c | 100 |
| | 100 | | 100 |

## Cash at bank account

| | £ | | £ |
|---|---|---|---|
| Capital introduced | 50,000 | Property purchased | 40,000 |
| Loan received | 30,000 | Purchase of stock | 5,000 |
| Sale of stock | 7,000 | Sundry expense | 100 |
| Debtors | 14,000 | Drawings | 600 |
| | | Creditors | 10,000 |
| | | Rent | 350 |
| | | Rates | 600 |
| | | Electricity | 150 |
| | | Repairs | 100 |
| | | Balance c/d | 44,100 |
| | 101,000 | | 101,000 |
| Balance b/d | 44,100 | | |

## Owner's capital account

| | £ | | £ |
|---|---|---|---|
| | | Cash at bank account | 50,000 |

## Loan account

| | £ | | £ |
|---|---|---|---|
| | | Cash at bank account | 30,000 |

## Property account

| | £ | | £ |
|---|---|---|---|
| Cash at bank account | 40,000 | | |

## Creditors account

| | £ | | £ |
|---|---|---|---|
| Cash at bank account | 10,000 | Purchases of stock | 10,000 |
| Balance c/d | nil | | |
| | 10,000 | | 10,000 |

## Debtors account

| | £ | | £ |
|---|---|---|---|
| Sales | 14,000 | Cash at bank account | 14,000 |
| | | Balance c/d | nil |
| | 14,000 | | 14,000 |

**Drawings account**

| | £ | | £ |
|---|---|---|---|
| Cash at bank account | 600 | Balance c/d | 600 |
| | 600 | | 600 |
| Balance b/d | 600 | | |

Close the books for the period and draw up an opening trial balance.

## 3.4 SOLUTION

**Step 1**    The individual balances for profit and loss account items have already been transferred to the profit and loss account, which appears below:

**Profit and loss account**

| | £ | | £ |
|---|---|---|---|
| Purchases | 15,000 | Sales | 21,000 |
| Sundry expenses | 100 | | |
| Rent expense | 350 | | |
| Rates expense | 600 | | |
| Electricity expense | 150 | | |
| Repairs expense | 100 | | |
| Balance c/d | 4,700 | | |
| | 21,000 | | 21,000 |
| | | Balance b/d | 4,700 |

**Step 2**    Clear the final balance on the profit and loss account (the net profit or loss for the period) to the capital account.

**Step 3**    Clear the balance on the drawings account to the capital account.

**Profit and loss account**

| | £ | | £ |
|---|---|---|---|
| Capital account | 4,700 | Balance b/d | 4,700 |

**Drawings account**

| | £ | | £ |
|---|---|---|---|
| Balance b/d | 600 | Capital account | 600 |
| | 600 | | 600 |

**Owner's capital account**

|  | £ |  | £ |
|---|---|---|---|
| Drawings | 600 | Cash at bank account | 50,000 |
| Balance c/d | 54,100 | Net profit (P&L a/c) | 4,700 |
|  | 54,700 |  | 54,700 |
|  |  | Balance b/d | 54,100 |

**Opening trial balance**

|  | £ | £ |
|---|---|---|
| Cash at bank | 44,100 |  |
| Loan |  | 30,000 |
| Property | 40,000 |  |
| Capital |  | 54,100 |
|  | 84,100 | 84,100 |

## ACTIVITY 2

Using the closing trial balance and final accounts of Jason and Co (Section 1 above) prepare an opening trial balance at 1 June 20X6.

*For a suggested answer, see the 'Answers' section at the end of the book.*

## CONCLUSION

Preparing the final accounts is a question of rearranging the information in the trial balance or ETB and presenting it in an acceptable format for a sole trader. As always, a methodical approach will guarantee you a correct answer.

After the financial statements are prepared, the income and expense ledger accounts should be cleared out to the income statement ledger account. This itself is cleared out to the capital account, along with the drawings ledger account. The balance on the capital account together with other balances on asset and liability ledger accounts form the opening trial balance for the next period.

## SELF TEST QUESTIONS

|  |  | *Paragraph* |
|---|---|---|
| 1 | What is carriage inwards? | 1 |
| 2 | How are sales returns reported in the profit and loss account? | 1 |
| 3 | Why must the books be closed at the period end? | 3.1 |
| 4 | To which account should the balance on the drawings account be cleared, when closing the books? | 3.2 |

## PRACTICE QUESTION

**K KONG**

The following balances were extracted from the records of K Kong at the end of his first year of trading:

**Trial balance as at 31 December 20X6**

| Account | Debit £ | Credit £ |
|---|---|---|
| Sales | | 9,000 |
| Purchases | 6,900 | |
| Rent | 300 | |
| Stationery | 70 | |
| Insurance | 50 | |
| Fixtures and fittings, cost | 700 | |
| Debtors | 2,500 | |
| Creditors | | 900 |
| Cash at bank | 1,100 | |
| Drawings | 1,020 | |
| Capital introduced | | 2,740 |
| | 12,640 | 12,640 |

You are given the following additional information:

(a)     Rent was £100 per quarter payable in arrears.  The property has been rented since 1 January 20X6.

(b)     £10 of the insurance paid covered a period in 20X7.

(c)     Goods unsold at 31 December 20X6 had cost K Kong £750.

(d)     The fixtures and fittings were expected to last for ten years and would then be sold for £50.  Depreciation is to be on the straight-line basis.

(e)     An allowance for debtors of £100 is to be created.

**Requirement 1:**

Prepare an extended trial balance showing the figures that will appear in the financial statements.

**Requirement 2**

Prepare the trading and profit and loss account of K Kong for the year ending 31 December 20X6 and a balance sheet at that date, using the format below:

*For a suggested answer, see the 'Answers' section at the end of the book.*

# Chapter 9

# INCOMPLETE RECORDS AND CLUBS AND SOCIETIES

In real life, and in questions, the accounting records may be incomplete. This may be because the records have been lost or destroyed, or because full records were not kept in the first place. There are many different techniques utilised in the preparation of accounts from incomplete records. In an exam question you will have to select the most appropriate ones for the information given to you. Most of the examples in this chapter are based on the accounts of a sole trader and clubs and societies, but exactly the same techniques are used to prepare the accounts of partnerships and limited companies with incomplete records.

## CONTENTS

1 Calculation of profit from information about the balance sheet only

2 Preparation of final accounts from limited records

3 Using ratios and percentages

4 Club and society accounts

## LEARNING OUTCOMES

At the end of this chapter you should be able to:

- derive missing figures from incomplete records.

## 1 CALCULATION OF PROFIT FROM INFORMATION ABOUT THE BALANCE SHEET ONLY

### 1.1 DISTINCTION BETWEEN INCOMPLETE AND LIMITED ACCOUNTING RECORDS

| Definition | **Limited accounting records** are records kept by a business of certain transactions but additional information is required to prepare financial statements. |
| --- | --- |

| Definition | **Incomplete accounting records** are records which the business has not fully completed or where no records at all have been kept of transactions. |
| --- | --- |

Many businesses fall into each of the above categories. Many businesses keep limited accounting information such as daily records of cash received, invoices paid (i.e. some form of purchase day book) and wages paid. They leave it to the accountant who prepares the annual financial statements to make sense of the information and to ask for other information at that time.

With limited accounting records, the accountant thus has (generally) sufficient information to prepare the accounts but no ledger accounts have been prepared. We will look at the procedures used to prepare financial statements in this situation later in the chapter.

A business that has kept very little information on its daily transactions is providing the accountant with the task of preparing financial statements from incomplete data. In this section we will see how limited the data can be and yet still it is possible to prepare financial statements. However these financial statements are more prone to error because of the incomplete records.

In practice, the term incomplete records is used to cover both situations.

## 1.2 CALCULATION OF THE NET ASSET POSITION AND THE PROFIT FOR A BUSINESS WHICH HAS INCOMPLETE ACCOUNTING RECORDS

The most basic incomplete records situation of all is where one is required to calculate net profit, given details only of capital at the beginning and end of the year and of drawings.

**Example**

The capital position of a business is as follows:

|  | 31 December | |
| --- | --- | --- |
|  | 20X6 | 20X7 |
|  | £ | £ |
| Motor vehicle: | | |
| Cost | 2,000 | 2,000 |
| Depreciation | (800) | (1,200) |
|  | 1,200 | 800 |
| Stock | 2,040 | 2,960 |
| Debtors | 865 | 1,072 |
| Bank | 1,017 | 1,964 |
| Cash | 351 | 86 |
|  | 5,473 | 6,882 |
| Creditors | 1,706 | 1,905 |
|  | 3,767 | 4,977 |

Drawings for the year have been estimated at £3,000. An estimate of net profit for the year is required.

**Solution**

From the basic balance sheet equation capital equals assets less liabilities. Hence the opening and closing capital account balances are £3,767 and £4,977 respectively. Net profit may be calculated by completing his capital account.

**Capital account**

| 20X7 | | £ | 20X7 | | £ |
|---|---|---|---|---|---|
| | Drawings | 3,000 | 1 Jan | Balance b/d | 3,767 |
| 31 Dec | Balance c/d | 4,977 | | Net profit (bal fig) | 4,210 |
| | | 7,977 | | | 7,977 |
| | | | 20X8 | | |
| | | | 1 Jan | Balance b/d | 4,977 |

Note that the net profit figure is very much an estimate and depends on the reliability of the drawings and the opening and closing net asset positions.

It also assumes that no new capital has been introduced by the owners during the year.

**Alternative solution**

An alternative method of calculation is:

| | £ |
|---|---|
| Net assets this year end | 4,977 |
| Net assets last year end | 3,767 |
| Increase in net assets | 1,210 |
| Less:  Capital introduced by owners | – |
| Add:  Drawings | 3,000 |
| Profit for the year | 4,210 |

The alternative method emphasises that profit represents an increase in the net assets of the business unless it is withdrawn by the owners.

**Conclusion**      Profit for the year = Increase in net assets – Capital introduced + Drawings.

# ACTIVITY 1

On 1 January 20X5 B Freen commenced business.  At that date he purchased a shop premises for £14,000 and paid £2,000 for interior fittings.  He also paid £4,000 into the business bank account.  On 31 December 20X6 he realised the need for a profit figure for the two years he had been in business, but his records were completely inadequate.  At this date the assets he possessed in addition to the premises and fittings were:

| | £ |
|---|---|
| Stock | 6,000 |
| Debtors | 1,040 |
| Motor lorry purchased 30 June 20X6 for | 8,000 |
| Cash at bank | 2,500 |

He owed £1,400 to trade creditors and had borrowed £10,000 from a friend.  Interest accrued but unpaid on the loan amounted to £200.  Freen estimated that he was withdrawing £300 a month from the business.

**Required:**

Compute the net profit for the two years valuing the fixed assets at cost less depreciation (on a straight line basis): on premises at 2% p.a. and on fittings at 5% p.a. and on the motor lorry at 20% p.a.

*For a suggested answer, see the 'Answers' section at the end of the book.*

## 1.3  SUMMARY

A business that has information about assets owned at the year end, but no information on income and expenditure items cannot prepare a detailed profit and loss account. The profit for the year can be found by:

- preparing a summarised balance sheet: profit will be the balancing figure

- using the accounting equation:

> Profit for the year = Increase in net assets – Capital introduced + Drawings.

# 2  PREPARATION OF FINAL ACCOUNTS FROM LIMITED RECORDS

## 2.1  CASH AND BANK TRANSACTIONS

In the first example above no details were given of transactions taking place during the year.  If basic information regarding receipts and payments is provided, it is possible to build up to a balance sheet and profit and loss account, although some important assumptions may well need to be made.

## 2.2  BASIC PROCEDURE FOR LIMITED RECORDS

The procedure suggested below is a full procedure suitable for a wide range of limited records questions and may be set out in basic steps.  We will see later how some of these steps can be cut back on for examination purposes.

| | |
|---|---|
| **Step 1** | Set aside a sheet for the trading and profit and loss account and a sheet for the balance sheet.  Some information can be inserted straight into the final accounts. |
| **Step 2** | Prepare the opening balance sheet from information on assets and liabilities. |
| **Conclusion** | The opening capital account balance can be calculated as a balancing figure (Capital = Assets less Liabilities). |
| **Step 3** | Insert the opening balances in T-accounts. For example: |

| *Balance* | *Account* |
|---|---|
| Cash at bank | Cash at bank (bank) |
| Cash in hand | Cash in hand (cash) |
| Debtors | Sales ledger control account |
| Creditors | Purchases ledger control account |
| Accrued expenses | Separate account for each expense category |
| Prepayments | Separate account for each expense category |

| | |
|---|---|
| **Step 4** | Information is almost certain to be given as regards cash and bank transactions.  Accordingly the cash and bank accounts can be prepared, making use of double entry principles and completing the entries by debiting and crediting whichever accounts are appropriate. |

**Notes**

(a) Cash withdrawn is cash taken out of the bank (Cr bank) and into cash in hand (Dr cash).

(b) Cash banked operates in the opposite direction – it is a reduction of cash (Cr cash) and an increase in money at bank (Dr bank).

Depending on the degree of incompleteness, cash is likely to contain one or two missing items of information. This aspect of the problem will be receiving more attention later.

**Step 5**    Insert into the accounts the closing balances provided in the question in respect of debtors, creditors, accrued expenses and prepayments. In simple questions the respective transfers to profit and loss may be calculated as balancing items.

### Sales ledger control account

|  | £ |  | £ |
|---|---|---|---|
| Opening debtors b/d | X | Cash | X |
| Sales (bal fig) | X | Closing debtors c/d | X |
|  | X |  | X |

### Purchases ledger control account

|  | £ |  | £ |
|---|---|---|---|
| Cash | X | Opening trade creditors b/d | X |
| Bank | X | Purchases (bal fig) | X |
| Closing trade creditors c/d | X |  |  |
|  | X |  | X |

### Rates account (assuming paid in advance)

|  | £ |  | £ |
|---|---|---|---|
| Opening prepayment b/d | X | Profit and loss (bal fig) | X |
| Bank | X | Closing prepayment c/d | X |
|  | X |  | X |

**Step 6**    Carry out any further adjustments as required, such as dealing with doubtful debts and depreciation.

**Example**

A business has a cash float of £50 and the following expenses are paid out of the till before cash is banked:

|  | £ |
|---|---|
| Purchases | 20 |
| Wages | 100 |
| Expenses | 80 |

The bank statement shows that the takings banked in the period were £4,000.

Write up the cash account and find the value of cash sales.

**Solution**

### Cash

|  | £ |  | £ |
|---|---|---|---|
| Balance b/d | 50 | Purchases | 20 |
| Cash takings (sales) (bal fig) | 4,200 | Wages | 100 |
|  |  | Expenses | 80 |
|  |  | Bankings | 4,000 |
|  |  | Balance c/d | 50 |
|  | 4,250 |  | 4,250 |

## ACTIVITY 2

The following information relates to a business's transactions for a month:

|  | £ |
|---|---|
| Opening cash | 100 |
| Closing cash | 50 |
| Opening debtors | 460 |
| Closing debtors | 420 |
| Cash expenses | 750 |
| Bankings | 4,220 |
| Cash drawings | 1,200 |
| Cash sales | 2,500 |
| Credit sales | 3,700 |
| Irrecoverable debts written off | 50 |
| Discounts allowed | 70 |

Write up the cash account and sales ledger control account to identify cash received from debtors.

*For a suggested answer, see the 'Answers' section at the end of the book.*

## 2.3 COMPREHENSIVE EXAMPLE

Yatton does not keep proper books of account. You ascertain that his bank payments and receipts during the year to 31 December 20X8 were as follows:

### Bank account

|  | £ |  | £ |
|---|---|---|---|
| Balance 1 Jan 20X8 | 800 | Cash withdrawn | 200 |
| Cheques for sales | 2,500 | Purchases | 2,500 |
| Cash banked | 3,000 | Expenses | 800 |
|  |  | Drawings | 1,300 |
|  |  | Delivery van |  |
|  |  | (bought 1 Oct 20X8) | 1,000 |
|  |  | Balance 31 Dec 20X8 | 500 |
|  | 6,300 |  | 6,300 |

From a cash notebook you ascertain that:

|  | £ |
|---|---:|
| Cash in hand 1 January 20X8 | 70 |
| Cash takings | 5,200 |
| Purchases paid in cash | 400 |
| Expenses paid in cash | 500 |
| Cash in hand 31 December 20X8 | 30 |
| Drawings by proprietor in cash | Unknown |

You discover that assets and liabilities were as follows:

|  | 1 Jan 20X8 | 31 Dec 20X8 |
|---|---:|---:|
|  | £ | £ |
| Debtors | 300 | 450 |
| Trade creditors | 800 | 900 |
| Expense creditors | 100 | 150 |
| Stock on hand | 1,400 | 1,700 |

Yatton says that he has no hope of receiving an amount of £100 due from one customer and that an allowance for 10% of debtors would be prudent. Depreciation on the van is to be provided at the rate of 20% per annum.

**You are required** to prepare a trading and profit and loss account for the year to 31 December 20X8 and a balance sheet at that date.

## 2.4 SOLUTION TO COMPREHENSIVE EXAMPLE

**Step 1** The sheets set aside for the final accounts can be inserted with main headings and certain information such as opening and closing stock can be inserted.

**Step 2** The preparation of the opening balance sheet is usually achieved by drawing up a statement of opening capital using information given in the question about the opening balances. A careful scrutiny of the question reveals:

*Workings*

(W1) **Statement of opening capital**

|  | Dr | Cr |
|---|---:|---:|
|  | £ | £ |
| Bank | 800 |  |
| Cash | 70 |  |
| Debtors | 300 |  |
| Trade creditors |  | 800 |
| Expense creditors |  | 100 |
| Stock | 1,400 |  |
|  | 2,570 | 900 |
|  | 900 |  |
|  | 1,670 |  |

Thus debits (assets) exceed credits (liabilities) by £1,670. Accordingly Yatton's business has net assets of £1,670, represented on the balance sheet by his opening capital account.

**Step 3**     Insert the opening balances into T-accounts if construction of the accounts is required. Leave plenty of space between the ledger accounts.

Thus a ledger account for Bank is not required as the question has already provided this. Accounts for stock and capital are not required as the information can be inserted immediately into the final accounts.

**(W2)** **Cash**

| | £ | | £ |
|---|---|---|---|
| Balance b/d | 70 | | |

**(W3)** **Sales ledger control account**

| | £ | | £ |
|---|---|---|---|
| Balance b/d | 300 | | |

**(W4)** **Purchases ledger control account**

| | £ | | £ |
|---|---|---|---|
| | | Balance b/d | 800 |

**(W5)** **Creditors – expenses**

| | £ | | £ |
|---|---|---|---|
| | | Balance b/d | 100 |

**Step 4**     Prepare the cash account, and post the cash and bank entries to the other accounts.

**(W2)** **Cash**

| | £ | | £ |
|---|---|---|---|
| Balance b/d | 70 | Bank | 3,000 |
| Bank | 200 | Purchases ledger control account | 400 |
| Sales ledger control account | 5,200 | Expenses | 500 |
| | | Drawings (bal fig) | 1,540 |
| | | Balance c/d | 30 |
| | 5,470 | | 5,470 |

**(W3)** **Sales ledger control account**

| | £ | | £ |
|---|---|---|---|
| Balance b/d | 300 | Bank | 2,500 |
| | | Cash | 5,200 |

**(W4)** **Purchases ledger control account**

| | £ | | £ |
|---|---|---|---|
| Bank | 2,500 | Balance b/d | 800 |
| Cash | 400 | | |

**(W5)** **Creditors – expenses**

| | £ | | £ |
|---|---|---|---|
| Bank | 800 | Balance b/d | 100 |
| Cash | 500 | | |

**(W6)**                             **Drawings**

|  | £ | £ |
|---|---|---|
| Bank | 1,300 |  |
| Cash | 1,540 |  |

**(W7)**                             **Van cost**

|  | £ | £ |
|---|---|---|
| Bank | 1,000 |  |

Two points are worth noting at this stage:

(a)      The commentary above is designed to show what happens after each step; there is no question of writing out each account on more than one occasion.

(b)      If a question gives full details of the bank account (as this one does), there is no need to write it out again as part of your workings.

**Step 5**      Insert the closing balances and calculate the transfers to profit and loss.

**(W4)**                 **Purchase ledger control account**

|  | £ |  | £ |
|---|---|---|---|
| Bank | 2,500 | Balance b/d | 800 |
| Cash | 400 | Trading and profit and loss |  |
| Balance c/d | 900 |    (bal fig) | 3,000 |
|  | 3,800 |  | 3,800 |

**(W5)**                 **Creditors – expenses**

|  | £ |  | £ |
|---|---|---|---|
| Bank | 800 | Balance b/d | 100 |
| Cash | 500 | Trading and profit and loss |  |
| Balance c/d | 150 |    (bal fig) | 1,350 |
|  | 1,450 |  | 1,450 |

The sales ledger control account has not yet been closed, as there is an adjustment for irrecoverable debts still to be made.

**Step 6**      Carry out any further adjustments. These will be familiar, and the principles behind them are unchanged.

**Bad debts**

**(W3)**             **Sales ledger control account**

|  | £ |  | £ |
|---|---|---|---|
| Balance b/d | 300 | Bank | 2,500 |
| Trading and profit and loss |  | Cash | 5,200 |
|    (bal fig) | 7,850 | Irrecoverable debts | 100 |
|  |  | Balance c/d (£450 – £100) | 350 |
|  | 8,150 |  | 8,150 |

**(W8)**                 **Irrecoverable debts**

| | £ | | £ |
|---|---|---|---|
| Sales ledger control account | 100 | Profit and loss | 135 |
| Provision for doubtful debts | 35 | | |
| | 135 | | 135 |

**(W9)**            **Provision for doubtful debts**

| | £ | | £ |
|---|---|---|---|
| Balance c/d (10% × £350) | 35 | Balance b/d | Nil |
| | | Irrecoverable debts | 35 |
| | 35 | | 35 |

**Depreciation**

**(W7)**                 **Van cost**

| | £ | | £ |
|---|---|---|---|
| Bank | 1,000 | Balance c/d | 1,000 |

**(W10)**            **Van accumulated depreciation**

| | £ | | £ |
|---|---|---|---|
| Balance c/d | 50 | Profit and loss | 50 |

Charge 20% × 3 months × £1,000 = £50

**Drawings**

**(W6)**                 **Drawings**

| | £ | | £ |
|---|---|---|---|
| Bank | 1,300 | Capital | 2,840 |
| Cash | 1,540 | | |
| | 2,840 | | 2,840 |

The remaining figures can be inserted into the final accounts.

**Yatton**
**Trading and profit and loss account for year ended 31 December 20X8**

|  | £ | £ |
|---|---:|---:|
| Sales (W3) |  | 7,850 |
| Cost of sales: |  |  |
|    Opening stock | 1,400 |  |
|    Purchases (W4) | 3,000 |  |
|  | 4,400 |  |
| Less: Closing stock | 1,700 |  |
|  |  | 2,700 |
| Gross profit |  | 5,150 |
| Expenses (W5) | 1,350 |  |
| Irrecoverable debts (W8) | 135 |  |
| Depreciation of van (W10) | 50 |  |
|  |  | 1,535 |
| Net profit |  | 3,615 |

**Yatton**
**Balance sheet as at 31 December 20X8**

|  | £ | £ | £ |
|---|---:|---:|---:|
| Fixed assets: |  |  |  |
|    Van at cost |  |  | 1,000 |
|    Depreciation to date (W10) |  |  | 50 |
|  |  |  | 950 |
| Current assets: |  |  |  |
|    Stocks |  | 1,700 |  |
|    Debtors (W3) | 350 |  |  |
|    Less: Allowance for doubtful debts | 35 |  |  |
|  |  | 315 |  |
| Cash at bank |  | 500 |  |
| Cash in hand |  | 30 |  |
|  |  | 2,545 |  |
| Less: Current liabilities: |  |  |  |
|    Trade creditors | 900 |  |  |
|    Expense creditors | 150 |  |  |
|  | 1,050 |  |  |
|  |  |  | 1,495 |
|  |  |  | 2,445 |
| Capital account: |  |  |  |
|    Capital at 1 January 20X8 (W1) |  |  | 1,670 |
|    Add: Profit for year |  |  | 3,615 |
|  |  |  | 5,285 |
| Less: Drawings in year (W6) |  |  | 2,840 |
|  |  |  | 2,445 |

## 2.5 SUMMARY

A methodical approach is required to assemble the incomplete information into a set of accounts and to find the missing figures on the way.

The steps to achieve this are:

(1) Draft a proforma balance sheet and profit and loss account – slot in figures as you find them.

(2) Calculate opening capital using opening net assets.

(3) Use T-account workings for debtors, creditors and expenses with accruals or prepayments: insert opening balances.

(4) Use T-account workings for cash and bank: insert cash transactions into the T-accounts from Step 3 when completing the cash and bank accounts.

(5) Insert closing entries in all T-account workings and calculate the transfers to profit and loss account.

# 3 USING RATIOS AND PERCENTAGES

## 3.1 INTRODUCTION

In the example above, drawings was the only unknown in the cash account. What happens if there are **two** unknowns in the cash account – for example, drawings and takings? We can still construct the financial statements provided we are given some additional information.

## 3.2 GROSS PROFIT PERCENTAGE

**Definition**     **Gross profit percentage** = $\dfrac{\text{Gross profit}}{\text{Sales}} \times 100$

For instance, if we know that sales total £8,000 and the gross profit percentage is 25%, the following can be deduced:

|  | £ | % |
|---|---|---|
| Sales | 8,000 (given) | 100 |
| Less: Cost of sales | 6,000 | 75 |
| Gross profit | 2,000 | 25 (given) |

**Example**

Assume that we are told that the gross profit percentage is 30% and gross profit £6,000. What are sales and cost of sales?

**Solution**

|  | £ | % |
|---|---|---|
| Sales | 20,000 | 100 |
| Less: Cost of sales | 14,000 | 70 |
| Gross profit | 6,000 (given) | 30 (given) |

The percentages provided may have been calculated by reference to a similar business or from the previous years' results of this business.

## 3.3 MARGINS AND MARK-UPS

The gross profit percentage in the previous examples is also known as the **profit margin**. The percentage of profit is given by reference to sales.

Alternatively information on the **mark-up** may be given.

**Definition**     **Mark-up percentage** $= \dfrac{\text{Gross profit}}{\text{Cost of sales}} \times 100$

Thus, if we know that cost of sales is £6,000 and the mark-up is one-third, we can set out the following:

|  | £ | Ratio |
|---|---|---|
| Sales |  |  |
| Cost of sales (given) | 6,000 | 3 |
| Gross profit |  | 1 |

The 'ratio' is an alternative to using percentages. One-third is awkward to work with in percentage terms.

In ratio terms gross profit is one part to three parts costs.

Sales are therefore four parts (1 + 3), so total sales $= \dfrac{4}{3} \times £6,000 = £8,000$.

|  | £ | Ratio |
|---|---|---|
| Sales | 8,000 | 4 |
| Cost of sales | 6,000 | 3 |
| Gross profit | 2,000 | 1 |

### Example

The sales of a business are £280,000 and there is a mark up on cost of 40%. What are the figures for cost of sales and gross profit?

### Solution

|  | £ | % |
|---|---|---|
| Sales | 280,000 | 140 |
| Cost of sales (280,000 × 100/140) | 200,000 | 100 |
| Gross profit (280,000 × 40/140) | 80,000 | 40 |

## 3.4 CONVERTING MARGINS TO MARK-UPS AND VICE VERSA

Suppose we have been told that sales are £60,000 and the mark-up is 25%. The information given can be set out:

|  | £ | % |
|---|---|---|
| Sales | 60,000 |  |
| Cost of sales |  | 100 |
| Gross profit |  | 25 |

Laying out the information as above should show that gross profit and cost of sales can still be worked out. In percentage terms sales are 125% (100 + 25). Profit is therefore $\frac{25}{125} \times £60,000 = £12,000$.

|  | £ | % |
|---|---|---|
| Sales | 60,000 | 125 |
| Cost of sales | 48,000 | 100 |
| Gross profit | 12,000 | 25 |

**Conclusion**  To convert mark-up to margin (where figures are percentages):

$$\text{Margin} = \frac{\text{Mark - up}}{\text{Mark - up} + 100}$$

To convert margin to mark-up:

$$\text{Mark-up} = \frac{\text{Margin}}{100 - \text{Margin}}$$

**Example**

Kendal, a sole trader, has provided you with the following information relating to the year ended 31 December 20X5.

(a)  He has not made a note of drawings or of cash received.  The following items were paid from takings prior to banking:

|  |  |
|---|---|
| Purchases | £760 |
| Sundry expenses | £400 |

(b)  Kendal has estimated that his gross profit percentage is 20%.

(c)  His summarised bank account was as follows:

**Bank**

| 20X5 |  | £ | 20X5 |  | £ |
|---|---|---|---|---|---|
| 1 Jan | Balance b/d | 1,700 |  | Rent | 1,000 |
|  | Bankings | 16,940 |  | Electricity | 235 |
|  |  |  |  | Purchases | 16,140 |
|  |  |  |  | Drawings | 265 |
|  |  |  | 31 Dec | Balance c/d | 1,000 |
|  |  | 18,640 |  |  | 18,640 |

(d)  Assets and liabilities were as follows:

|  | 31 Dec 20X5 | 31 Dec 20X4 |
|---|---|---|
|  | £ | £ |
| Stock | 4,800 | 5,600 |
| Debtors | 1,650 | 2,100 |
| Creditors: |  |  |
| Goods | 1,940 | 1,640 |
| Electricity | 65 | - |
| Cash float | 2,400 | 170 |

(e)  He started paying rent in 20X5.  A year's rent was paid in advance on 1 April 20X5.

**You are required** to prepare:

(a)   a trading and profit and loss account for the year ended 31 December 20X5

(b)   a balance sheet at that date.

**Solution**

| | |
|---|---|
| **Step 1** | Sheets are reserved for the profit and loss account and balance sheet. In particular the trading account becomes a key working in situations where a margin or mark-up is given. Insert the opening and closing stock figures (if given) and also the margin percentages. |
| **Step 2** | Up till now the opening balance sheet has been completed in order to derive the opening capital balance. This working will now be done after the sales and purchases ledger control accounts have been completed as it only helps in finding one figure to go into the final accounts. |
| | We need to recognise that there may be time pressure in the examination and therefore we should spend our time first on the control accounts. |
| **Step 3** | Insert the opening balances in T-accounts. |
| **Step 4** | Deal with the information given as regards cash and bank transactions. Note that the bank account is not included in the workings, full details being given in the question. |
| | In addition, no ledger accounts have been shown for the various expenses. Instead workings have been shown on the face of the profit and loss account e.g. rent. |
| | There is a rent prepayment of £250 (three months rent). The expense is therefore £750. The derivation of the £750 (1,000 – 250) has been shown in brackets by the narrative on the profit and loss account. |
| | Where **simple** adjustments are to be made, this method allows the speedier preparation of the solution. Continue to use T-accounts if you need to. |
| **Step 5** | Insert the closing balances into the accounts. At this point the figure for purchases can be calculated. |
| | Having reached this far, a little more thought is now required. |
| | The position as regards unknowns can be summarised as follows: |

|  |  | |
|---|---|---|
| **Debtors** | – | The figures for sales and receipts from debtors are unknown. |
| **Cash** | – | The figures for drawings and receipts from debtors are unknown. |

This is where the gross profit percentage is utilised as follows:

|  |  | £ | £ | % |
|---|---|---|---|---|
| Sales |  |  | 22,500 | 100 |
| Less: Cost of goods sold: |  |  |  |  |
| Opening stock |  | 5,600 (given) |  |  |
| Purchases |  | 17,200 (calculation) |  |  |
|  |  | 22,800 |  |  |
| Less: Closing stock |  | 4,800 (given) |  |  |
|  |  |  | 18,000 | 80 |
| Gross profit |  |  | 4,500 | 20 (given) |

The sales figure has now been derived, leaving only one unknown in the debtors' account – receipts from debtors, which is calculated as a balancing figure.

The resulting double entry (Dr Cash £22,950, Cr Sales ledger control £22,950) means that there is now only one unknown in the cash account, the drawings figure.

## Workings

(W1)

### Cash

|  | £ |  | £ |
|---|---|---|---|
| Balance b/d | 170 | Bank | 16,940 |
| Debtors | 22,950 | Creditors – goods | 760 |
|  |  | Creditors – expenses | 400 |
|  |  | Drawings (bal fig) | 2,620 |
|  |  | Balance c/d | 2,400 |
|  | 23,120 |  | 23,120 |

(W2)

### Sales ledger control

|  | £ |  | £ |
|---|---|---|---|
| Balance b/d | 2,100 | Cash (bal fig) | 22,950 |
| Trading and profit and loss | 22,500 | Balance c/d | 1,650 |
|  | 24,600 |  | 24,600 |

(W3)

### Purchases ledger control

|  | £ |  | £ |
|---|---|---|---|
| Bank | 16,140 | Balance b/d | 1,640 |
| Cash | 760 | Trading and profit and loss |  |
| Balance c/d | 1,940 | (bal fig) | 17,200 |
|  | 18,840 |  | 18,840 |

(W4)

### Drawings

|  | £ |  | £ |
|---|---|---|---|
| Bank | 265 | Capital | 2,885 |
| Cash | 2,620 |  |  |
|  | 2,885 |  | 2,885 |

**(W5) Statement of opening capital**

|  | Dr | Cr |
|---|---|---|
|  | £ | £ |
| Bank | 1,700 |  |
| Stock | 5,600 |  |
| Debtors | 2,100 |  |
| Creditors – goods |  | 1,640 |
| Cash | 170 |  |
|  | 9,570 | 1,640 |
|  | 1,640 |  |
|  | 7,930 |  |

**(a) Trading and profit and loss account for the year ended 31 December 20X5**

|  | £ | £ | % |
|---|---|---|---|
| Sales |  | 22,500 | 100 |
| Opening stock | 5,600 |  |  |
| Purchases | 17,200 |  |  |
|  | 22,800 |  |  |
| Closing stock | 4,800 |  |  |
| Cost of sales |  | 18,000 | 80 |
| Gross profit |  | 4,500 | 20 |
| Rent (1,000 – 250) | 750 |  |  |
| Electricity (235 + 65) | 300 |  |  |
| Sundry | 400 |  |  |
|  |  | 1,450 |  |
| Net profit |  | 3,050 |  |

**(b)                              Balance sheet as at 31 December 20X5**

|  | £ | £ |
|---|---|---|
| Current assets: |  |  |
| Stock |  | 4,800 |
| Debtors |  | 1,650 |
| Prepayment |  | 250 |
| Bank |  | 1,000 |
| Cash |  | 2,400 |
|  |  | 10,100 |
| Less:   Current liabilities: |  |  |
| Creditors: |  |  |
| Goods | 1,940 |  |
| Expenses | 65 |  |
|  |  | 2,005 |
|  |  | 8,095 |
| Capital account: |  |  |
| Opening capital |  | 7,930 |
| Add:  Net profit |  | 3,050 |
|  |  | 10,980 |
| Less:  Drawings |  | 2,885 |
|  |  | 8,095 |

## 3.5 VARIATIONS ON THE THEME

No two incomplete records questions are quite the same, although the differences between them are often fairly small.  Two examples of possible variations are:

(a)    Suppose that stock were destroyed in a fire and that there was enough information to calculate sales, purchases and opening stock.  The gross profit percentage would enable sales to be converted to cost of sales.  Closing stock could then be calculated as a balancing figure.

(b)    Suppose that a business always received a rebate from its suppliers amounting to 1% of purchases, and that in the current year the rebate amounted to £172.  Clearly this tells us that purchases were £17,200.  If cash paid to suppliers was unknown, it could be calculated as a balancing figure.

# 4    CLUB AND SOCIETY ACCOUNTS

Club and society treasurers usually keep a simple cash book to record the income and expenditure over the accounting period.

An analysis of the cash book would result in a receipts and payments account being prepared.

However as such, non-profit making organisations need to account using the accruals or matching concept, then the receipts and payments account together with adjustments for accruals and prepayments and the treatment of depreciation of tangible assets would form the basis of a club's income and expenditure account for its financial year.

In addition to this, important financial statement and balance sheet would also be prepared.  The Balance Sheet of a club or society would include terminology that is unique to such organisations, that of the accumulated fund.

The accumulated fund is derived from the basic accounting equation:-

Assets less Liabilities

= Accumulated Fund

This fund represents the member's interest in the club or society.  Many of the concepts that apply there are those that you have covered in your previous studies in this text.

### Development

Preparation of a set of final accounts for a club.

The example that follows is based on a question that recently appeared in an ICB Level 3 examination.

*Example*

Harthill Hockey Club had the following assets and liabilities at 1 January 2007:

Net book value of fixed assets:

| | |
|---|---|
| Pavilion | £75,000 |
| Machinery | £22,000 |
| Equipment | £6,800 |
| | |
| Bank | £4,250 |
| Creditor for machine maintenance | £750 |
| | |
| Accruals: | |
| Heat and light | £450 |
| Ground rent | £490 |
| Prepayments Insurance | £510 |

Subscriptions in arrears and advance were £100 and £120 respectively.

The receipts and payments for the year ended 31 December 2007 showed:-

(This is simply a summary of the Club's Cash Book)

|  | £ |
|---|---|
| Bank Balance 1/1/07 | 4,250 |
| **Income:** | |
| Christmas Draw | 1,800 |
| Raffles | 750 |
| Jumble Sale | 1,400 |
| Subscriptions | 1,001 |
| Refreshments | 869 |
| Sponsorship | 2,520 |
| | 12,590 |
| **Expenditure:** | |
| Refreshments | 1,250 |
| Heat and light | 900 |
| Ground rent | 1,400 |
| Insurance | 1,100 |
| New equipment fence/nets | 4,200 |
| Ground maintenance | 690 |
| Maintenance machinery | 960 |
| | 10,500 |
| Bank Balance 31/12/07 | £2,090 |

- **Additional Information**

  At 31 December 2007:

  Insurance was prepaid by £610

  Heat and light was accrued £210 and £450 was outstanding for ground rent

  Subscriptions of £100 were outstanding as overdue and £80 had been paid in advance

  Creditor machinery maintenance £175

  Depreciation Policy:

  Machinery 10% on net book value

  Equipment 20% on net book value

  It was now agreed to depreciate the pavilion 2% on cost.

  **Task**

  Prepare the Income and Expenditure Account for year ended 31 December 2007, together with a Balance Sheet for presentation to the members of Harthill Hockey Club.

**Step 1**

Calculate the opening accumulated fund.

Assets Less Liabilities = Accumulated Fund

Assets:   £

| | |
|---|---:|
| Pavilion | 75,000 |
| Machinery | 22,000 |
| Equipment | 6,800 |
| Bank | 4,250 |
| Pre-payments | 510 |
| Subscriptions in arrears (due from members) | 100 |
| | £108,660 |

Less:  Liabilities

| | |
|---|---:|
| Creditors | 750 |
| Subscriptions in advance | 120 |
| Accruals:- | |
|     Heat and light | 450 |
|     Ground rent | 490 |
| | 1,810 |

| | |
|---|---:|
| **Accumulated Fund** | **£106,850** |

This figure will be needed as the opening fund to be shown on the Balance Sheet.

**Step 2**

There are various figures shown in the receipts and payments account that require adjustment when preparing the income and expenditure account, to apply to accruals concept.

(1)   Subscriptions (member's contribution)

It is often the case that member's subscriptions at the end of the year may be in advance or arrears.  Here we have opening and closing values for subscriptions in arrears and advance.

The best approach to determine the figure required for the income and expenditure account is to construct a "T" account.

**Subscriptions a/c**

| | | | | | |
|---|---|---|---|---|---|
| 1/1/07 | Balance B/d | 100 | 1/1/07 | Balance B/d | 120 |
| 31/12/07 | Balance C/d | | 31/12/07 | Bank | 1,001 |
| | (in advance) | 80 | 31/12/07 | Balance C/d | 100 |
| 31/12/07 | I&E a/c | 1,041 | | (outstanding) | |
| | | | | | |
| 1/1/08 | Balance B/d | 100 | 1/1/08 | Balance B/d | 80 |

The account now shows that the club has a current asset (DR balance) subscriptions overdue from members and a current liability (CR balance) subscriptions received in advance from members.

These values will appear on the club balance sheet, and the amount transferred to the income and expenditure account for the year accounts for these adjustments.

(2)     The accruals and pre-payments are also best dealt with by the use of a series of "T" accounts.

### Heat and Light

| | | | | | |
|---|---|---|---|---|---|
| 31/12/07 | Bank | 900 | 1/1/07 | Balance B/d | 450 |
| 31/12/07 | Balance C/d | | 31/12/07 | I&E a/c | 660 |
| | (accruals) | 210 | | | |
| | | | 1/1/08 | Balance B/d | 210 |

The account now shows the closing liability, the accrual and the amount to be transferred to the income and expenditure account.

### Ground Rent

| | | | | | |
|---|---|---|---|---|---|
| 31/12/07 | Bank | 1,400 | 1/1/07 | Balance B/d | 490 |
| 31/12/07 | Balance C/d | | 31/12/07 | I&E a/c | 1,360 |
| | (accruals) | 450 | | | |
| | | | 1/1/08 | Balance B/d | 450 |

Again, here we can see the closing liability in the form of the accrual, and the amount transferred to the income and expenditure account.

### Machine Maintenance

| | | | | | |
|---|---|---|---|---|---|
| 31/12/07 | Bank | 960 | 1/1/07 | Balance B/d | 750 |
| 31/12/07 | Balance C/d | | 31/12/07 | I&E a/c | 385 |
| | (closing creditor) | 175 | | | |
| | | | 1/1/08 | Balance B/d | 175 |

The closing liability is again clearly shown here, together with the transfer to the income and expenditure account.

There is a pre-payment to adjust for on insurance.

**Insurance Account**

| | | | | | |
|---|---|---|---|---|---|
| 1/1/07 | Balance B/d | 510 | 31/12/07 | Balance C/d | 610 |
| 31/12/07 | Bank | 1,100 | | (pre-payment) | |
| | | | 31/12/07 | I&E A/c | 1,000 |
| | | | | | |
| 1/1/08 | Balance B/d | 610 | | | |

Here we can see the closing pre-payment is a (DR) balance brought down of £610.

This will appear as a Current Asset on the balance sheet.

The transfer to I&E account is also shown in the account.

(3)   **Depreciation**

We need to determine the charge for the year.

Pavilion £75,000

2% on Cost =                                          £1,500

Machinery £22,000

10% on NBV =                                        £2,200

| Equipment | | |
|---|---|---|
| at 1/1/07 | £6,800 | |
| Additions | | |
| in year | 4,200 | |
| | 11,000 | |
| 20% on NBV | | £2,200 |
| | | £5,900 |

The Income and Expenditure account and the Balance Sheet can now be prepared:-

**Balance Sheet as at 31 December 2007**

|  |  | NBV |
|---|---|---|
| **Fixed Assets** | | |
| Pavilion | | 73,500 |
| Machinery | | 19,800 |
| Equipment | | 8,800 |
| | | 102,100 |
| **Current Assets** | | |
| Bank | 2,090 | |
| Pre-payment | 610 | |
| Subs in arrears | 100 | |
| | 2,800 | |
| **Less Current Liabilities** | | |
| Creditors & Accruals | 835 | |
| Subs in advance | 80 | |
| | 915 | |
| Net Current Assets | | 1,885 |
| Net Assets | | £103,985 |
| | | |
| Financed By: | | |
| Accumulated Fund 1/07 | | 106,850 |
| Less excess expenditure over income for year | | (2,865) |
| | | £103,985 |

**Harthill Hockey Club**
**Income and Expenditure Account**
**for the year ended 31 December 2007**

| Income | £ | £ |
|---|---|---|
| Subscriptions | | 1,041 |
| Christmas Draw | | 1,800 |
| Raffles | | 750 |
| Jumble Sale | | 1,400 |
| Sponsorship | | 2,520 |
| | | 7,511 |
| **Expenditure** | | |
| Refreshments: | | |
| Income | 869 | |
| Expenditure | 1,250 | |
| | | 381 |
| Heat and Light | | 660 |
| Ground Rent | | 1,360 |
| Insurance | | 1,000 |
| Ground maintenance | | 690 |
| Machinery maintenance | | 385 |
| Depreciation: | | |
| Machinery | | 2,200 |
| Equipment | | 2,200 |
| Pavilion | | 1,500 |
| | | £10,376 |

Excess of Expenditure over Income  =  **£2,865**

You will note that there is also new terminology on the Income and Expenditure account that of:-

> excess of expenditure over income for the year (i.e. deficit), however, when a surplus is made this would read excess of income over expenditure for the year.

## 4.1   SUMMARY

Using mark-ups and gross profit percentages you can reconstruct a trading account and use these figures in your other workings:

**Sales** – a debit entry in the sales ledger control account (if they are all sales on credit).

**Cost of sales** can be used to find any of its components: **opening stock, closing stock** or **purchases**. Purchases is a credit entry in the purchase ledger control account.

## CONCLUSION

No two incomplete records situations are exactly the same whether this is in practice or in examination questions. For examination questions what is required is a knowledge of the techniques covered in this chapter for reconstructing financial statements from a variety of types of incomplete information together with a thorough grasp and application of double entry bookkeeping. It is very likely that you will be asked to complete a clubs and society question in the ICB exam, so pay particular attention to the illustrative question in this chapter.

The six step approach set out in the chapter is a good starting point in most questions although all six steps may not always be required. You should then be aware of the use of the cash and bank accounts, sales and purchases control accounts and any margins, mark-ups or other ratios that are given in the question. A good tip is that if a margin or mark-up is given in the question then it is highly likely that the only way to calculate either sales or purchases will be by applying this percentage to the information in the question.

## KEY TERMS

**Limited accounting records** – records kept by a trader of certain transactions but additional information is required to prepare financial statements.

**Incomplete accounting records** – records which the trader has not fully completed or where no records at all have been kept of transactions.

**Mark-up** – gross profit calculated as a percentage of cost of sales.

**Margin** – gross profit calculated as a percentage of sales.

## SELF TEST QUESTIONS

|  |  | *Paragraph* |
|---|---|---|
| 1 | How can the profit of a business be measured if opening and closing net assets and drawings are known? | 1.3 |
| 2 | What is the sales ledger control account? | 2.2 |
| 3 | What are the six basic steps for the approach to an incomplete records question? | 2.2 |
| 4 | How is the gross profit percentage calculated? | 3.2 |
| 5 | How is a mark-up percentage calculated? | 3.3 |
| 6 | How is a cost mark-up converted to a profit margin? | 3.4 |
| 7 | If stock were destroyed in a fire but sales, purchases and opening stock could be calculated, how would the figure for stock destroyed be estimated? | 3.5 |

## PRACTICE QUESTION

### B LETITSLIDE

B Letitslide is in business but does not keep proper books of account. In order to prepare his trading and profit and loss account for the year ended 31 December 20X5 you are given the following information:

|  | 20X5 1 Jan £ | 20X5 31 Dec £ |
|---|---|---|
| Stock on hand | 1,310 | 1,623 |
| Debtors | 268 | 412 |
| Creditors for goods | 712 | 914 |
| Creditors for expenses | 116 | 103 |

In addition, you are able to prepare the following summary of his cash and bank transactions for the year:

**Cash account**

|  | £ |  | £ |
|---|---|---|---|
| Balance 1 Jan | 62 | Payments into bank | 3,050 |
| Shop takings | 4,317 | Purchases | 316 |
| Cheques cashed | 200 | Expenses | 584 |
|  |  | Drawings | 600 |
|  |  | Balance 31 Dec | 29 |
|  | 4,579 |  | 4,579 |

**Bank account**

|  | £ |  | £ |
|---|---|---|---|
| Balance 1 Jan | 840 | Cash withdrawn | 200 |
| Cheques from customers | 1,416 | Purchases | 2,715 |
| Cash paid in | 3,050 | Expenses | 519 |
|  |  | Drawings | 400 |
|  |  | Delivery van |  |
|  |  | (purchased 1 Sep) | 900 |
|  |  | Balance 31 Dec | 572 |
|  | 5,306 |  | 5,306 |

In addition, Mr Letitslide says that he had taken goods for personal consumption and estimates those goods cost £100.

In considering the debtors, Mr Letitslide suggests that there is no hope of receiving an amount of £30 from one customer There are other doubtful debts and a provision is to be made of 5% of the debtors after writing off the irrecoverable debt of £30.

### Required:

Allowing depreciation on the delivery van of 20% per annum, prepare the accounts as requested and a balance sheet as at 31 December 20X5.

*For a suggested answer, see the 'Answers' section at the end of the book.*

## ADDITIONAL QUESTION 1

### CYGNUS

Cygnus is a sole trader selling antiques from a rented shop. He has not kept proper accounting records for the year ended 31 January 20X1, in spite of his accountant's advice after the preparation of his accounts for the year ended 31 January 20X0.

His assets and liabilities at 31 January 20X0 and 31 January 20X1 were as follows:

|  | Reference to notes | | 31 January | |
|---|---|---|---|---|
|  |  |  | 20X0 | 20X1 |
|  |  | £ | £ | £ |
| Assets |  |  |  |  |
| Shop equipment |  |  |  |  |
| Cost |  | 14,800 |  |  |
| Less Depreciation | 2 | 6,900 | 7,900 | To be calculated |
| Stock |  |  | 146,400 | 128,700 |
| Trade debtors |  |  | 14,400 | 15,700 |
| Rent in advance | 3 |  | 1,000 | To be calculated |
| Cash at bank |  |  | – | 4,850 |
| Cash in hand |  |  | 800 | 900 |
| Liabilities |  |  |  |  |
| Loan – Draco | 4 |  | 24,000 | 12,000 |
| Trade creditors |  |  | 12,100 | 14,200 |
| Accrued expenses | 5 |  | 2,300 | To be calculated |
| Bank overdraft |  |  | 2,600 | See summary below |

The following summary shows bank receipts and payments by Cygnus.

| Receipts | Notes | £ | Cash book summary | Notes | Payments £ |
|---|---|---|---|---|---|
| Sales revenue banked |  | 131,600 | Opening balance |  | 2,600 |
| Proceeds of sale of shop equipment | 2 | 300 | Payments for purchases | 3 | 81,400 |
|  |  |  | Rent paid |  | 8,250 |
|  |  |  | Purchase of shop equipment | 2 | 1,800 |
|  |  |  | Sundry expenses | 5 | 18,600 |
|  |  |  | Interest on loan | 4 | 2,400 |
|  |  |  | Repayment of loan | 4 | 12,000 |
|  |  |  | Closing balance |  | 4,850 |
|  |  | 131,900 |  |  | 131,900 |

Before banking the shop takings, Cygnus took various amounts as drawings.

**Notes**

(1)     Cygnus fixes his selling prices by doubling the cost of all items purchased.

(2)     During the year, Cygnus sold for £300 equipment that had cost £800, and had a written down value at 1 February 20X0 of £200. He purchased further equipment on 1 August 20X0 for £1,800.

       Depreciation is charged at 10% per year on the straight-line basis, with no depreciation in the year of sale and proportionate depreciation in the year of purchase.

(3)     Rent is payable quarterly in advance on 1 January, 1 April, 1 July and 1 October each year. On 1 July 20X0, the annual rent was increased from £6,000 to £9,000.

(4)     The loan from Draco carries interest at 10% per year payable annually on 31 December. On 31 December 20X0, Cygnus repaid £12,000 of the loan. The balance is repayable on 31 December 20X4.

(5)     The accrued expenses at 31 January 20X0 consist of the £200 interest accrued on Draco's loan (see Note 4) and sundry expenses of £2,100. At 31 January 20X1, accruals for sundry expenses amounted to £3,300.

**Required:**

Prepare for Cygnus a trading and profit and loss account for the year ended 31 January 20X1 and a balance sheet as at that date.

*For a suggested answer, see the 'Answers' section at the end of the book.*

                                                                      

## ADDITIONAL QUESTION 2

### AMY AND BARBARA

Amy and Barbara are in partnership together. They have just completed their second year of trading and have asked for your help in preparing their final accounts for the year ended 31 December 20X6.

The partners have not been able to keep proper accounting records, but they are able to provide you with the following information.

At 1 January 20X6 the business had the following balances:

|  | Dr £ | Cr £ |
|---|---|---|
| Vehicles at cost | 48,000 | |
| Equipment at cost | 90,000 | |
| Provisions for depreciation | | |
|   Vehicles | | 12,000 |
|   Equipment | | 18,000 |
| Stock | 37,500 | |
| Trade debtors | 120,000 | |
| Prepayments | | |
|   Advertising | 3,000 | |
|   Insurance | 6,000 | |
| Cash at bank | 15,000 | |
| Trade creditors | | 22,500 |
| Accruals | | |
|   Heating and lighting | | 4,500 |
|   Rent and rates | | 1,500 |
| Capital accounts: Amy | | 120,000 |
|             Barbara | | 75,000 |
| Current accounts: Amy | | 34,500 |
|             Barbara | | 31,500 |
| | 319,500 | 319,500 |

The business also made payments during the year for the following:

| | £ |
|---|---|
| Carriage inwards | 6,750 |
| Vehicle running expenses | 20,250 |
| Insurance | 7,500 |
| Heating and lighting | 10,500 |
| Telephone | 5,250 |
| Advertising | 3,375 |
| Rent and rates | 22,500 |
| Office supplies | 1,875 |
| Suppliers | 300,000 |
| | 378,000 |

**Additional information**

(i)     Stock as at 31 December 20X6 was valued at £55,500.

(ii)    Receipts from customers were £600,000 and there was £82,500 outstanding from customers at 31 December 20X6.

(iii)   Settlement discounts of £7,500 were given to customers.

(iv)    The business owed £15,000 to suppliers as at 31 December 20X6.

(v)     Insurance of £1,500 was paid in advance at 31 December 20X6.

(vi)    During the year irrecoverable debts of £22,500 were written off.

(vii)   Invoices totalling £3,375 relating to heating and lighting were unpaid at 31 December 20X6.

(viii)  Depreciation on vehicles is to be provided at 25% of their written down value.

(ix)    Depreciation on equipment is to be provided at 20% on its original cost.

(x)     Interest on capital account balances is to be allowed at 10%.

(xi)    Cash drawings during the year were: Amy £90,000; Barbara £45,000.

(xii)   Interest on drawings is to be charged as follows: Amy £3,000; Barbara £1,500.

(xiii)  Amy and Barbara have an agreement to share the profits in the ratio 2:1.

**Required:**

Prepare the following statements for the partnership:

(a)     the trading, profit and loss and appropriation account for the year ended 31 December 20X6

(b)     the partners' current accounts for the year ended 31 December 20X6

(c)     the balance sheet as at 31 December 20X6.

(You are advised to show any necessary supporting workings.)

*For a suggested answer, see the 'Answers' section at the end of the book.*

# Chapter 10

# PARTNERSHIP ACCOUNTS

With partnerships, there is some new terminology to learn but more importantly there are a number of special accounting entries that have to be dealt with.

Partnership accounts are covered by two chapters. Firstly, the basic techniques specific to partnership accounting are looked at. These basics are then built upon in the subsequent chapter when changes in partnerships are investigated.

## CONTENTS

## LEARNING OUTCOMES

At the end of this chapter you should be able to:

*   identify the key features of a partnership

*   outline the advantages and disadvantages of operating as a partnership, compared with operating as a sole trader or limited company

*   outline the conventional methods of dividing profit and maintaining equity between partners

*   draft an appropriation account for a partnership

*   distinguish between partners' capital and current accounts

*   record the partners' share of profits and losses and their drawings in the ledger accounts

*   record introductions and withdrawals in the ledger accounts

- draft the trading and profit and loss account and appropriation account and the balance sheet for a partnership from a trial balance incorporating period end adjustments including:

  - accruals and prepayments

  - depreciation

  - irrecoverable debts and provisions for debtors

  - closing stock.

# 1    PARTNERSHIPS – KEY FEATURES, ADVANTAGES AND DISADVANTAGES

## 1.1    IDENTIFICATION OF PARTNERSHIP

A partnership exists whenever two or more people trade together with the intention of making a profit.  No legal formalities are needed to create a partnership, although most partnerships will have a partnership agreement.  If no agreement exists then the partnership agreement set out in the Partnership Act of 1890 comes into effect.  This states that all profits and losses should be shared equally between the partners.

## 1.2    THE PARTNERSHIP AGREEMENT

**Definition**      A **partnership agreement**, which need not necessarily be in written form, will govern the relationships between the partners.

Important matters to be covered include:

(a)    name of firm, the type of business, and duration

(b)    capital to be introduced by partners

(c)    distribution of profits between partners

(d)    drawings by partners

(e)    arrangements for dissolution, or on the death or retirement of partners

(f)    settling of disputes

(g)    preparation and audit of accounts.

## 1.3    THE ADVANTAGES AND DISADVANTAGES OF OPERATING AS A PARTNERSHIP, RELATIVE TO SOLE TRADING OR AS A COMPANY

Comparing a partnership to sole trading, the advantages of operating as a partnership are as follows:

(a)    Business risks are spread among more than one person.

(b)    Individual partners can develop special skills upon which the other partners can rely rather than being a jack of all trades.

(c)    Certain partners may be able to draw upon larger capital resources to set up the partnership or expand the partnership.

The disadvantages are:

(a)    There may be disputes between partners on such matters as the direction the business is taking or how much money individual partners are taking out of the business. Some partners may feel they are contributing more time and effort to the partnership than others and not being sufficiently financially rewarded as a result.

(b)    A partner is 'jointly and severally liable' for his partners. This means that if one partner is being sued in relation to the business of the partnership, the other partners share in the responsibility.

A partnership has some advantages over a company as the arrangement is less formal than setting up a company requiring the issue of shares and the appointment of directors. If the partners wish to dissolve the business that is an easier matter to achieve by a partnership rather than a company.

The advantage of a company is that the owners of the business – the shareholders – may be protected from the creditors of the company as regards the payment of outstanding debts.

## 1.4    SUMMARY

Relative to sole trading, a partnership can give access to the wider skills and capital resources of several partners, although disputes amongst partners and the problems which can arise from joint and several liability are disadvantages

Partnerships have fewer formalities than companies but do not have the protection of limited liability.

# 2    DIVISION OF PROFITS AND THE PARTNERS' CAPITAL AND CURRENT ACCOUNTS

## 2.1    DIVISION OF PROFITS

The partnership agreement will detail how the profits of the firm are to be divided amongst the partners. However, if the partners do not have a partnership agreement, verbal or written, the rules laid down in the Partnership Act 1890 will apply. The rules are:

- residual profits are shared equally

- there are no salaries paid to partners

- there is no interest paid on partners' capital invested in the business

- interest at 5% per annum is payable on partners' loans to the business.

The division of profit stated in the partnership agreement may be quite complex in order to reflect the expected differing efforts and contributions of the partners. For example, some or all of the partners may be entitled to a salary to reflect the differing management involvement in the business. Interest on capital may be provided to reflect the differing amounts of capital contributed. The profit shares may differ to reflect seniority or greater skills.

It is important to appreciate however that all of the above examples are means of dividing the profits of the partnership and are not expenses of the business. A partnership salary is merely a device for calculating the division of profit; it is not a salary in the normal meaning of the term.

## 2.2 ACCOUNTING DISTINCTIONS BETWEEN PARTNERSHIPS AND SOLE TRADERS

The accounting techniques developed for sole traders are generally applicable to partnerships, but there are certain important differences:

| Item | Sole trader's books | Partnership's books |
|---|---|---|
| Capital introduced | Capital account | Partners' fixed capital accounts |
| Drawings and share of the profit | Capital account | Partners' current accounts |
| Division of profits | Inapplicable – one proprietor only | Appropriation account |

## 2.3 CAPITAL ACCOUNTS

At the commencement of the partnership an agreement will have to be reached as to the amount of capital to be introduced. This could be in the form of cash or other assets. Whatever the form of assets introduced and debited to asset accounts, it is normal to make the credit entry to fixed capital accounts. These are so called because they are not then used to record drawings or shares of profits but only major changes in the relations between partners. In particular, fixed capital accounts are used to deal with:

(a)     capital introduced or withdrawn by new or retiring partners

(b)     revaluation adjustments (these are discussed further in the next chapter).

The balances on fixed capital accounts do not necessarily bear any relation to the division of profits. However, to compensate partners who provide a larger share of the capital, it is common for notional interest on capital accounts to be paid to partners. This is dealt with through the appropriation account (see section 3).

## 2.4 CURRENT ACCOUNTS

These are used to deal with the regular transactions between the partners and the firm i.e. matters other than those sufficiently fundamental to be dealt with through the capital accounts. Most commonly these are:

(a)     share of profits, interest on capital and partners' salaries usually computed annually

(b)     monthly drawings against the annual share of profit.

**2.5 RECORDING THE PARTNERS' SHARES OF PROFITS/LOSSES AND THEIR DRAWINGS IN THE LEDGER ACCOUNTS AND BALANCE SHEET PRESENTATION**

**Example 1**

Nab and Crag commenced business in partnership on 1 January 20X6, contributing as fixed capital £5,000 and £10,000 cash respectively. All profits and losses are shared equally. The profit for the year ended 31 December 20X6 amounted to £10,000. Drawings for Nab and Crag amounted to £3,000 and £4,000 respectively.

**You are required** to prepare the capital and current accounts and balance sheet extracts.

**Partners' capital accounts**

|  | | Nab | Crag | | | | Nab | Crag |
|---|---|---|---|---|---|---|---|---|
|  | | £ | £ | | | | £ | £ |
|  | | | | 20X6 | | | | |
|  | | | | 1 Jan | Cash | | 5,000 | 10,000 |

**Partners' current accounts**

|  | | Nab | Crag | | | | Nab | Crag |
|---|---|---|---|---|---|---|---|---|
|  | | £ | £ | | | | £ | £ |
| 20X6 | | | | 20X6 | | | | |
| 1 Dec | Drawings | 3,000 | 4,000 | 31 Dec | Share of profits | | 5,000 | 5,000 |
|  | Balance c/d | 2,000 | 1,000 | | | | | |
|  | | 5,000 | 5,000 | | | | 5,000 | 5,000 |
|  | | | | 20X7 | | | | |
|  | | | | 1 Jan | Balance b/d | | 2,000 | 1,000 |

The above accounts are presented in a columnar format. This is quite common in a partnership set of books as each partner will have similar transactions during the year. A columnar format allows two (or more) separate accounts to be shown using the same narrative. It is important to remember though that each partner's account is separate from the other partner(s).

**Balance sheet at 31 December 20X6 (extract)**

|  | Capital accounts | Current accounts | |
|---|---|---|---|
|  | £ | £ | £ |
| Partners' accounts: | | | |
| Nab | 5,000 | 2,000 | 7,000 |
| Crag | 10,000 | 1,000 | 11,000 |
|  | 15,000 | 3,000 | 18,000 |

Note that the current account balances of £2,000 and £1,000 will be credited in the following year with profit shares and debited with drawings.

One of the main differences between the capital section of the balance sheet of a sole trader and a partnership, is that the partnership balance sheet will often only give the closing balances whereas the sole trader's movements in capital are shown. The main reason for the difference is simply one of space. Movements in the capital and current accounts for a few partners cannot be easily accommodated on the face of the balance sheet.

**Example 2**

The information is the same as in Example 1, except that Nab's drawings are £5,300. The current accounts now become

### Partners' current accounts

|  |  | Nab £ | Crag £ |  |  | Nab £ | Crag £ |
|---|---|---|---|---|---|---|---|
| 20X6 |  |  |  | 20X6 |  |  |  |
|  | Drawings | 5,300 | 4,000 |  | Share of profits | 5,000 | 5,000 |
| 31 Dec | Balance c/d |  | 1,000 | 31 Dec | Balance c/d | 300 |  |
|  |  | 5,300 | 5,000 |  |  | 5,300 | 5,000 |
| 20X7 |  |  |  | 20X7 |  |  |  |
| 1 Jan | Balance b/d | 300 |  | 1 Jan | Balance b/d |  | 1,000 |

Note that Nab's current account is overdrawn. How do we present this in the balance sheet?

### Balance sheet at 31 December 20X6 (extract)

|  | Capital accounts £ | Current accounts £ | £ |
|---|---|---|---|
| Partners' accounts: |  |  |  |
| Nab | 5,000 | (300) | 4,700 |
| Crag | 10,000 | 1,000 | 11,000 |
|  | 15,000 | 700 | 15,700 |

## ACTIVITY 1

Tor and Hill have been in partnership for two years, sharing profits in the ratio 2:1. Figures for profit and drawings are as follows:

|  |  | Year ending 31 December | |
|---|---|---|---|
|  |  | 20X4 £ | 20X5 £ |
| Drawings: | Tor | 2,000 | 2,500 |
|  | Hill | 1,500 | 1,500 |
| Residual profit |  | 9,000 | 12,000 |

**You are required** to prepare the partners' current accounts for 20X4 and 20X5, bringing down balances at the end of each year.

*For a suggested answer, see the 'Answers' section at the end of the book.*

## 2.6  SUMMARY

Partners' drawings and share of the annual profit is recorded in their current accounts. Their capital accounts are used to record fixed capital introduced or withdrawn and revaluation adjustments.

## 3 THE APPROPRIATION ACCOUNT

### 3.1 INTRODUCTION

**Definition** The **appropriation account** is a ledger account dealing with the allocation of net profit between the partners. In practice it is often included as the final part of the trading and profit and loss account.

It can also be presented as a statement in columnar form.

An important point is that all allocations of profit to partners in their capacity as partners, and during the time they actually are partners, are made through the appropriation account. This applies even though such allocations may be described as partners' salaries, interest on capital or a share of profits.

### 3.2 USING THE APPROPRIATION ACCOUNT

Pike and Scar are in partnership and have the following profit-sharing arrangements:

(a) interest on capital is to be provided at a rate of 8% pa

(b) Pike and Scar are to receive salaries of £6,000 and £8,000 pa respectively

(c) the balance of profit or loss is to be divided between Pike and Scar in the ratio 3 : 2.

Net profit for the year amounts to £20,000 and capital account balances are Pike £12,000 and Scar £9,000.

**You are required** to prepare:

(a) a statement showing the allocation of profit between the partners; and

(b) relevant entries in the trading and profit and loss and appropriation account.

**Solution**

(a) **Allocation of net profit of £20,000**

|  | Pike | | Scar | | Total |
|---|---|---|---|---|---|
|  | £ | | £ | | £ |
| Interest on capital | 960 | | 720 | | 1,680 |
| Salaries | 6,000 | | 8,000 | | 14,000 |
| Balance of profits (£20,000 – £15,680) | | | | | |
| In ratio 3 : 2 | 2,592 | (3/5) | 1,728 | (2/5) | 4,320 |
| Totals | 9,552 | | 10,448 | | 20,000 |

Note that this is only a calculation of the allocation of profit and not part of the double entry bookkeeping system, merely providing the figures for the appropriation account.

(b)     Extract from trading and profit and loss and appropriation account for the year ended 20X1

|  | £ | £ |
|---|---|---|
| Sales |  | x |
| Cost of sales |  | x |
| Gross profit |  | x |
| Expenses |  | x |
| Net profit |  | 20,000 |
| Allocated to: |  |  |
| Pike | 9,552 |  |
| Scar | 10,448 |  |
|  |  | 20,000 |

The profit and loss appropriation account is closed by transferring the profit shares to the credit of the partners' current accounts. The double entry is therefore

| Debit | Credit | With |
|---|---|---|
| Profit and loss appropriation account | Pike's current account | £9,552 |
| Profit and loss appropriation account | Scar's current account | £10,448 |

For the purposes of examinations (and in practice) parts (a) and (b) above can be amalgamated as follows

**Extract from trading and profit and loss and appropriation account for the year ended 20X1**

|  | £ | £ |
|---|---|---|
| Sales |  | x |
| Cost of sales |  | x |
| Gross profit |  | x |
| Expenses |  | x |
| Net profit for year |  | 20,000 |

**Appropriation statement**

|  | Pike £ | Scar £ | Total £ |
|---|---|---|---|
| Interest on capital | 960 | 720 | 1,680 |
| Salaries | 6,000 | 8,000 | 14,000 |
| Balance of profits (£20,000 – £15,680) in ratio 3 : 2 | 2,592 (3/5) | 1,728 (2/5) | 4,320 |
| Totals | 9,552 | 10,448 | 20,000 |

The debits actually being made are as before (£9,552 and £10,448).

## ACTIVITY 2

Flame and Smoke are in partnership and have the following profit-sharing arrangements:

(a)     Interest on capital is provided at a rate of 8% pa.

(b)     Flame and Smoke are to receive salaries of £6,000 and £8,000 pa.

(c)     The balance of profit or loss is to be divided between Flame and Smoke in the ratio 3:2.

The balances on the capital accounts of the partners stand at Flame: £6,000 and Smoke: £4,000. The net profit for the year is £3,680.

**You are required** to show the allocation of profit between the partners.

---

*For a suggested answer, see the 'Answers' section at the end of the book.*

## 3.3   PARTNERS' SALARIES

One point which regularly causes difficulties is the partners' salaries.  The key is to remember at the outset that a partner's salary is an appropriation of profit, whereas a salary paid to an employee is an expense.

Accordingly a salary to which a partner is entitled, is included as part of the appropriation statement.  Questions sometimes state that a partner has withdrawn his salary.  In this case:

(a)     include the salary in the appropriation statement as usual; and

(b)     quite separately treat the withdrawal of the salary as drawings.

| Debit | Credit | With |
|---|---|---|
| Partner's current account | Bank | Amount withdrawn |

## 3.4   GUARANTEED MINIMUM PROFIT SHARE

In certain partnership agreements a partner may be guaranteed a minimum share of profits.  The appropriation of profit would proceed in the normal way.  If the result is that the partner has less than this minimum, the deficit will be made good by the other partners (normally in profit-sharing ratio). Sometimes the guarantee is given by one partner only, who will then bear the whole of the deficit.

**Example**

Tessa, Laura and Jane are in partnership and have the following profit-sharing arrangements:

(a)     Tessa and Laura are to receive salaries of £20,000 and £30,000 respectively

(b)     balance of profit or loss is to be divided in the ratio: Tessa 1, Laura 2, Jane 3

(c)     Tessa is guaranteed a minimum profit share of £25,000.

The net profit for the year is £68,000.

**You are required** to show the appropriation account for the year.

**Solution**

### Appropriation account

|  | Tessa £ | Laura £ | Jane £ | Total £ |
|---|---|---|---|---|
| Net profit |  |  |  | 68,000 |
| Salaries | 20,000 | 30,000 |  | (50,000) |
|  |  |  |  | 18,000 |
| Balance of profits in ratio 1 : 2 : 3 | 3,000 | 6,000 | 9,000 | (18,000) |
|  | 23,000 | 36,000 | 9,000 |  |
| Adjustment | 2,000 |  |  |  |
| Laura 2/5 × 2,000 |  | (800) |  |  |
| Jane 3/5 × 2,000 |  |  | (1,200) |  |
| Totals | 25,000 | 35,200 | 7,800 | 68,000 |

## 3.5  INTEREST ON DRAWINGS

Occasionally there is a provision in a partnership agreement for a notional interest charge on the drawings by each partner.  The interest charges are merely a negative profit share – they are a means by which total profits are allocated between the partners.

The reason for an interest on drawings provision is that those partners who draw out more cash than their colleagues in the early part of an accounting period should suffer a cost.

**Example**

Dick and Dastardly are in partnership.  The capital and current accounts as at 1 January 20X7 show:

|  | Capital £ | Current £ |
|---|---|---|
| Dick | 50,000 | 2,500 |
| Dastardly | 20,000 | 3,000 |

The partnership agreement provides for the following:

(a)  profits and losses are shared between Dick and Dastardly in percentages 60 and 40

(b)  interest on capital at 10% per annum is allowed

(c)  interest on drawings is charged at 12% per annum.

Drawings for the year to 31 December 20X7 are:

|  | Dick | Dastardly |
|---|---|---|
|  | £ | £ |
| 1 February 20X7 | 5,000 | 2,000 |
| 30 September 20X7 | 2,000 | 5,000 |

The profit for the year is £20,000.

**You are required** to prepare the appropriation account and the current accounts for the year ended 31 December 20X7.

### Solution

#### Appropriation account for the year ended 31 December 20X7

|  | Dick | Dastardly |  |
|---|---|---|---|
|  | £ | £ | £ |
| Profit for the year |  |  | 20,000 |
| Add: Interest on drawings (see working) | (610) | (370) | 980 |
|  |  |  | 20,980 |
| Less: Interest on capital: |  |  |  |
| 50,000 × 10% | 5,000 |  |  |
| 20,000 × 10% |  | 2,000 | (7,000) |
|  |  |  | 13,980 |
| Balance in profit-sharing ratio: |  |  |  |
| 13,980 × 60% | 8,388 |  |  |
| 13,980 × 40% |  | 5,592 | (13,980) |
| Total allocation | 12,778 | 7,222 | 20,000 |

#### Current accounts

|  |  | Dick | Dastardly |  |  | Dick | Dastardly |
|---|---|---|---|---|---|---|---|
|  |  | £ | £ |  |  | £ | £ |
| 20X7: |  |  |  | 20X7: |  |  |  |
| 1 Feb | Drawings | 5,000 | 2,000 |  | Balance b/d | 2,500 | 3,000 |
| 30 Sep | Drawings | 2,000 | 5,000 | 31 Dec | Share of profits | 12,778 | 7,222 |
|  | Balance c/d | 8,278 | 3,222 |  |  |  |  |
|  |  | 15,278 | 10,222 |  |  | 15,278 | 10,222 |

#### *Workings*

|  |  | Dick | Dastardly |
|---|---|---|---|
|  |  | £ | £ |
| Interest on drawings: |  |  |  |
| 1 February 20X7 | 5,000 × 12% × 11/12 | 550 |  |
|  | 2,000 × 12% × 11/12 |  | 220 |
| 30 September 20X7 | 2,000 × 12% × 3/12 | 60 |  |
|  | 5,000 × 12% × 3/12 |  | 150 |
|  |  | 610 | 370 |

| | | |
|---|---|---|
| **Conclusion** | The appropriation account shows how the net profit for the year has been divided amongst the partners. Appropriations may take the form of: | |

- interest on capital

- 'salaries'

- a share of the remaining profit (in the agreed ratio)

- interest on drawings (occasionally).

# 4 DRAFTING THE FINANCIAL STATEMENTS FOR A PARTNERSHIP FROM THE TRIAL BALANCE

You should now be in a position to follow through from the trial balance stage a full example of partnership accounts.

**Example**

You are provided with the following information regarding the partnership of Dacre, Hutton and Tod.

(a) The trial balance at 31 December 20X6 is as follows:

| | Dr £ | Cr £ |
|---|---|---|
| Sales | | 50,000 |
| Stock at 1 January 20X6 | 6,000 | |
| Purchases | 29,250 | |
| Carriage inwards | 250 | |
| Carriage outwards | 400 | |
| Creditors | | 4,000 |
| Cash at bank | 3,900 | |
| Current accounts: | | |
| Dacre | | 900 |
| Hutton | | 750 |
| Tod | | 1,350 |
| Capital accounts: | | |
| Dacre | | 4,000 |
| Hutton | | 5,000 |
| Tod | | 6,000 |
| Drawings: | | |
| Dacre | 2,000 | |
| Hutton | 3,000 | |
| Tod | 5,000 | |
| Sundry expenses | 2,800 | |
| Debtors | 13,000 | |
| Shop fittings: | | |
| Cost | 8,000 | |
| Accumulated depreciation | | 1,600 |
| | 73,600 | 73,600 |

(b)    Closing stock is valued for accounts purposes at £5,500.

(c)    Depreciation of £800 is to be provided on the shop fittings.

(d)    The profit-sharing arrangements are as follows:

   (i)     interest on capital is to be provided at a rate of 10% per annum

   (ii)    Dacre and Tod are to receive salaries of £3,000 and £4,000 per annum respectively

   (iii)   the balance of profit or loss is to be divided between Dacre, Hutton and Tod in the ratio of 3 : 8 : 4.

**You are required** to prepare final accounts together with current accounts of the partners.

**Solution**

**Dacre, Hutton and Tod**
**Trading and profit and loss account for the year ended 31 December 20X6**

|  | £ | £ |
|---|---|---|
| Sales | | 50,000 |
| Opening stock | 6,000 | |
| Purchases | 29,250 | |
| Carriage inwards | 250 | |
|  | 35,500 | |
| Less:  Closing stock | 5,500 | |
|  | | 30,000 |
| Gross profit | | 20,000 |
| Sundry expenses | 2,800 | |
| Carriage outwards | 400 | |
| Depreciation | 800 | |
|  | | 4,000 |
| Net profit | | 16,000 |
| Allocated to: | | |
| Dacre | 4,900 | |
| Hutton | 4,500 | |
| Tod | 6,600 | |
|  | | 16,000 |

## Balance sheet as at 31 December 20X6

|  | Cost £ | Acc dep'n £ | £ |
|---|---|---|---|
| **Fixed assets** | | | |
| Shop fittings | 8,000 | 2,400 | 5,600 |
| **Current assets** | | | |
| Stock | | 5,500 | |
| Debtors | | 13,000 | |
| Cash | | 3,900 | |
| | | 22,400 | |
| **Current liabilities** | | | |
| Creditors | | 4,000 | |
| Net current assets | | | 18,400 |
| | | | 24,000 |

## Partners' accounts

|  | Capital accounts £ | Current accounts £ | £ |
|---|---|---|---|
| Dacre | 4,000 | 3,800 | 7,800 |
| Hutton | 5,000 | 2,250 | 7,250 |
| Tod | 6,000 | 2,950 | 8,950 |
| | 15,000 | 9,000 | 24,000 |

## Partners' current accounts

|  |  | Dacre £ | Hutton £ | Tod £ |  |  |  | Dacre £ | Hutton £ | Tod £ |
|---|---|---|---|---|---|---|---|---|---|---|
| 20X6: | | | | | 20X6: | | | | | |
| | Drawings | 2,000 | 3,000 | 5,000 | 1 Jan | Balance b/d | | 900 | 750 | 1,350 |
| 31 Dec | Balance | | | | | P&L app | | 4,900 | 4,500 | 6,600 |
| | c/d | 3,800 | 2,250 | 2,950 | | | | | | |
| | | 5,800 | 5,250 | 7,950 | | | | 5,800 | 5,250 | 7,950 |
| | | | | | 20X7: | | | | | |
| | | | | | 1 Jan | Balance b/d | | 3,800 | 2,250 | 2,950 |

### Workings and commentary

The adjustments for stock and depreciation should be familiar by now.

The new development is that, having calculated the profit for the period, it has to be appropriated between Dacre, Hutton and Tod. To calculate their respective shares an appropriation statement is used

| | Dacre | Hutton | Tod | Total |
|---|---|---|---|---|
| | £ | £ | £ | £ |
| Interest on capital | 400 | 500 | 600 | 1,500 |
| Salaries | 3,000 | – | 4,000 | 7,000 |
| Balance of profit (£16,000 – £8,500) in ratio 3 : 8 : 4 | 1,500 | 4,000 | 2,000 | 7,500 |
| | 4,900 | 4,500 | 6,600 | 16,000 |

This gives us the figures for the double entry

Dr  Profit and loss appropriation

Cr  Partners' current accounts

**A final point**

The majority of examination questions specify separate capital and current accounts. Occasionally you may be faced with a question specifying only one account for each partner. Such an account acts as a capital and current account combined.

**Conclusion**     Adopt a stepwise approach to the preparation of partnership accounts, as follows:

1       Draw up a proforma balance sheet and profit and loss account and enter figures as soon as you calculate them.

2       Work through any adjustments required.

3       Complete the profit and loss account and appropriate the profit as per the partnership agreement.

4       Open up partners' current accounts; enter the opening balances, appropriations of profit and drawings.

5       Find the new balances on the partners' current accounts.

6       Complete the balance sheet.

# KEY TERMS

**Partnership** – exists whenever two or more people trade together with the intention of making a profit.

**Partnership agreement** – which need not necessarily be in written form, will govern the relationships between the partners.

**Joint and several liability** – each partner has unlimited liability for all of the losses incurred by the business. Usually losses will be shared in the profit sharing ratio, but if one or more partners become insolvent, then the loss must be borne by the other partners.

**Partners' capital accounts** – records the long-term investment by the partners in the business.

**Partners' current accounts** – used to deal with the regular transactions between the partners and the firm, such as profits and drawings.

**Partners' appropriation account** – a ledger account dealing with the allocation of net profit between the partners.

**Partners' salaries** – an appropriation of profit. They are not an expense of the business.

**Profit-sharing ratio** – the agreed ratio in which the residual profits of the partnership are shared between the partners.

**Residual profits** – the net profit of the partnership adjusted for interest on capital and drawings and salaries.

# SELF TEST QUESTIONS

|   |   | *Paragraph* |
|---|---|---|
| 1 | What is a partnership? | 1.1 |
| 2 | What are the differences between capital and current accounts? | 2.3 & 2.4 |
| 3 | Is interest on drawings an expense of the partnership? | 3.5 |

## ADDITIONAL QUESTION

### OWEN AND GRIFFITHS

Owen and Griffiths are in partnership, sharing profits equally after Owen has been allowed a salary of £5,000 per year. No interest is charged on drawings or allowed on current accounts, but interest of 10% pa is allowed on the opening capital account balances for each year. Their bookkeeper has been having trouble balancing the books and has eventually produced the following list of balances as at 31 December:

|  | £ |
|---|---|
| Capital account: | |
| Owen | 9,000 |
| Griffiths | 10,000 |
| 10% loan account: | |
| Griffiths | 5,000 |
| Williams | 6,000 |
| Current account balance on 1 January: | |
| Owen | 1,000 |
| Griffiths | 2,000 |
| Drawings: | |
| Owen | 6,500 |
| Griffiths | 5,500 |
| Sales | 113,100 |
| Sales returns | 3,000 |
| Closing stock | 17,000 |
| Cost of goods sold | 70,000 |
| Sales ledger control account | 30,000 |
| Purchase ledger control account | 25,000 |
| Operating expenses | 26,100 |
| Fixed assets at cost | 37,000 |
| Provision for depreciation | 18,000 |
| Bank overdraft | 3,000 |
| Suspense account | |

You ascertain the following information:

(a)     The sales ledger control account does not agree with the list of balances from the ledger.  The following errors, when corrected, will remove the difference:

   (i)     the sales returns day book has been undercast by £100

   (ii)    a contra entry with the creditors ledger for £200 has been omitted from the control accounts

   (iii)   an invoice for £2,000 was incorrectly entered in the sales day book as £200.

(b)     A fully depreciated fixed asset, original cost £5,000, was sold during the year.  The proceeds of £1,000 were entered in the bank account only, and no other entries in connection with the disposal were made.

(c)     It is agreed that hotel bills for £500 paid by Griffiths from his personal bank account are proper business expenses.  Owen has taken goods out of the business for his own use, costing £1,000.  No entry has been made for either of these items.

(d)     No interest of any kind has yet been paid or recorded.

(e)     Any remaining balance on the suspense account cannot be traced, and is to be treated in the most suitable manner.

**You are required:**

(a)     to prepare a trial balance and establish the balance on the suspense account

(b)     to incorporate the necessary adjustments, showing your workings clearly in any way you feel appropriate

(c)     to prepare final accounts for presentation to the partners.

*For a suggested answer, see the 'Answers' section at the end of the book.*

# Chapter 11

# PARTNERSHIP CHANGES

**This chapter covers the accounting techniques to record changes in a partnership.**

---

## CONTENTS

1    Introduction

2    Recording introductions and withdrawals of capital in the ledger accounts

3    Partnership changes requiring revaluations

4    Partnership changes and goodwill

---

## LEARNING OUTCOMES

At the end of this chapter you should be able to:

- explain why a revaluation is required after an admission, a change in the profit sharing ratio or a retirement

- revalue the partnership after such a change and calculate the goodwill

- make appropriate entries in the ledger accounts

- draft the partnership balance sheet after a change in the partnership.

---

## 1    INTRODUCTION

### 1.1    TYPES OF PARTNERSHIP CHANGE

**Definition**    **Partnership changes** may occur in three quite different situations:

(a)    when a partner leaves, dies or retires

(b)    when a new partner enters the partnership

(c)    when existing partners change their profit-sharing arrangements.

---

From the accounting viewpoint there are two aspects:

(a)     dividing profits between old and new partners when the change occurs during the course of the financial period (covered in this section)

(b)     the problem of valuing partnership assets, especially goodwill, at the time of the change (sections 3 and 4).

## 1.2     DIVISION OF PROFITS IN A PARTNERSHIP CHANGE

There will be many occasions when a partnership change does not take place at a convenient date (such as the accounting year end!).

For the purpose of dividing profits equitably between the partners concerned, it is necessary to apportion (or allocate) profits between those arising before the change, and those arising afterwards.

In most cases where the trade is not of a seasonal nature, sales occur at an even rate during the year.  It will then be reasonable to apportion sales on a time basis.  Having apportioned the profit between the different parts of the year, it is then allocated between the partners according to their arrangements for sharing profits during those periods.  This is demonstrated below.

### Example

Gavel and Kirk are in partnership, sharing profits in the ratio 3:2, after Gavel has received a salary of £2,000 per annum. The accounting year-end of the partnership is 31 December.  On 30 June 20X6 Blea is admitted to the partnership.  The new profit-sharing arrangements provide for Gavel's salary of £2,000 per annum to be maintained, and for Blea to receive a salary of £3,000 per annum.  The balance is to be shared between Gavel, Kirk and Blea in the ratio 2:2 :1.

The net profit for the year to 31 December 20X6 is £22,000.

**You are required** to show the transfer to the partners' current accounts for the year ended 31 December 20X6.

### Solution

Assuming that the net profit of £22,000 accrues evenly over the year, it may be apportioned on a time basis as follows:

|  |  | £ |
|---|---|---|
| 1 January 20X6 to 30 June 20X6 | $\frac{6}{12} \times £22,000$ | 11,000 |
| 1 July 20X6 to 31 December 20X6 | $\frac{6}{12} \times £22,000$ | 11,000 |
|  |  | 22,000 |

The net profit relating to each six-month period is allocated according to the profit-sharing arrangements operating during that period.

**Statement of allocation of profit**

| | Gavel | Kirk | Blea | Total |
|---|---|---|---|---|
| **Six months to 30 June 20X6** | £ | £ | £ | £ |
| Salary: | | | | |
| Gavel  6/12 × £2,000 | 1,000 | – | – | 1,000 |
| Balance of profit  (£11,000 – £1,000) | | | | |
| in ratio 3 : 2 | 6,000 | 4,000 | – | 10,000 |
| | 7,000 | 4,000 | – | 11,000 |

**Six months to 31 December 20X6**

| | Gavel | Kirk | Blea | Total |
|---|---|---|---|---|
| Salary: | £ | £ | £ | £ |
| Gavel  6/12 × £2,000 | 1,000 | – | – | 1,000 |
| Blea  6/12 × £3,000 | – | – | 1,500 | 1,500 |
| Balance of profit  (£11,000 – £2,500) | | | | |
| in ratio 2 : 2 : 1 | 3,400 | 3,400 | 1,700 | 8,500 |
| | 4,400 | 3,400 | 3,200 | 11,000 |
| Totals – 12 months | 11,400 | 7,400 | 3,200 | 22,000 |

Remember that the salaries are expressed at an annual rate!  Interest on capital percentages are also expressed at an annual rate so a similar problem of time apportionment could apply elsewhere.

**Partners' current accounts – Extract**

| | Gavel | Kirk | Blea | | Gavel | Kirk | Blea |
|---|---|---|---|---|---|---|---|
| | £ | £ | £ | | £ | £ | £ |
| | | | | Profit and loss | | | |
| | | | | appropriation: | | | |
| | | | | To 30 June | 7,000 | 4,000 | – |
| | | | | To 31 Dec | | | |
| | | | | 20X6 | 4,400 | 3,400 | 3,200 |

## 1.3 APPORTIONMENT OF PROFIT – SOME COMPLICATIONS

Unless otherwise instructed, it is acceptable to apportion profits on a time basis. Occasionally the question may specify some alternative basis.

**Example**

Assume that in the previous example the net profit of £22,000 was arrived at as follows:

| | £ | £ |
|---|---|---|
| Sales (£96,000 in six months to 30 June 20X6) | | 160,000 |
| Cost of sales | | 118,000 |
| Gross profit | | 42,000 |
| Selling and distribution expenses | 5,500 | |
| Administrative expenses | 12,500 | |
| Financial expenses | 2,000 | |
| | | 20,000 |
| Net profit | | 22,000 |

**You are required** to show the apportionment of profit between the two parts of the year. Assume that gross profit and selling expenses are to be apportioned on a turnover basis and all other items on a time basis. The allocation of profit between the partners is not required.

**Solution**

|  | £ |
|---|---|
| Turnover: | |
| Six months to 30 June 20X6 | 96,000 |
| Six months to 31 December 20X6 | 64,000 |
| | 160,000 |

The ratio of turnover is therefore 96:64 or 3:2. Costs directly related to sales should be split in this ratio (i.e. cost of sales and selling expenses). Other costs which can be taken to accrue evenly over the year should be split equally.

| | Six months to 30 June 20X6 | | Six months to 31 December 20X6 | | Total | |
|---|---|---|---|---|---|---|
| | £ | £ | £ | £ | £ | £ |
| Gross profit (3:2) | | 25,200 | | 16,800 | | 42,000 |
| Selling expenses (3:2) | 3,300 | | 2,200 | | 5,500 | |
| Administrative expenses (1:1) | 6,250 | | 6,250 | | 12,500 | |
| Financial expenses (1:1) | 1,000 | | 1,000 | | 2,000 | |
| | | 10,550 | | 9,450 | | 20,000 |
| Net profit | | 14,650 | | 7,350 | | 22,000 |

The apportionment of net profit is therefore:

|  | £ |
|---|---|
| Six months to 30 June 20X6 | 14,650 |
| Six months to 31 December 20X6 | 7,350 |
| | 22,000 |

As can be seen, in a seasonal business, where sales fluctuate greatly from month to month, the apportionment of a net profit on a time basis may give a misleading picture.

## ACTIVITY 1

The net profit of Harry, Barry and Gary for the year ended 31 December 20X8 was arrived at as follows:

|  |  | £ |
|---|---|---|
| Sales (£30,000 in the 4 months to 1 May 20X8) | | 180,000 |
| Less: Cost of sales | | 90,000 |
| | | 90,000 |
| Gross profit | | |
| Selling and distribution expenses | 12,000 | |
| Administrative expenses | 3,000 | |
| | | 15,000 |
| Net profit | | 75,000 |

Gary joined the partnership on 1 May 20X8. The partners have agreed to apportion gross profit and selling and distribution expenses on the basis of sales and administrative expenses on a time basis.

The profit-sharing ratios are:

| | |
|---|---|
| 1 January to 30 April 20X8 | Harry 2: Barry 1 |
| 1 May to 31 December 20X8 | Harry 2: Barry 1: Gary 1 |

There are no salaries or interest payable to the partners.

**You are required** to calculate each partner's share of profit for 20X8.

*For a suggested answer, see the 'Answers' section at the end of the book.*

### 1.4 SUMMARY

In the year of a partnership change, the profits for the year have to be split into pre-acquisition and post-acquisition portions with reference to the date of the change. The relevant portions will then be divided amongst the old partners in the old profit-sharing ratio and the new partners in the new profit-sharing ratio.

## 2 RECORDING INTRODUCTIONS AND WITHDRAWALS OF CAPITAL IN THE LEDGER ACCOUNTS

### 2.1 INTRODUCTIONS AND WITHDRAWALS OF CAPITAL

**Definition**      **Introductions of capital** refers to the introduction of cash or other assets into the partnership. This is usual on admission of a new partner who will be expected to 'buy' her way in to the partnership.

**Definition**      **Withdrawals of capital** refers to cash or other assets taken out of the business in settlement of amounts owing to the partners on their capital and current accounts. This will occur when a partner leaves the partnership.

Partners may need to introduce or withdraw capital at times other than when there are partnership changes and the accounting treatment will be the same.

For the sake of clarity, two unrealistic assumptions will be made in this section, namely that at the date of partnership changes:

(a) all tangible assets (e.g. stock, fixed assets) are stated in the accounts at their current value

(b) goodwill is ignored.

These unrealistic assumptions will be removed in sections 3 and 4 below, but first two possible causes of a change in the partnership will be considered: – the retirement of an existing partner and the admission of a new partner.

## 2.2 RETIREMENT OF AN EXISTING PARTNER

When a partner retires, it is important, first of all, to ensure that his current account is credited with his share of profits and debited with his drawings up to the date of retirement. The balances on his current and capital accounts are then transferred to a loan account and become a liability of the business. The manner and timing of the payment of this liability are likely to be regulated by the partnership agreement. In practice, the amount will probably be paid in instalments, with allowance for interest on the unpaid balance. Since the former partner is no longer a partner of the business, the interest cannot be regarded as an appropriation of profit and must be regarded as an expense of the partnership (in the same way, as interest on a bank overdraft).

### Example

Birk, How and Stile have been in partnership for many years. Birk retired from the partnership on 1 July. At 30 June the summarised balance sheet showed the following position:

|  |  |  | £ |
|---|---|---|---|
| Sundry assets |  |  | 27,296 |

| Partners' accounts | Capital accounts | Current accounts | |
|---|---|---|---|
|  | £ | £ | |
| Birk | 12,000 | 1,735 | 13,735 |
| How | 8,000 | 2,064 | 10,064 |
| Stile | 3,000 | 497 | 3,497 |
|  | 23,000 | 4,296 | 27,296 |

It is assumed that the current account balances reflect profit shares and drawings up to 30 June. At that date, the balances on Birk's capital and current accounts should be transferred to a loan account and regarded as a liability of the partnership. A balance sheet at 1 July would then appear:

|  |  |  | £ |
|---|---|---|---|
| Sundry assets |  |  | 27,296 |
| Less: Loan account – Birk |  |  | 13,735 |
| Net assets |  |  | 13,561 |

| Partners' accounts | Capital accounts | Current accounts | |
|---|---|---|---|
|  | £ | £ | |
| How | 8,000 | 2,064 | 10,064 |
| Stile | 3,000 | 497 | 3,497 |
|  | 11,000 | 2,561 | 13,561 |

Birk is now a creditor of the partnership as he is no longer a partner.

### Example

Strode wishes to retire from his partnership. The balances on his capital and current accounts, after accounting for his share of the profits and his drawings, are £9,000 Cr and £1,000 Cr respectively. He wishes to keep his car, which is in the partnership books at a cost of £8,000 less depreciation of £6,000, to be paid £3,000 in cash and for the rest to remain on loan.

You are required to show the double entry to record the withdrawal of capital by Strode on his retirement.

**Solution**

|  |  | £ | £ |
|---|---|---|---|
| Dr | Capital account | 9,000 |  |
| Dr | Current account | 1,000 |  |
| Dr | Car: depreciation | 6,000 |  |
|  | Cr    Car: cost |  | 8,000 |
|  | Cr    Cash |  | 3,000 |
|  | Cr    Loan |  | 5,000 |

The £10,000 owed to Strode is partly settled by means of a car at its net book value of £2,000 and £3,000 cash. Therefore, £5,000 still remains on loan.

## 2.3 ADMISSION OF A NEW PARTNER

A new partner will often be required to bring in cash as a contribution to the fixed capital of the partnership. This cash is therefore credited to the partner's capital account.

**Example**

Facts as in the previous Birk, How and Stile example. Tarn is admitted to the partnership on 3 July. He brings in cash of £2,500 as his fixed capital. The partners' current accounts would not be affected, but the capital accounts would appear as follows:

**Partners' capital accounts**

|  | Birk<br>£ | How<br>£ | Stile<br>£ | Tarn<br>£ |  | Birk<br>£ | How<br>£ | Stile<br>£ | Tarn<br>£ |
|---|---|---|---|---|---|---|---|---|---|
| 2 July:<br>Loan<br>account | 12,000 | – | – | – | 1 July:<br>Bal b/d | 12,000 | 8,000 | 3,000 | · |
|  |  |  |  |  | 3 July:<br>Cash | – | – | – | 2,50( |

A summarised balance sheet at 3 July would then show the following position:

|  |  | £ |
|---|---|---|
| Sundry assets  (£13,561 + £2,500) |  | 16,061 |

| Partners' accounts | Capital accounts<br>£ | Current accounts<br>£ |  |
|---|---|---|---|
| How | 8,000 | 2,064 | 10,064 |
| Stile | 3,000 | 497 | 3,497 |
| Tarn | 2,500 | – | 2,500 |
|  | 13,500 | 2,561 | 16,061 |

If Tarn had contributed his capital share in the form of an asset other than cash, for example a car valued at £2,500, the double entry would have been:

| Debit | Credit | With |
|---|---|---|
| Motor car account | Tarn's capital account | £2,500 |

The only effect on the balance sheet would then be the make-up of the sundry assets figure of £16,061 as between fixed and current assets.

## 2.4  SUMMARY

Withdrawals of capital are recorded as:

Dr Capital (and current) account

Cr Cash / other assets / loan (if the amount due is to be settled later)

Introductions of capital are recorded as:

Dr Cash / other assets

Cr Capital account

# 3  PARTNERSHIP CHANGES REQUIRING REVALUATIONS

## 3.1  INTRODUCTION

Two unrealistic assumptions have been made so far.

(a)  No notice was taken of any difference between the current value of individual tangible assets and the amount at which they were stated in the books of account.  On a change in partnership-sharing arrangements, such an account must be taken as partners are entitled to share capital profits in the same ratio as they share revenue profits.

Thus, just as we time-apportion profits between periods before and after the change, so we need to take account of capital gains or losses at the date of change.  This topic is explored further in this section.

(b)  Goodwill was ignored.  Its nature and measurement will be dealt with in the next section.

## 3.2  WHY A REVALUATION IS REQUIRED ON A PARTNERSHIP CHANGE

Any change in a partnership (and remember a change can be an admission of a new partner, the retirement of an old partner or a change in profit sharing ratios) affects partners' rights to profits and assets.  The entitlement to a one third share in profits means an entitlement to a one third share in the assets which exist in the partnership as well.

To the extent that the current worth of the assets is different from their book value, a profit or loss will have accrued on the asset from the date of acquisition of the asset to the date of the partnership change.  This profit or loss will need to be allocated to each partner in the old profit sharing ratio as the partnership change triggers off new profit sharing ratios.

The gain/loss is computed by revaluing the net assets at the date of change.

## 3.3 ENTRIES IN THE LEDGER ACCOUNTS IN RESPECT OF REVALUATIONS

Wherever there is a change in profit-sharing arrangements, a partnership will take account of changes in the value of its tangible assets.

In this instance, use will be made of a temporary revaluation account to calculate the overall gain or loss on the revaluation; this will then be shared between the old partners in their old profit-sharing ratios in the capital accounts.

The initial bookkeeping entries are as follows:

| Debit | Credit | With |
|---|---|---|
| Assets | Revaluation | Increases in asset values |
| Revaluation | Assets | Decreases in asset values |
| Liabilities | Revaluation | Decreases in liability values |
| Revaluation | Liabilities | Increases in liability values |

At this stage the balance on the revaluation account will represent the overall surplus or deficiency on the revaluation, which will be shared between the old partners in their old profit-sharing ratios:

| Debit | Credit | With |
|---|---|---|
| Revaluation | Partner's capital accounts | Surplus on revaluation |
| or | | |
| Partners' capital accounts | Revaluation | Deficit on revaluation |

**Example**

Trooper, Tremlett and Arkle are in partnership; sharing profits in the ratio 4:3:3. As at 1 January 20X6 Randall is to be admitted to the partnership, thereafter profits are to be shared equally. Randall is to introduce capital of £30,000.

The partnership's balance sheet as at 31 December 20X5 shows the following:

|  | £ | £ |
|---|---|---|
| Fixed assets: | | |
| Property | | 70,000 |
| Plant and machinery | | 30,000 |
| Fixtures and fittings | | 25,000 |
| | | 125,000 |
| Current assets: | | |
| Stock | 35,000 | |
| Debtors | 28,000 | |
| Bank | 17,000 | |
| | 80,000 | |
| Less: Current liabilities: | | |
| Creditors | 27,250 | |
| | | 52,750 |
| | | 177,750 |

|  | Capital £ | Current £ | Total £ |
|---|---|---|---|
| Partners' accounts: |  |  |  |
| Trooper | 50,000 | 2,000 | 52,000 |
| Tremlett | 53,750 | 4,000 | 57,750 |
| Arkle | 65,000 | 3,000 | 68,000 |
|  | 168,750 | 9,000 | 177,750 |

For the purposes of the revaluation the assets of the partnership are to be revalued as follows:

|  | £ |
|---|---|
| Property | 80,000 |
| Plant and machinery | 27,500 |
| Fixtures and fittings | 32,100 |
| Stock | 36,350 |
| Debtors | 27,750 |

**You are required** to show:

(a)    the revaluation account

(b)    the partners' capital accounts

(c)    the balance sheet of the partnership as at 1 January 20X6.

**Solution**

(a)

### Revaluation

|  | £ | £ |  | £ |
|---|---|---|---|---|
| Plant and machinery |  | 2,500 | Property | 10,000 |
| Debtors |  | 250 | Fixtures and fittings | 7,100 |
| Profit on revaluation: |  |  | Stock | 1,350 |
| Trooper (4) | 6,280 |  |  |  |
| Tremlett (3) | 4,710 |  |  |  |
| Arkle (3) | 4,710 |  |  |  |
|  |  | 15,700 |  |  |
|  |  | 18,450 |  | 18,450 |

(b)

### Partners' capital accounts

|  | Trooper £ | Tremlett £ | Arkle £ | Randall £ |  | Trooper £ | Tremlett £ | Arkle £ | Randall £ |
|---|---|---|---|---|---|---|---|---|---|
| Balance c/d | 56,280 | 58,460 | 69,710 | 30,000 | Balance b/d | 50,000 | 53,750 | 65,000 |  |
|  |  |  |  |  | Revalu- ation | 6,280 | 4,710 | 4,710 |  |
|  |  |  |  |  | Bank |  |  |  | 30,000 |
|  | 56,280 | 58,460 | 69,710 | 30,000 |  | 56,280 | 58,460 | 69,710 | 30,000 |

(c)                 **Trooper, Tremlett, Arkle and Randall**
**Balance sheet as at 1 January 20X6**

| | £ | £ |
|---|---:|---:|
| Fixed assets: | | |
| Property | | 80,000 |
| Plant and machinery | | 27,500 |
| Fixtures and fittings | | 32,100 |
| | | 139,600 |
| Current assets: | | |
| Stock | 36,350 | |
| Debtors | 27,750 | |
| Bank | 47,000 | |
| | 111,100 | |
| Less: Current liabilities: | | |
| Creditors | 27,250 | |
| | | 83,850 |
| | | 223,450 |

| | Capital £ | Current £ | Total £ |
|---|---:|---:|---:|
| Partners' accounts | | | |
| Trooper | 56,280 | 2,000 | 58,280 |
| Tremlett | 58,460 | 4,000 | 62,460 |
| Arkle | 69,710 | 3,000 | 72,710 |
| Randall | 30,000 | – | 30,000 |
| | 214,450 | 9,000 | 223,450 |

Note that the capital accounts were adjusted for the change in asset values as it is a capital transaction. In particular the revaluation does not create realised profits (i.e. they are not in the form of cash) and thus partners cannot increase their drawings out of their current accounts.

## ACTIVITY 2

The following revaluations were made to the net assets of Blagden and MacDonald on admission of Kirkman:

| | | £ |
|---|---|---:|
| Plant and machinery | increased by | 5,000 |
| Debtors | decreased by | 1,000 |
| Stock | decreased by | 1,000 |
| Property | increased by | 17,000 |

The profit-sharing ratio prior to Kirkman's admission was Blagden 3 : McDonald 2. After Kirkman's admission it was Blagden 2 : MacDonald 2 : Kirkman 1.

**You are required** to write up the revaluation account indicating each partner's share of any profit or loss on revaluation.

*For a suggested answer, see the 'Answers' section at the end of the book.*

## 3.4 SUMMARY

All increases and decreases in the value of assets and liabilities at the date of a partnership change are included in the revaluation account:

- increases in assets will be credit entries

- increases in liabilities will be debit entries.

The balance on the revaluation account is shared amongst the old partners in their old profit-sharing ratio.

# 4 PARTNERSHIP CHANGES AND GOODWILL

## 4.1 THE NATURE OF GOODWILL

**Definition**     **Goodwill** is the difference between the value of the business as a whole and the aggregate of the fair values of the net assets.

When a business changes hands, the price paid will commonly exceed the value of the net assets owned by the business, even when these are valued at market prices. This difference is an intangible asset referred to as goodwill. It is generated by the business as it continues to operate and comprises a number of factors, such as reputation for quality, a good location, experience and technical know-how. Such factors all mean that the business is in a good position to continue in the future and to make profits, and it is this that a purchaser is prepared to pay for, over and above the value of the net assets of the business.

## 4.2 MEASUREMENT OF GOODWILL

There can be no precise valuation of goodwill, which has to be essentially the result of an exercise of judgement of the worth of the business as a whole by the parties involved.

In examination questions, the examiner will either tell you the valuation to be placed on the goodwill, or give sufficient information to enable you to calculate the figure. The most likely possibilities are as follows.

(a)     Goodwill is valued at £12,000.  Self-explanatory.

(b)     X introduces £3,000 in payment for his share of one quarter of the goodwill.  If a quarter share is valued at £3,000, then the total value for goodwill is £12,000.

(c)     Goodwill is to be valued at three times last year's profit of £4,000.  Three times last year's profit is £12,000, giving the total value for goodwill.

(d)     The business is worth £200,000 and the fair value of the tangible net assets is £160,000.  Goodwill is therefore £40,000.

## 4.3 ADJUSTMENTS IN RESPECT OF GOODWILL

There are two main situations as regards goodwill:

(a)     the partners wish to include goodwill as an asset in their balance sheet; or

(b)     the partners do not wish to include goodwill as an asset in their balance sheet but the effect of goodwill needs to be reflected in their capital accounts. This is more likely to be the requirement in examination questions.

## 4.4 GOODWILL INCLUDED AS AN ASSET IN THE BALANCE SHEET

In this situation use can be made of the revaluation account in the normal fashion:

| Debit | Credit | With |
|-------|--------|------|
| Goodwill | Revaluation | Increase in the value of goodwill |
| Revaluation | Goodwill | Decrease in the value of goodwill |

If goodwill has not previously been incorporated in the books, the entry is:

| Debit | Credit | With |
|-------|--------|------|
| Goodwill | Revaluation | The agreed value of goodwill |

Again the revaluation account acts as a 'holding account' with the balance being split between the partners in the profit share ratio and cleared out to the capital accounts.

## 4.5 EXAMPLE

Laid, Back and Gower are in partnership sharing profits 5:3:2. As at 1 January 20X7 Gooch is to be admitted to the partnership; thereafter profits are to be shared equally. Gooch is to introduce capital of £40,000, of which £10,000 represents a payment for his share of the goodwill, which is subsequently to be disclosed in the books.

The partnership's balance sheet as at 31 December 20X6 shows the following:

|  | £ | £ |
|---|---|---|
| Fixed assets: | | |
| Property | | 42,500 |
| Plant and machinery | | 16,750 |
| Fixtures and fittings | | 12,800 |
| | | 72,050 |
| Current assets: | | |
| Stock | 15,800 | |
| Debtors | 29,471 | |
| Bank | 18,623 | |
| | 63,894 | |
| Less: Current liabilities: | | |
| Creditors | 24,713 | |
| | | 39,181 |
| | | 111,231 |
| Partners' capital accounts: | | |
| Laid | | 61,237 |
| Back | | 18,476 |
| Gower | | 31,518 |
| | | 111,231 |

For the purposes of the revaluation the assets of the partnership are to be revalued as follows:

|  | £ |
|---|---|
| Property | 75,000 |
| Plant and machinery | 21,250 |
| Fixtures and fittings | 11,000 |

**You are required** to show:

(a)    the revaluation account

(b)    the partners' capital accounts

(c)    the balance sheet of the partnership as at 1 January 20X7.

**Solution**

(a)

**Revaluation account**

|  | £ | £ |  | £ |
|---|---|---|---|---|
| Fixtures and fittings |  | 1,800 | Property | 32,500 |
| Profit on revaluation: |  |  | Plant and machinery | 4,500 |
| Laid (5) | 37,600 |  | Goodwill | 40,000 |
| Back (3) | 22,560 |  |  |  |
| Gower (2) | 15,040 |  |  |  |
|  |  | 75,200 |  |  |
|  |  | 77,000 |  | 77,000 |

***Working – Goodwill***

If Gooch is introducing £10,000 for his share of the goodwill (one quarter thereof) the total value of goodwill must be £40,000.

(b)

**Partners' capital accounts**

|  | Laid £ | Back £ | Gower £ | Gooch £ |  | Laid £ | Back £ | Gower £ | Gooch £ |
|---|---|---|---|---|---|---|---|---|---|
| Balance |  |  |  |  | Balance |  |  |  |  |
| c/d | 98,837 | 41,036 | 46,558 | 40,000 | b/d | 61,237 | 18,476 | 31,518 |  |
|  |  |  |  |  | Bank |  |  |  | 40,000 |
|  |  |  |  |  | Reval- |  |  |  |  |
|  |  |  |  |  | uation | 37,600 | 22,560 | 15,040 |  |
|  | 98,837 | 41,036 | 46,558 | 40,000 |  | 98,837 | 41,036 | 46,558 | 40,000 |

**Laid, Back, Gower and Gooch**
**Balance sheet as at 1 January 20X7**

|  | £ | £ |
|---|---|---|
| Fixed assets: | | |
| Goodwill | | 40,000 |
| Property | | 75,000 |
| Plant and machinery | | 21,250 |
| Fixtures and fittings | | 11,000 |
| | | 147,250 |
| Current assets: | | |
| Stock | 15,800 | |
| Debtors | 29,471 | |
| Bank | 58,623 | |
| | 103,894 | |
| Less: Current liabilities: | | |
| Creditors | 24,713 | |
| | | 79,181 |
| | | 226,431 |
| Partners' capital accounts: | | |
| Laid | 98,837 | |
| Back | 41,036 | |
| Gower | 46,558 | |
| Gooch | 40,000 | |
| | | 226,431 |

## 4.6 GOODWILL IS THE ONLY ASSET THAT REQUIRES REVALUATION

Quite often, it is only goodwill which requires to be revalued. The book value of the tangible assets may be fairly close to their market value and thus the time and expense involved in making valuations is too much compared to the benefits.

If only goodwill is being revalued, the revaluation account need not be used. The revaluation increase (or decrease) can be transferred from the goodwill account to the partner's capital accounts.

## ACTIVITY 3

The Faldo, Woosnam partnership is to admit Newcomer into the partnership as at 1 July 20X6. Faldo and Woosnam currently share profits 3:1 after annual salaries of £100,000 each.

As from 1 July 20X6 the profit sharing ratio will be Faldo 3, Woosnam 2, Newcomer 2, after annual salaries of £120,000 each.

The partnership balance sheet as at 30 June 20X6 shows:

|  | £ |
|---|---|
| Net assets | 45,000 |

| Partners' accounts | Capital | Current | Total |
|---|---|---|---|
|  | £ | £ | £ |
| Faldo | 20,000 | 8,000 | 28,000 |
| Woosnam | 12,000 | 5,000 | 17,000 |
|  | 32,000 | 13,000 | 45,000 |

Goodwill which does not currently appear on the balance sheet is estimated to be worth £280,000. Newcomer is to pay £90,000 capital into the business. Goodwill is to remain as an asset in the books.

**You are required** to show the partnership balance sheet as at 1 July 20X6 after the admission of Newcomer.

*For a suggested answer, see the 'Answers' section at the end of the book.*

## 4.7 GOODWILL NOT INCLUDED AS AN ASSET IN THE BALANCE SHEET

In many cases goodwill will not be shown on the balance sheet after a partnership change despite the fact that a new partner, for example, has paid for a share. The reasons for this are:

(a) **Subjective nature of valuation**

The value attached to goodwill on a partnership change is either a matter of negotiation between the partners or derived from a formula in the partnership agreement.

It only represents a value attached to the asset at the time of the change. In changing business conditions in the future its value may be very different.

(b) **Taxation**

For capital gains tax purposes it is generally disadvantageous to record partnership goodwill as an asset.

This will not change the need to make entries; the old partners by allowing another person into partnership are sharing their business with him. They are thus selling some of the past goodwill to him and this fact needs to be recorded in the capital accounts.

The approach to be adopted in this instance is to open up temporarily an account for goodwill, using the following journal entries:

| Debit | Credit | With |
|---|---|---|
| Goodwill | Old partners' capital accounts | Their share of the goodwill (using old profit-sharing ratio) |
| New partner's capital accounts | Goodwill | Their share of the goodwill (using new profit-sharing ratio) |

In simple terms this can be described as:

- write up goodwill in the old profit-sharing ratios (OPSR); and

- write it down in the new profit-sharing ratios (NPSR).

**Example**

Alpha, Beta and Gamma are in partnership sharing profits 7:2:1. As at 1 January 20X8 Delta is to be admitted to the partnership; thereafter profits are to be shared 3:3:3:1. Delta is to introduce capital of £50,000, of which £12,000 represents a payment for his share of the goodwill, not to be disclosed in the books.

An extract from the partnership balance sheet as at 31 December 20X7 shows the following:

| | £ |
|---|---|
| Capital accounts: | |
| Alpha | 36,761 |
| Beta | 27,304 |
| Gamma | 29,287 |
| | 93,352 |

Assuming that there are no other revaluations necessary to other assets you are required to show:

(a) partners' capital accounts; and

(b) goodwill account.

**Solution**

(a) **Partners' capital accounts**

| | Alpha £ | Beta £ | Gamma £ | Delta £ | | Alpha £ | Beta £ | Gamma £ | Delta £ |
|---|---|---|---|---|---|---|---|---|---|
| | | | | | Balance | | | | |
| Goodwill | 36,000 | 36,000 | 36,000 | 12,000 | b/d | 36,761 | 27,304 | 29,287 | |
| Balance | | | | | Bank | | | | 50,000 |
| c/d | 84,761 | 15,304 | 5,287 | 38,000 | Goodwill | 84,000 | 24,000 | 12,000 | |
| | 120,761 | 51,304 | 41,287 | 50,000 | | 120,761 | 51,304 | 41,287 | 50,000 |

(b) **Goodwill**

| | £ | | £ |
|---|---|---|---|
| Alpha (7) | 84,000 | Alpha (3) | 36,000 |
| Beta (2) | 24,000 | Beta (3) | 36,000 |
| Gamma (1) | 12,000 | Gamma (3) | 36,000 |
| | | Delta (1) | 12,000 |
| | 120,000 | | 120,000 |

*Working*

If Delta is introducing £12,000 for his share of the goodwill (one-tenth thereof) the total value of goodwill must be £120,000.

### Commentary

Goodwill invariably appears as a complication in questions involving partnerships. The key is to follow the requirements of the question.

Confusion often arises in the case of goodwill not shown in the books in the sense that it appears most unfair that Delta, in the previous example, for instance pays in £50,000 on admission to the partnership and yet ends up with only £38,000 on his capital account. However, the point to remember is that the balance sheet does not include goodwill.

If goodwill were subsequently to be included in the books, say on 2 January 20X8, Delta's capital account would be credited with his share of the goodwill (1/10 × £120,000 = £12,000).

Similarly, if the partnership were dissolved, Delta would be entitled to a one-tenth share in the profit on the disposal of the partnership, which would include the valuation placed on the goodwill.

In any event the key is to follow the requirement in the question, which is likely to treat the partners fairly.

## ACTIVITY 4

The balances on Ratner's and Hogg's capital accounts are £12,500 and £8,600 when they take on a third partner, Friar. Friar contributes £10,000 in cash as her fixed capital. Goodwill is valued at £20,000 at the date of Friar's admission, and is to remain in the books as an asset.

The partners have agreed to share profits and losses equally after Friar is admitted, as was the case prior to the partnership change.

**You are required** to write up the partners' capital accounts and the goodwill account, bringing down balances after the partnership change.

*For a suggested answer, see the 'Answers' section at the end of the book.*

## 4.8   SUMMARY

The double entries in respect of goodwill are as follows:

If goodwill is to remain as an asset in the balance sheet:

> Dr  Goodwill

>> Cr  Revaluation (if other assets are being revalued)

>>> or

>> Cr  Capital accounts in the old profit-sharing ratio

If goodwill is not to remain as an asset in the balance sheet:

> Dr  Capital accounts in the new profit-sharing ratio

>> Cr  Capital accounts in the old profit-sharing ratio

# SELF TEST QUESTIONS

*Paragraph*

| | | |
|---|---|---|
| 1 | What are the three types of partnership change? | 1.1 |
| 2 | Where does the capital account of a partner go to when he retires? | 2.2 |
| 3 | Why is it necessary to revalue assets at the date of the partnership change? | 3.2 |
| 4 | If goodwill is to be valued at three times last year's profit of £4,000, what is the value of goodwill? | 4.2 |

## ADDITIONAL QUESTION 1

### AL, BERT AND HALL

Al and Bert are in partnership, sharing profits equally. At 30 June they have balances on their capital accounts of £12,000 (Al) and £15,000 (Bert). On that day they agree to bring in their friend Hall as a third partner. All three partners are to share profits equally from now on. Hall is to introduce £20,000 as capital into the business. Goodwill on 30 June is agreed at £18,000.

**You are required:**

(a) to show the partners' capital accounts for 30 June and 1 July on the assumption that the goodwill, previously unrecorded, is to be included in the accounts

(b) to show the additional entries necessary to eliminate goodwill again from the accounts

(c) to explain briefly what goodwill is. Why are adjustments necessary when a new partner joins a partnership?

*For a suggested answer, see the 'Answers' section at the end of the book.*

## ADDITIONAL QUESTION 2

### RED, BLUE AND YELLOW

Red, Blue and Yellow are in partnership. Red has decided to retire from the partnership at the end of the day on 31 March 20X9. You have been asked to finalise the partnership accounts for the year ended 31 March 20X9 and to make the entries necessary to account for the retirement of Red from the partnership on that day.

You have been given the following information:

(a) The profit for the year ended 31 March 20X9 was £53,060.

(b) The partners are entitled to the following salaries per annum:

Red    £9,000

Blue    £8,000

Yellow   £6,500

(c) Interest on capital is to be paid at a rate of 12% on the balance at the beginning of the year on the capital accounts. No interest is paid on the current accounts.

(d)     Cash drawings in the year amounted to:

Red          £19,000

Blue         £15,000

Yellow       £14,500

(e)     The balances on the current and capital accounts at 1 April 20X8 were as follows:

| Capital accounts | | Current accounts | |
|---|---|---|---|
| Red | £14,000 Cr | Red | £1,250 Cr |
| Blue | £13,000 Cr | Blue | £1,080 Cr |
| Yellow | £11,000 Cr | Yellow | £935 Cr |

(f)     The profit-sharing ratios in the partnership are currently:

Red          4/10

Blue         3/10

Yellow       3/10

On the retirement of Red, Blue will put a further £20,000 of capital into the business. The new profit-sharing ratios will be:

Blue         6/10

Yellow       4/10

(g)     The goodwill in the partnership is to be valued at £45,000 on 31 March 20X9. No separate account for goodwill is to be maintained in the books of the partnership. Any adjusting entries in respect of goodwill are to be made in the capital accounts of the partners.

(h)     The partners have had the assets of the partnership valued at 31 March 20X9. The book value of the assets at that date and the valuation are as follows:

|  | Book value | Valuation |
|---|---|---|
|  | £ | £ |
| Land and buildings | 139,000 | 164,000 |
| Debtors | 18,000 | 13,000 |

The valuations are to remain in the books of the new partnership.

(i)     Any amounts to the credit of Red on the date of her retirement should be transferred to a loan account.

**Required:**

(a)     Prepare the partners' capital accounts as at 31 March 20X9 showing the adjustments that need to be made on the retirement of Red from the partnership.

(b)     Prepare an appropriation account for the partnership for the year ended 31 March 20X9.

(c)     Prepare the partners' current accounts for the year ended 31 March 20X9.

(d)     Show the balance on Red's loan account as at 31 March 20X9.

*For a suggested answer, see the 'Answers' section at the end of the book.*

# Chapter 12

# INTERPRETATION OF FINANCIAL STATEMENTS

Financial statements are prepared for a variety of people and purposes. For example:

- shareholders need to assess the stewardship of their directors

- investors need to assess the investment potential of a company's shares

- managers need to assess the past and potential performance of individual products or departments.

These different needs require the financial statements to be analysed and interpreted. Part of this analysis will involve the calculation of ratios, but the key performance criteria at this stage is to interpret those ratios. In an exam situation this will involve outlining the possible causes of change within a business, and then outlining the possible effects of those changes.

## CONTENTS

1   Analysis of accounting statements and use of ratios

2   Ratio calculation and analysis

3   Profitability ratios

4   Working capital ratios

5   Solvency ratios

6   Interpretation of financial statements

## LEARNING OUTCOMES

At the end of this chapter you should be able to:

- calculate the following ratios: profitability, liquidity, efficiency, investor, financial

- analyse and interpret the ratios to give an assessment of a company's performance in comparison with:

    (i)    a company's previous period's financial statements

    (ii)   another similar company for the same period

    (iii)  industry average ratios

- identify and discuss the limitations of ratio analysis

- prepare a financial analysis report of a company in a suitable format.

# 1 ANALYSIS OF ACCOUNTING STATEMENTS AND USE OF RATIOS

## 1.1 THE INTERNAL AND EXTERNAL USERS OF ACCOUNTING INFORMATION

Users of accounting information have been discussed in an earlier chapter. The main users we will normally be concerned with are management, lenders and shareholders (including potential shareholders).

## 1.2 RELEVANT INFORMATION

The various users of financial statements require information for quite different purposes. There are a large number of ratios, not all of which will be relevant to a particular situation. It is therefore important to determine the precise information needs of the user, and the decisions he has to take after analysing the relevant information.

The needs of the three particular users may be summarised:

| User | Required for |
|------|--------------|
| Management | Control of costs, improved profitability |
| Lenders | Borrowing and credit purposes |
| Shareholders and investment analysts | Investment decisions – buying and selling shares |

Ask yourself the questions 'What decision is being made?' and 'What information is relevant to that decision?'.

## 1.3 THE SHORTCOMINGS OF INTERPRETATION

The main function for many users is to estimate the future. However, an estimate can only be made by interpretation of the past. There is thus a significant shortcoming in any interpretation as to its effectiveness in estimating the future.

Even if the needs of the user are more concerned with historical stewardship of the business, there are limitations of interpretation as the information presented to the user is of necessity summarised in some form. The summarisation process may have the effect of distorting the nature of some of the information. For example, creditors will be classified into those payable within one year and those payable beyond one year. Two loans which have two days difference in their payment date may well as a consequence be classified under separate headings. The user, unless he is provided with further information will tend to take the two resultant totals at face value.

Finally, it should be noted that the emphasis on information produced by an undertaking is financial. In many cases, non-financial data would be useful in order to see a complete picture of the state of the organisation. Non-financial data includes for example the number of employees in the organisation and the type of skills they possess or indicators of efficiency with which the organisation addresses complaints from customers.

## 1.4 TECHNIQUES OF INTERPRETATION

The syllabus at this level of accounting emphasises the use of ratios to interpret information but this is only one stage in the interpretation process. A most important first step is to understand the environment in which the business operates.

Factors that need to be considered include:

- markets in which the business operates

- general economic conditions

- size of business in relation to competitors.

## 1.5 RATIO CALCULATION

In the context of examination questions much of this information is not available and thus we start at the calculation of ratios stage.

When calculating ratios, the two main points to bear in mind are:

- calculate only those ratios which are relevant to the needs of the user

- state the definitions used.

Some ratios can be calculated in alternative ways and therefore it is important to define the terms used.

## 1.6 RATIO ANALYSIS

Having calculated the ratios, the results must be analysed. Consideration needs to be given to such matters as:

- If a ratio has been computed over a number of time periods does it show a worsening or an improving situation?

- Can the ratio be compared to an objective standard? That is can it be compared with an 'ideal' ratio?

- Do all the ratios when taken together support the conclusions drawn from each individual ratio?

The final stage of interpretation is the critical review.

The limitations of the data used to calculate the ratios need to be considered so that a prudent overall conclusion can be reached.

The information gathered by calculating ratios will allow comparisons with:

(a)     the performance of the business in previous years

(b)     the budgeted or planned performance in the current year

(c)     the performance of similar businesses.

The ratios themselves do not tell one what to do, but they do help to point one in the right direction. Ratios should, therefore, make it easier to make better decisions.

## 1.7 SHORTCOMINGS OF RATIO ANALYSIS

It must be emphasised that accounting ratios are only a means to an end; they are not an end in themselves. By comparing the relationship between figures, they merely highlight significant features or trends in the accounts. Indeed, they may well create more problems than they solve. The real art of interpreting accounts lies in defining the reasons for the features and fluctuations disclosed. To do this effectively, the interested party may need more information and a deeper insight into the affairs of the business.

He should also bear in mind the following:

(a) The date at which the accounts are drawn up. Accurate information can only be obtained with any degree of certainty from up-to-date figures. Furthermore, seasonal variations in the particular trade should be taken into account. Final accounts tend to be drawn up at the end of seasonal trade when the picture they present is of the business at its strongest point financially.

(b) The accuracy of the position shown in the balance sheet. The arrangement of certain matters can be misleading and present a more favourable picture e.g. such 'window-dressing' operations as:

(i) making a special effort to collect debts just before the year-end in order to show a larger cash balance and lower debtors than is normal

(ii) ordering goods to be delivered just after the year-end so that stocks and creditors can be kept as low as possible.

(c) Interim accounts. Whenever possible interested parties should examine accounts prepared on a monthly basis, as a clearer picture of the trends and fluctuations will emerge from these than from the annual financial statements.

(d) Accounting ratios are based on accounting information and are, therefore, only as accurate as the underlying accounting information. At a time, as at present, when traditional accounting procedures are coming in for heavy criticism, students should remember that ratios based on those procedures can be easily criticised.

(e) Ratios based on historic cost accounts do not give a true picture of trends from year to year. An apparent increase in profit may not be a 'true' increase, because of the effects of inflation.

(f) Financial statements only reflect those activities that can be expressed in money terms. They do not give a complete picture of the activities of a business.

(g) The accounting ratios of one company must be compared with those of another similar company in order to draw meaningful conclusions. These conclusions will only be meaningful if that other company's trade is similar.

However, even comparing the financial statements of apparently similar businesses can be misleading because:

(a) Businesses may use different accounting policies. For example, some businesses measure fixed assets at historic cost while others revalue them.

(b) Ratios may not be calculated according to the same formula. For example, there are several possible definitions of gearing and return on capital employed.

(c) Large organisations can achieve economies of scale (e.g. by negotiating extended credit periods or discounts for bulk buying with suppliers). These measures may not be available to smaller businesses.

(d) Companies within the same industry can serve completely different markets and there may be differences in sales mix and product range. These can affect profitability ratios such as profit margin and expenses to sales.

## 1.8 INTERPRETATION AND 'NOT-FOR-PROFIT' ORGANISATIONS

Most public sector bodies now prepare commercial style accounts and may be required to comply with generally accepted accounting principles and applicable accounting standards. These accounts can be interpreted using ratio analysis and observation in exactly the same way as the accounts of a commercial organisation.

When interpreting the accounts of a public sector body you should bear in mind the following major differences between private sector and public sector organisations.

|  | Private sector | Public sector |
| --- | --- | --- |
| Primary objective | To make profits | To provide a service (economy, effectiveness, efficiency) |
| Stewardship responsibilities | To investors (shareholders) | To the general public |

The main users of the accounts of private sector organisations are investors and potential investors, lenders and potential lenders and management. The main users of the accounts of public sector organisations are:

(a) taxpayers

(b) those who benefit from their activities

(c) electors.

Other users may include:

(a) central government

(b) employees

(c) lenders of funds

(d) pressure groups.

As always, you should interpret the accounts in the light of the objective of the organisation and the needs of those who are interested in its accounts (these should normally be stated or implied in the question).

**Conclusion** When calculating ratios:

- be aware of the needs of the users of the accounts

- calculate only those ratios relevant to those needs

- always state the definitions used.

Remember that ratios cannot be used in isolation. They must always be interpreted in relation to other information e.g.:

- comparative figures

- budgeted figures

- performance of similar businesses.

# 2 RATIO CALCULATION AND ANALYSIS

## 2.1 TYPES OF RATIOS

Ratios fall into several groups, the relevance of particular ratios depending on the purpose for which they are required. The groups to be considered here are:

- profitability ratios

- working capital ratios

- medium and long-term solvency ratios

- investor ratios.

## 2.2 ILLUSTRATION

Each of the above ratios will be illustrated by reference to the following example. In each case the ratio will be defined and explained, calculated and then interpreted.

### Summarised balance sheets at 30 June

|  | 20X7 | | 20X6 | |
|---|---|---|---|---|
|  | £000 | £000 | £000 | £000 |
| Fixed assets (net book value) |  | 130 |  | 139 |
| Current assets: |  |  |  |  |
| Stock | 42 |  | 37 |  |
| Debtors | 29 |  | 23 |  |
| Bank | 3 |  | 5 |  |
|  | 74 |  | 65 |  |
| Creditors: Amounts falling due within one year: |  |  |  |  |
| Trade creditors | 36 |  | 55 |  |
| Taxation | 10 |  | 10 |  |
|  | 46 |  | 65 |  |
| Net current assets |  | 28 |  | – |
| Total assets less current liabilities |  | 158 |  | 139 |
| Creditors: Amounts falling due after more than one year: |  |  |  |  |
| 5% secured loan stock |  | 40 |  | 40 |
| 8% Preference shares (£1 shares) |  | 25 |  | 25 |
|  |  | 93 |  | 74 |
| Ordinary share capital (50p shares) |  | 35 |  | 35 |
| Share premium account |  | 17 |  | 17 |
| Revaluation reserve |  | 10 |  | – |
| Profit and loss account |  | 31 |  | 22 |
|  |  | 93 |  | 74 |

**Summarised profit and loss account for the year ended 30 June**

|  | 20X7 | | 20X6 | |
| --- | --- | --- | --- | --- |
|  | £000 | £000 | £000 | £000 |
| Sales |  | 209 |  | 196 |
| Opening stock | 37 |  | 29 |  |
| Purchases | 162 |  | 159 |  |
|  | 199 |  | 188 |  |
| Closing stock | 42 |  | 37 |  |
|  |  | 157 |  | 151 |
| Gross profit |  | 52 |  | 45 |
| Interest | 2 |  | 2 |  |
| Preference share dividend | 2 |  | 2 |  |
| Depreciation | 9 |  | 9 |  |
| Sundry expenses | 14 |  | 11 |  |
|  |  | 27 |  | 24 |
| Net profit |  | 25 |  | 21 |
| Taxation |  | 10 |  | 10 |
| Net profit for the year |  | 15 |  | 11 |
| Dividends paid |  | 6 |  | 5 |

# 3 PROFITABILITY RATIOS

## 3.1 INTRODUCTION

There are several ratios which attempt to assess the profitability of a business. These are more conveniently expressed in percentage form and look at various aspects of a business's operations.

## 3.2 GROSS PROFIT PERCENTAGE

**Definition**     **Gross profit** is expressed as a percentage of sales. It is also known as the **gross profit margin**.

This is a very popular ratio and is used by even the smallest of businesses. In the illustration the ratios for the two years are as follows:

20X7                         20X6

$$\frac{52}{209} \times 100 = 24.9\% \qquad \frac{45}{196} \times 100 = 23.0\%$$

What can be learned from these figures? Clearly, the gross profit percentage has improved but it is not known why. Nor is it obvious whether these figures are better or worse than those which would be expected in a similar type of business. Before coming to definite conclusions one would need further information. For example, most businesses sell a wide range of products, usually with different gross profit percentages (or profit margins). It may be that in 20X7 the sales mix changed and that a larger proportion of items with a high profit percentage were sold, thus increasing the overall gross profit percentage of the business.

## 3.3 PERCENTAGE CHANGE IN SALES

**Definition**     Increase or decrease in sales/turnover expressed as a percentage of the earliest year's turnover.

It is relevant to consider the change in sales at this point. The percentage growth in sales is:

$$\frac{209 - 196}{196} \times 100 = 6.6\%$$

This may not be a significant increase. A larger increase might have given some evidence of the type of changes in trading conditions that have occurred.

## 3.4 NET PROFIT PERCENTAGE

**Definition**     $\frac{\text{Net profit}}{\text{Sales}} \times 100$. This is also known as the **net profit margin**.

*20X7*                                    *20X6*

$$\frac{25}{209} \times 100 = 11.9\%$$        $$\frac{21}{196} \times 100 = 10.7\%$$

What conclusions can be drawn from this apparent improvement? Very few! Since net profit equals gross profit less expenses, it would be useful to tabulate, for each of the two years, the various expenses and express them as a percentage of sales. A suitable tabulation might be:

|  | *20X7* | | *20X6* | |
| --- | --- | --- | --- | --- |
|  | £000 | % | £000 | % |
| Sales | 209 | 100.0 | 196 | 100.0 |
| Cost of sales | 157 | 75.1 | 151 | 77.0 |
| Gross profit | 52 | 24.9 | 45 | 23.0 |
| Interest | (2) | (1.0) | (2) | (1.1) |
| Preference dividend | (2) | (1.0) | (2) | (1.1) |
| Depreciation | (9) | (4.3) | (9) | (4.5) |
| Sundry expenses | (14) | (6.7) | (11) | (5.6) |
| Net profit | 25 | 11.9 | 21 | 10.7 |

Given a detailed trading and profit and loss account, the above type of summary could be very useful. Care must be taken in interpreting the results, particularly since sales (£) are used as the denominator. An increase in sales (£) could be due to a combination of price and quantity effects.

## 3.5 RETURN ON CAPITAL EMPLOYED (ROCE)

**Definition**     Profit is expressed as a percentage of the capital invested in the business. Due to its importance the ROCE is sometimes referred to as the **primary ratio**.

This is an important ratio as it relates profit to the capital invested in a business. Finance for a business is only available at a cost – loan stock finance requires interest payments and further finance from shareholders requires either the immediate payment of dividends or the expectation of higher dividends in the future. Therefore a business needs to maximise the profits per £ of capital employed.

There are several ways of measuring ROCE, but the essential point is to relate the profit figure used to its capital base. The profit figure used must match with the capital employed figure.

**Definition**　　**Total capital employed** in the business

$$\frac{\text{Profit before interest and tax}}{\text{Share capital} + \text{Reserves} + \text{Long term liabilities}} \times 100$$

The denominator could alternatively be calculated as total assets less current liabilities. This is the profit available for all of the providers of finance as a percentage of all of the sources of finance.

**Definition**　　**Equity shareholders' capital employed**

$$\frac{\text{Profit after interest and preference dividend but before tax}}{\text{Ordinary share capital} + \text{Reserves}} \times 100$$

This is the profit available to the ordinary shareholder (before tax) as a percentage of the ordinary shareholder's capital. This is sometimes called **return on owner's equity** (ROOE).

**Example**

Using the figures in the illustration in Section 2.2, calculate ROCE for 20X6 and 20X7 using each of these alternatives.

**Solution**

**Total capital employed**

　　　*20X7*　　　　　　　　　　　　　　*20X6*

$$\frac{29}{158} \times 100 = 18.4\%$$　　　　　　$$\frac{25}{139} \times 100 = 18.0\%$$

**Equity capital employed**

　　　*20X7*　　　　　　　　　　　　　　*20X6*

$$\frac{25}{93} \times 100 = 26.9\%$$　　　　　　$$\frac{21}{74} \times 100 = 28.4\%$$

(The ordinary shareholders' funds is the capital and reserves total minus the preference shares.)

There is a slight improvement in total ROCE and a falling off in equity ROCE.

A reason for the variation is the revaluation of fixed assets during the year. This has the effect of increasing the denominator in 20X7 relative to 20X6 and creates an unfair comparison as it is likely that the fixed assets were worth more than their book value last year as well. It is not common, however, for UK companies to revalue their assets every year so that comparisons from year to year can be difficult.

The differences in returns for equity compared to total capital employed are large. It means that equity shareholders have had a significant increase in their return because of the company's using fixed interest finance to enlarge the capital employed in the business.

## 3.6   STRUCTURE OF OPERATING RATIOS

ROCE can be broken down into a further pattern of operating ratios as shown in the diagram below:

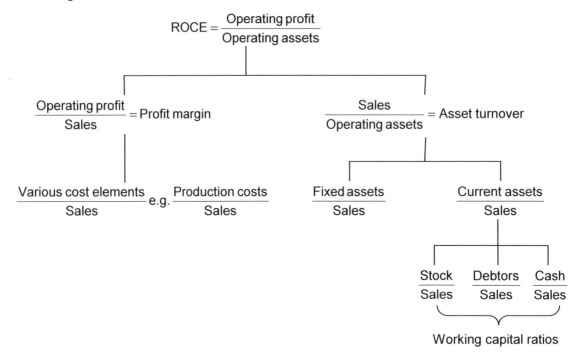

## 3.7   ANALYSIS OF ROCE

As can be seen from the diagram the initial breakdown of ROCE is into two further ratios:

- profit margin

- rate of asset utilisation or asset turnover.

**Note:** The product of these two gives the return on capital employed:

$$\frac{\text{Operating profit}}{\text{Sales}} \times \frac{\text{Sales}}{\text{Operating assets}} = \frac{\text{Operating profit}}{\text{Operating assets}} = \text{ROCE}$$

In the example for 20X7 using total capital employed:

$$\text{ROCE} = \frac{£29,000}{£158,000} = 18.3\%$$

$$\text{Profit margin} = \frac{\text{Operating profit}}{\text{Sales}} = \frac{£29,000}{£209,000} = 13.9\%$$

$$\text{Asset turnover} = \frac{\text{Sales}}{\text{Operating assets}} = \frac{£209,000}{£158,000} = 1.32$$

$$13.9\% \times 1.32 \times 100 = 18.3\%$$

As ROCE is made up of the product of profit margin and asset turnover then any initial analysis of ROCE over a period will normally involve calculation of these two further ratios.

**Conclusion**   $\dfrac{\text{Operating profit}}{\text{Sales}} \times \dfrac{\text{Sales}}{\text{Operating assets}} = \dfrac{\text{Operating profit}}{\text{Operating assets}} = \text{ROCE}$

## 3.8 ASSET TURNOVER

**Definition**     **Asset turnover** is calculated as $\dfrac{\text{Sales}}{\text{Operating assets}}$

The resultant figure indicates how many £s of sales are being made for every £1 of operating assets or capital employed.

In our example asset turnover for each of the two years is:

20X6     $= \dfrac{£196,000}{£139,000} = 1.41$

20X7     $= \dfrac{£209,000}{£158,000} = 1.32$

This shows that for every £1 invested in the business in 20X6 £1.41 of sales were being made whilst this has fallen to £1.32 of sales for every £1 invested in 20X7.

The profit margin can also be considered for each of the two years:

20X6     $= \dfrac{£25,000}{£196,000} = 12.8\%$

20X7     $= \dfrac{£29,000}{£209,000} = 13.9\%$

The initial analysis of ROCE (using total capital employed) might therefore be that it has increased over the two year period due to an increase in profit margin and indeed despite a reduction in the efficient use of the assets as measured by asset turnover.

**Tutorial note:** If this analysis of ROCE is to be carried out it is important that the same profit figure and capital employed figure is used in all three ratios otherwise the result will be meaningless.

## 3.9 FIXED ASSET TURNOVER

**Definition**     **Fixed asset turnover** is calculated as $\dfrac{\text{Sales}}{\text{Fixed assets}}$

The resultant figure indicates the amount of £ sales being made for every £1 investment in fixed assets.

This measures the efficiency of just the fixed asset utilisation rather than all of the assets in total.

In our example the fixed asset turnover is:

20X6     $= \dfrac{£196,000}{£139,000} = 1.41$

20X7     $= \dfrac{£209,000}{£130,000} = 1.61$

This indicates that there has been a substantial increase in the efficiency of the utilisation of the fixed assets although not of the overall assets over the two year period. This is also despite the fact that there has been a revaluation of the fixed assets in 20X7.

**Conclusion**   From the analysis it becomes clear that the subdivision of the key ratio, return on capital employed, is limited only by the detail in the data available. The important point to remember is that if ROCE is to be sub-analysed, care must be taken with the profit and capital employed figures used.

# 4   WORKING CAPITAL RATIOS

## 4.1   INTRODUCTION

The working capital (net current assets) of a business can be considered in total and also broken down into their component elements.

## 4.2   THE CURRENT RATIO

**Definition**   The **current ratio** is the ratio of current assets to current liabilities.

*20X7*                               *20X6*

$$\frac{74}{46} = 1.61 \qquad\qquad \frac{65}{65} = 1.0$$

The current ratio is sometimes referred to as the working capital ratio.

## 4.3   THE LIQUIDITY (OR QUICK) RATIO (ACID TEST RATIO)

**Definition**   The **liquidity ratio** is the ratio of current assets excluding stock to current liabilities.

*20X7*                               *20X6*

$$\frac{32}{46} = 0.7 \qquad\qquad \frac{28}{65} = 0.43$$

Stock is excluded from this ratio as it is much less liquid than cash and even debtors.

## 4.4   ANALYSIS

Both of these ratios show a strengthening.

The extent of the change between the two years seems surprising and would require further investigation.

It would also be useful to know how these ratios compare with those of a similar business, since typical ratios for supermarkets are quite different from those for heavy engineering firms.

What can be said is that in 20X7 the current liabilities were well covered by current assets. Liabilities payable in the near future (creditors), however, are only half covered by cash and debtors (a liquid asset, easily convertible to cash).

Conventional wisdom has it that an ideal current ratio is 2 and an ideal quick ratio is 1. It is very tempting to draw definite conclusions from limited information or to say that the current ratio **should** be 2, or that the liquidity ratio **should** be 1. However, this is not very meaningful without taking into account the type of ratio expected in a similar business.

It should also be noted that a high current or liquidity ratio is not necessarily a good thing. It may indicate that working capital is not being used efficiently. This in itself can be investigated by calculation of ratios for each individual element of working capital.

## 4.5 STOCK TURNOVER RATIO

Companies have to strike a balance between being able to satisfy customers' requirements out of stock and the cost of having too much capital tied up in stock.

**Definition** The **stock turnover ratio** is the cost of sales divided by the average level of stock during the year. Using the example:

*20X7*          *20X6*

$$\frac{157}{\frac{1}{2}(37+42)} = 4.0 \text{ times pa} \qquad \frac{151}{\frac{1}{2}(29+37)} = 4.6 \text{ times pa}$$

The stock turnover ratio has fallen.

*Note:* The average of opening and closing stocks is used here, but examination questions frequently do not provide the opening stock figure and the **closing** stock has to be taken instead of the average stock. In any case, the average of opening and closing stock will not necessarily give the true average level of stock during the year if the stock fluctuates a lot from month to month.

Unless the nature of the business is known, it is not possible to say whether either 4.6 or 4.0 is satisfactory or unsatisfactory. A jeweller will have a low stock turnover ratio, but it is hoped that a fishmonger selling fresh fish has a very high turnover ratio.

An alternative calculation of the stock turnover ratio is to show the result in days. The calculation is:

$$\frac{\text{Average stock during the accounting period}}{\text{Cost of sales}} \times 365 \text{ (i.e. length of accounting period)}$$

*20X7*          *20X6*

$$\frac{\frac{1}{2}(37+42)}{157} \times 365 = 92 \text{ days} \qquad \frac{\frac{1}{2}(29+37)}{151} \times 365 = 80 \text{ days}$$

## 4.6 DEBT COLLECTION PERIOD (OR AVERAGE PERIOD OF CREDIT ALLOWED TO CUSTOMERS)

Businesses which sell goods on credit terms specify a credit period. Failure to send out invoices on time or to follow up late payers will have an adverse effect on the cash flow of the business.

**Definition** The **debt collection period** relates closing trade debts to the average daily credit sales. It shows the number of days that debtors are outstanding on average.

In the example:

|  | 20X7 | 20X6 |
|---|---|---|

Credit sales per day $\dfrac{£209,000}{365} = £573$     $\dfrac{£196,000}{365} = £537$

Closing trade debtors     £29,000     £23,000

Debt collection period $\dfrac{£29,000}{£573} = 50.6$ days     $\dfrac{£23,000}{£537} = 42.8$ days

Compared with 20X6 the debt collection period has worsened in 20X7.

If the average credit allowed to customers was, say, 30 days, then something is clearly wrong.  Further investigation might reveal delays in sending out invoices or failure to 'screen' new customers.

The quickest way to compute the debt collection period is to use the formula:

$$\frac{\text{Closing trade debtors}}{\text{Credit sales for year}} \times 365$$

*20X7*                     *20X6*

$\dfrac{29,000}{209,000} \times 365 = 50.6$ days     $\dfrac{23,000}{196,000} \times 365 = 42.8$ days

*Tutorial note:*  In this example it has been assumed that all sales are on credit.

## 4.7   AVERAGE PERIOD OF CREDIT ALLOWED BY SUPPLIERS

**Definition**     This relates closing creditors to average daily credit purchases.  It shows the number of days it takes the business to pay its creditors.

|  | 20X7 | 20X6 |
|---|---|---|

Credit purchases per day $\dfrac{162,000}{365} = £444$     $\dfrac{159,000}{365} = £436$

Closing trade creditors     £36,000     £55,000

Average period of credit
allowed by suppliers          81.1 days          126.3 days

*Tutorial note:*  Again it has been assumed here that all purchases are on credit.

The average period of credit allowed has fallen substantially from last year.  It is, however, in absolute terms still a high figure.

Often, suppliers request payment within 30 days.  The company is taking nearly three months.  Trade creditors are thus financing much of the working capital requirements of the business which is beneficial to the company.

However, there are three potential disadvantages of extending the credit period:

(i)     future supplies may be endangered

(ii)    possibility of cash discounts is lost

(iii)   suppliers may quote a higher price for the goods knowing the extended credit taken by the company.

The quick calculation is:

$$\frac{\text{Closing trade creditors}}{\text{Credit purchases for year}} \times 365$$

*20X7*

$$\frac{36,000}{162,000} \times 365 = 81.1 \text{ days}$$

*20X6*

$$\frac{55,000}{159,000} \times 365 = 126.3 \text{ days}$$

## 4.8   THE WORKING CAPITAL CYCLE

The investment made in working capital is largely a function of sales and, therefore, it is useful to consider the problem in terms of a firm's working capital (or **cash operating**) cycle.

**The cash operating cycle**

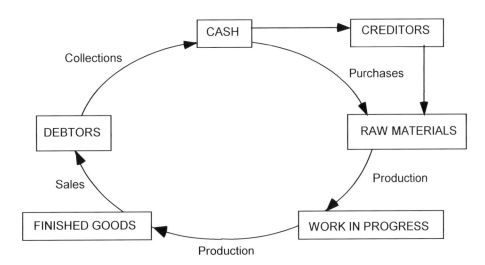

The cycle reflects a firm's investment in working capital as it moves through the production process towards sales.  The investment in working capital gradually increases, firstly being only in raw materials, but then in labour and overhead as production progresses.  This investment must be maintained throughout the production process, the finished goods holding period and up to the final collection of cash from trade debtors   Note that the net investment can be reduced by taking trade credit from suppliers.

The faster a firm can 'push' items around the operating cycle the lower its investment in working capital will be.  However, too little investment in working capital can lose sales since customers will generally prefer to buy from suppliers who are prepared to extend trade credit, and if items are not held in stock when required by customers, sales may be lost.

With some fairly basic financial information it is possible to measure the length of the working capital cycle for a given firm.

**Example**

Using the example in Section 2.2, determine the working capital cycle for 20X7.

**Solution**

(1)   Creditors:

Average payment collection period

$$\left(365 \times \frac{\text{Creditors}}{\text{Purchases}}\right) \qquad 365 \times \frac{36}{162} = \qquad (81\text{ days})$$

(2)   Debtors:

Average collection period

$$= \left(365 \times \frac{\text{Debtors}}{\text{Sales}}\right) \qquad 365 \times \frac{29}{209} = \qquad 51\text{ days}$$

(3)   Stock turnover:

$$= 365 \times \frac{\text{Stock}}{\text{Cost of goods sold}} \qquad 365 \times \frac{\frac{1}{2}(37 + 42)}{157} \qquad 92\text{ days}$$

Length of working capital cycle    62 days

**Conclusion**   The working capital of a business can be considered in total to assess liquidity and then broken down into its individual elements to assess the efficiency of the control of these elements.

# 5    SOLVENCY RATIOS

## 5.1   INTRODUCTION

Most companies will be financed by a variety of sources of finance, some by share capital and some by loan finance.  Typical examples of sources of finance are given below:

| Source of finance | Priority in relation to profit | Priority on liquidation |
|---|---|---|
| Secured loan stock (debentures) | Interest must be paid whether or not the company makes a profit | Secured by a fixed or floating charge – first claim on assets |
| Unsecured loan stock | Interest must be paid whether or not the company makes a profit | Ranks as unsecured creditor |
| Preference share capital (assumed non-participating) | If the company makes a profit, the preference dividend has a priority over the ordinary dividend | Cannot be repaid until all liabilities have been met.  Has priority over ordinary shareholders |

| Source of finance | Priority in relation to profit | Priority on liquidation |
|---|---|---|
| Ordinary share capital | Dividends paid after debenture interest and fixed preference dividends have been paid | Ranks behind all the above but usually entitled to surplus assets in a liquidation |

The aim of solvency ratios is to assess how much a business is financed by loan capital rather than owners' capital.

## 5.2 CAPITAL GEARING

Gearing is one of the most widely used terms in accounting. Unfortunately it can be defined and calculated in several different ways. It is essential to state the definition used.

Gearing is relevant to the long-term financial stability of a business. Two possible definitions will be considered, both based on book values of assets. Both of these consider the relationship between:

(a)    ordinary shareholders' funds (or equity interest)

(b)    fixed return capital – comprising loans and preference share capital.

## 5.3 EQUITY GEARING

**Definition**    $\dfrac{\text{Preference share capital plus loans}}{\text{Ordinary share capital and reserves}}$

*20X7*                                        *20X6*

$\dfrac{25 + 40}{118 - 25} \times 100 = 69.9\%$        $\dfrac{25 + 40}{99 - 25} \times 100 = 87.8\%$

## 5.4 TOTAL GEARING

**Definition**    $\dfrac{\text{Preference share capital plus loans}}{\text{Total long - term capital}}$

*20X7*                                        *20X6*

$\dfrac{65}{158} \times 100 = 41.1\%$        $\dfrac{65}{139} \times 100 = 46.8\%$

There is no real difference between the two types of calculation as the components of the numerator remain the same. Some prefer to use the equity gearing as it shows a more pronounced change if either fixed return capital or equity capital changes. Most use the second calculation as it is perhaps clearer to note the relationship of fixed interest finance to total finance.

There is no immediate cut-off between a low-geared company and a highly-geared company. Gearing is a matter of degree.

In our example there has been no increase or decrease in the amount of fixed interest finance. The only reason for the change in ratio is due to retained profit and revaluation for 20X7.

## 5.5 THE ADVANTAGES AND DISADVANTAGES OF RAISING FINANCE BY ISSUING DEBENTURES

Gearing may have an important effect on the distribution of profits. For example, consider two companies with the same profit record but different capital structures. The return of the ordinary shareholders can vary considerably.

|  | A Ltd £ | B Ltd £ |
|---|---|---|
| Capital structure: |  |  |
| 10% Loan stock | 20,000 | – |
| Ordinary share capital and reserves | 10,000 | 30,000 |
|  | 30,000 | 30,000 |

|  | Highly geared | No gearing |
|---|---|---|
| Year 1 – Profits £4,000 before interest |  |  |
| ∴ Returns: |  |  |
| 10% Interest | 2,000 | – |
| Ordinary shares – balance | 2,000 | 4,000 |
|  | 4,000 | 4,000 |
| Year 2 – Profits double to £8,000 before interest |  |  |
| ∴ Returns: |  |  |
| 10% Interest | 2,000 | – |
| Ordinary shares – balance | 6,000 | 8,000 |
|  | 8,000 | 8,000 |
| Therefore, increase in return to ordinary shareholders | 3 times | 2 times |

Thus, the doubling of the profits in year 2 has the effect of tripling the return to the equity shareholders in the highly-geared company. The effect would be even more dramatic if the profits fell below £2,000 because then there would be no return at all to the ordinary shareholders in A Ltd. Thus an investment in ordinary shares in a highly-geared company is a far more speculative investment than a purchase of ordinary shares in a low-geared company.

## 5.6 INTEREST COVER

**Definition** $\dfrac{\text{Profit before interest and tax}}{\text{Interest}}$

Interest on loan stock (debenture stock) must be paid whether or not the company makes a profit. The ratio emphasises the cover (or security) for the interest by relating profit before interest and tax to interest paid.

*20X7*                                             *20X6*

$\dfrac{29}{2}$ i.e. 14.5 times                    $\dfrac{25}{2}$ i.e. 12.5 times

From the point of view of medium- and long-term solvency, the company is in a strong position as regards the payment of interest. Profit would have to drop considerably before any problem of paying interest arose.

(It is assumed that the company could delay paying the preference dividend.)

**Conclusion**    The medium- to long-term solvency of a business will be of concern to most users of the financial statements. Therefore gearing ratios will be very important but to avoid confusion any calculation must be defined.

# 6 INTERPRETATION OF FINANCIAL STATEMENTS

## 6.1 INTRODUCTION

So far this chapter has concentrated on the calculation of a variety of ratios for different purposes and provision of information. It is now important to consider using these ratios in order to interpret a set of financial statements and to draw valid conclusions from the information contained in a set of financial statements.

## 6.2 EXAMPLE

A Ltd has been trading steadily for many years as ski boot manufacturers. In 20X4 a surge in skiing increased the level of A Ltd's turnover significantly. The summarised balance sheets of the last two years are given below:

|  | 20X4 | | 20X3 | |
|---|---:|---:|---:|---:|
|  | £000 | £000 | £000 | £000 |
| Fixed assets: | | | | |
| Intangible assets | | 30 | | 40 |
| Tangible assets: | | | | |
| Property | | 640 | | 216 |
| Plant | | 174 | | 142 |
| | | 844 | | 398 |
| Current assets: | | | | |
| Stock | 540 | | 140 | |
| Debtors | 440 | | 170 | |
| Investments | – | | 120 | |
| Cash at bank | 4 | | 150 | |
| | 984 | | 580 | |
| Creditors – Amounts falling due within one year: | | | | |
| Trade creditors | 520 | | 250 | |
| Taxation | 70 | | 80 | |
| Dividend proposed | 60 | | 20 | |
| | 650 | | 350 | |
| Net current assets | | 334 | | 230 |
| Total assets less current liabilities | | 1,178 | | 628 |
| Creditors – Amounts falling due after more than one year: | | | | |
| 10% debentures | | 120 | | – |
| | | 1,058 | | 628 |
| Capital and reserves: | | | | |
| Called up share capital: | | | | |
| Ordinary 50p shares | | 300 | | 250 |
| Revaluation reserve | | 270 | | – |
| Capital redemption reserve | | – | | 50 |
| Profit and loss account | | 488 | | 328 |
| | | 1,058 | | 628 |

Sales for 20X4 and 20X3 respectively were £1,600,000 and £1,150,000. Cost of goods sold for 20X4 and 20X3 respectively were £1,198,000 and £880,000.

Given that this is the only information available, you are required to comment as fully as you can on A Ltd's financial position.

## 6.3 SOLUTION

### Comments on A Ltd – Financial position

### Profitability and growth

|  | 20X4 | 20X3 |
|---|---|---|
|  | £ | £ |
| Sales | 1,600,000 | 1,150,000 |
| Cost of sales | 1,196,000 | 880,000 |
| Gross profit | 404,000 | 270,000 |

Profit and loss accounts have not been given but laying these out as far as they are available

### Profit margin:

$$\frac{\text{Gross profit}}{\text{Sales}} \times 100$$

| 25.25% | 23.48% |

### Return on capital employed:

$$\frac{\text{Gross profit}}{\text{Share capital} + \text{Reserves} + \text{Debt}} \times 100$$

| $\frac{404,000}{1,178,000}$ | $\frac{270,000}{628,000 + 270,000}$ |

(see note below)

| = 34.30% | = 30.07% |

(Average capital employed should be used but year-end figures have been taken so that a figure for 20X3 can be computed. It is assumed that property was worth £270,000 more than its book value in 20X3 also.)

### Asset turnover:

$$\frac{\text{Sales}}{\text{Share capital} + \text{Reserves} + \text{Debt}} \times 100$$

| $\frac{1,600,000}{1,178,000}$ | $\frac{1,150,000}{898,000}$ |

| = 1.36 | = 1.28 |

The ROCE figures have been computed in a rough and ready fashion but they indicate an improvement in 20X4 compared with 20X3. The gross profit/sales shows a (slight) improvement as does the efficiency measure of asset turnover. This would appear to be encouraging as the sales have grown considerably.

| 20X4 Sales | £1,600,000 |
|---|---|
| 20X3 Sales | £1,150,000 |
| Percentage increase | 39.13% |

**Solvency: long term**

*Gearing*

There was no debt in 20X3. The 10% debentures issued in 20X4 were to enable the investment to be made to finance growth. The year-end gearing is:

$$\frac{\text{Debt}}{\text{Capital employed (as above)}} \times 100 \quad = \quad \frac{120,000}{1,178,000} \times 100$$

$$= \quad 10.19\%$$

In absolute terms this is a low figure.

**Solvency: short term**

|  | 20X4 | 20X3 |
|---|---|---|

*Current ratio*

$$\frac{\text{Current assets}}{\text{Current liabilities}} \qquad \frac{984,000}{650,000} = 1.5 \qquad \frac{580,000}{350,000} = 1.7$$

*Quick ratio*

$$\frac{\text{Current assets - Stock}}{\text{Current liabilities}} \qquad \frac{444,000}{650,000} = 0.7 \qquad \frac{440,000}{350,000} = 1.3$$

Both ratios have shown a decline – particularly the quick ratio. Conventional opinion states that for many businesses an ideal current ratio is 2 and an ideal quick ratio is 1. However, the ideal ratio will depend on the type of business of a company. More important is the constancy of the ratio over time (assuming that the ratios reflect the efficient use of working capital).

The decline should not be viewed with alarm, particularly as the 20X3 figures include current assets which were surplus to the working capital requirements of the business at that time i.e., the investments and cash. Both these items have been spent in purchasing new fixed assets. The quick ratio is, however, now low and should be watched carefully.

**Working capital efficiency**

|  | 20X4 | 20X3 |
|---|---|---|

*Stock turnover*

$$\frac{\text{Cost of sales}}{\text{Year - end stocks}} \qquad \frac{1,196,000}{540,000} = 2.2 \text{ times pa} \qquad \frac{880,000}{140,000} = 6.3 \text{ times pa}$$

Year-end stock has been taken so that the 20X3 figure can be computed.

A very significant fall in stock turnover. This may indicate that:

(a)     the growth in sales has been made by offering many more types of boots, some of which are not selling quickly;  or

(b)     further growth in sales is expected so that the company has stepped up production to anticipate this.

A closer look at this area is required.

|  | 20X4 | 20X3 |
|---|---|---|

*Debtor collection period*

$$\frac{\text{Year - end trade debtors}}{\text{Sales}} \times 365 \qquad \frac{440,000}{1,600,000} = 100.4 \text{ days} \qquad \frac{170,000}{1,150,000} = 54.0 \text{ days}$$

54 days to collect debts is not very impressive – 100 days is potentially disastrous. Immediate action is required to ensure prompter payment although the situation may not be as bad as it appears if it is the case that the growth in sales took place shortly before the year end rather than throughout the year. Debtors at the year end would then not be typical of the sales throughout the whole year.

*Creditor collection period*

(Cost of sales will have to be used in this example in the absence of purchases figures.)

|  | 20X4 | 20X3 |
|---|---|---|

$$\frac{\text{Year - end trade creditors}}{\text{Cost of sales}} \times 365 \qquad \frac{520,000}{1,196,000} \times 365 = 159 \text{ days} \qquad \frac{250,000}{880,000} \times 365 = 104 \text{ days}$$

The creditor collection period was high in 20X3 but is now even higher. Clearly one of the ways in which the company's considerable growth has been financed has been through taking long periods of credit from its suppliers. This area may need further investigation as this policy may backfire at some point in the future with credit being refused or withdrawn.

*Working capital cycle*

|  | 20X4 | 20X3 |
|---|---|---|

*Stock turnover in days*

$$\frac{540,000}{1,196,000} \times 365$$

165 days

$$\frac{140,000}{880,000} \times 365$$

58 days

| | 20X4 | 20X3 |
|---|---|---|
| Debtors turnover in days | 100 days | 54 days |
| Creditors turnover in days | (159 days) | (104 days) |
| | 106 days | 8 days |

*Overall analysis*

The company has quite clearly had considerable growth over the past year. This has been financed by a small amount of loan capital but largely by a reduction in overall short-term liquidity and in particular an increase in time taken to pay creditors. This can be further seen from the drastic increase in the working capital cycle.

The growth appears to be profitable, indeed the ROCE and the profit margin has increased. The major concern for this company would therefore appear to be regarding its working capital control.

## ACTIVITY 1

The outline balance sheets of the Nantred Trading Co Ltd were as shown below:

**Balance sheets as at 30 September**

| | 20X5 £ | 20X5 £ | 20X6 £ | 20X6 £ |
|---|---|---|---|---|
| Fixed assets (at written down values): | | | | |
| Premises | 40,000 | | 98,000 | |
| Plant and equipment | 65,000 | | 162,000 | |
| | | 105,000 | | 260,000 |
| Current assets: | | | | |
| Stock | 31,200 | | 95,300 | |
| Trade debtors | 19,700 | | 30,700 | |
| Bank and cash | 15,600 | | 26,500 | |
| | 66,500 | | 152,500 | |
| Current liabilities: | | | | |
| Trade creditors | 23,900 | | 55,800 | |
| Corporation tax | 11,400 | | 13,100 | |
| Sundry | 17,000 | | 17,000 | |
| | 52,300 | | 85,900 | |
| Working capital | | 14,200 | | 66,600 |
| Net assets employed | | 119,200 | | 326,600 |
| Financed by: | | | | |
| Ordinary share capital | 100,000 | | 200,000 | |
| Reserves | 19,200 | | 26,600 | |
| Shareholders' funds | | 119,200 | | 226,600 |
| 7% debentures | | – | | 100,000 |
| | | 119,200 | | 326,600 |

The only other information available is that the turnover for the years ended 30 September 20X5 and 20X6 was £202,900 and £490,700, respectively, and that net profit before tax for 20X5 and 20X6 respectively was £21,500 and £37,500.

**Required:**

(a)    Calculate, for each of the two years, six suitable ratios to highlight the financial stability, liquidity and profitability of the company.

(b)    Comment on the situation revealed by the figures you have calculated in your answer to (a) above.

*For a suggested answer, see the 'Answers' section at the end of the book.*

# KEY TERMS

**Gross profit margin** – gross profit expressed as a percentage of sales. It is also known as the gross profit margin.

**Percentage change in sales** – increase or decrease in sales/turnover expressed as a percentage of the earliest year's turnover.

**Net profit percentage** – $\dfrac{\text{Net profit}}{\text{Sales}} \times 100$. This is also known as the net profit margin.

**Return on capital employed (ROCE)** – profit is expressed as a percentage of the capital invested in the business. Due to its importance the ROCE is sometimes referred to as the primary ratio.

**Total capital employed in the business** – the profit available for all of the providers of finance as a percentage of all of the sources of finance.

**Equity shareholders' capital employed** – the profit available to the ordinary shareholder (before tax) as a percentage of the ordinary shareholder's capital.

**Asset turnover** – indicates how many £s of sales are being made for every £1 of operating assets or capital employed.

**Fixed asset turnover** – indicates the amount of £ sales being made for every £1 investment in fixed assets.

**Current ratio** – the ratio of current assets to current liabilities.

**Liquidity (or quick) ratio** – the ratio of current assets (excluding stock) to current liabilities.

**Stock turnover ratio** – the cost of sales divided by the average level of stock during the year.

**Debt collection period** – relates closing trade debts to the average daily credit sales. It shows the number of days that debtors are outstanding on average.

**Average period of credit allowed by suppliers** – relates closing creditors to average daily credit purchases.

**Working capital cycle** – the period of time which elapses between the point at which cash begins to be expended on the production of a product and the collection of cash from the purchaser.

**Gearing** – relationship between a company's borrowings and its shareholder funds.

# SELF TEST QUESTIONS

|  |  | *Paragraph* |
|---|---|---|
| 1 | Name three different user groups of financial statements and state the particular interests of each group. | 1.2 |
| 2 | Distinguish between the gross profit margin and the net profit margin. | 3.2 & 3.4 |
| 3 | How do you calculate the return on capital employed for a company? | 3.5 |
| 4 | Which two ratios can be multiplied together to give the return on capital employed? | 3.7 |
| 5 | What does fixed asset turnover represent? | 3.9 |
| 6 | What are the two key ratios to assess a company's liquidity? | 4.2 & 4.3 |
| 7 | How would you assess whether a company's debt collection procedures were improving or deteriorating? | 4.6 |
| 8 | How is capital gearing determined? | 5.2 |

## PRACTICE QUESTION

### ELECTRICAL ENGINEERING

You are given summarised results of an electrical engineering business, as follows. All figures are in £000.

**Profit and loss account**

|  | *Year ended* | |
|---|---|---|
|  | *31.12.X1* | *31.12.X0* |
| Turnover | 60,000 | 50,000 |
| Cost of sales | 42,000 | 34,000 |
| Gross profit | 18,000 | 16,000 |
| Operating expenses | 15,500 | 13,000 |
|  | 2,500 | 3,000 |
| Interest payable | 2,200 | 1,300 |
| Profit before taxation | 300 | 1,700 |
| Taxation | 350 | 600 |
| (Loss) profit after taxation | (50) | 1,100 |

Dividends of £600,000 were paid in each year.

**Balance sheet**

| | | |
|---|---:|---:|
| Fixed assets | | |
| Intangible | 500 | – |
| Tangible | 12,000 | 11,000 |
| | 12,500 | 11,000 |
| Current assets | | |
| Stocks | 14,000 | 13,000 |
| Debtors | 16,000 | 15,000 |
| Bank and cash | 500 | 500 |
| | 30,500 | 28,500 |
| Creditors due within one year | 24,000 | 20,000 |
| Net current assets | 6,500 | 8,500 |
| Total assets less current liabilities | 19,000 | 19,500 |
| Creditors due after one year | 6,000 | 5,500 |
| | 13,000 | 14,000 |
| Capital and reserves | | |
| Share capital | 1,300 | 1,300 |
| Share premium | 3,300 | 3,300 |
| Revaluation reserve | 2,000 | 2,000 |
| Profit and loss | 6,400 | 7,400 |
| | 13,000 | 14,000 |

## Required:

(a) Prepare a table of the following 12 ratios, calculated for both years, clearly showing the figures used in the calculations:

        current ratio

        quick assets ratio

        stock turnover in days

        creditors turnover in days

        gross profit %

        net profit % (before taxation)

        interest cover

        dividend cover

        ROCE

        gearing

(b) Making full use of the information given in the question, of your table of ratios, and your common sense, comment on the actions of the management.

*For a suggested answer, see the 'Answers' section at the end of the book.*

## ADDITIONAL QUESTION

### HAWK

The directors of Hawk Limited wish to compare the company's most recent financial statements with those of the previous year. The company's financial statements are given below.

**Hawk Limited**
**Profit and loss accounts**

| | Year ended | |
| --- | --- | --- |
| | 31 March 20X1 £000 | 31 March 20X2 £000 |
| Sales revenue (80% on credit and 20% cash) | 1,800 | 2,500 |
| Cost of sales (see note below) | (1,200) | (1,800) |
| | | |
| Gross profit | 600 | 700 |
| Distribution costs | (160) | (250) |
| Administrative expenses | (200) | (200) |
| | | |
| Operating profit | 240 | 250 |
| Interest payable | (50) | (50) |
| | | |
| Profit before tax | 190 | 200 |
| Taxation | (44) | (46) |
| | | |
| Retained profit | 146 | 154 |

**Note:** Cost of sales figures are made up as follows:

| | Year ended | |
| --- | --- | --- |
| | 31 March 20X1 £000 | 31 March 20X2 £000 |
| Opening stock | 180 | 200 |
| Purchases (all on credit) | 1,220 | 1,960 |
| | | |
| | 1,400 | 2,160 |
| Less closing stock | (200) | (360) |
| | | |
| Cost of sales | 1,200 | 1,800 |

## Balance sheets

|  | As at | | | |
|---|---|---|---|---|
|  | 31 March 20X1 | | 31 March 20X2 | |
|  | £000 | £000 | £000 | £000 |
| Fixed assets – cost | 3,100 |  | 3,674 |  |
| Less accumulated depreciation | 1,214 |  | 1,422 |  |
|  | ——— | 1,886 | ——— | 2,252 |
| Current assets |  |  |  |  |
| Stock | 200 |  | 360 |  |
| Debtors – trade | 400 |  | 750 |  |
| Cash at bank | 100 |  | 120 |  |
|  | ——— |  | ——— |  |
|  | 700 |  | 1,230 |  |
|  | ——— |  | ——— |  |
| Less current liabilities |  |  |  |  |
| Creditors – trade | (210) |  | (380) |  |
| – sundry | (260) |  | (430) |  |
| Taxation | (48) |  | (50) |  |
|  | ——— |  | ——— |  |
|  | (518) |  | (860) |  |
|  | ——— |  | ——— |  |
| Net current assets |  | 182 |  | 370 |
|  |  | ——— |  | ——— |
| Total assets less current liabilities |  | 2,068 |  | 2,622 |
| 10% debentures |  | 500 |  | 500 |
|  |  | ——— |  | ——— |
|  |  | 1,568 |  | 2,122 |
|  |  | ——— |  | ——— |
| Capital and reserves |  |  |  |  |
| Issued ordinary share capital* | 1,000 |  | 1,200 |  |
| Share premium account* | 400 |  | 600 |  |
| Profit and loss account | 168 |  | 322 |  |
|  | ——— | 1,568 | ——— | 2,122 |
|  |  | ——— |  | ——— |
|  |  | 1,568 |  | 2,122 |
|  |  | ——— |  | ——— |

*The additional share capital was issued on 1 April 20X1

**Required:**

(a) Calculate, for each of the two years, eight accounting ratios which should assist the directors in their comparison, using closing figures for balance sheet items needed.

(b) Suggest possible reasons for the changes in the ratios between the two years.

*For a suggested answer, see the 'Answers' section at the end of the book.*

# Chapter 13

# ANSWERS TO END-OF-CHAPTER QUESTIONS

## CHAPTER 1

### ACTIVITY 1

State the accounting concept(s) being applied in each of these situations:

(1) Plant and machinery has a net book value of £24m, but it would only fetch £15m if it were to be sold.

Going concern. The accounts are prepared on the basis that the company will continue in business. The break-up value of plant and machinery is not relevant.

(2) The plant and machinery is being depreciated over five years.

Accruals concept. The cost of a machine is apportioned to the periods expected to benefit from its use.

(3) Stock is valued at £23m, even though it will probably sell for £35m.

Two concepts are being applied here:

- The historic cost concept requires these assets to be recorded at the £23m cost incurred in acquiring them.

- The prudence concept states that the £12m expected profit should not be recognised until it has been realised.

(4) John Ltd has just bought the trade and assets of a Sally, rival unincorporated business. John has changed Sally's accounting policies, bringing them into line with the rest of the business.

This is the consistency concept. Similar items should be treated in a similar manner throughout the company.

## ADDITIONAL QUESTION

### DEFINITIONS

(a)   **Accruals**

The accruals concept is that revenue and expenses are recognised in the profit and loss account as they are earned or incurred, not as the money from the revenue income is received or as the payments for the expenses are paid. It also includes the matching concept that accrued costs should be set against related accrued revenues in arriving at the profit or loss for a period.

*Example:* Rent due but not yet paid is recognised as an expense of the period to which it relates and is therefore set against revenue for the same period, as an accrued expense. Similarly, rent paid in advance for a period falling in a future accounting period is treated as a prepayment (a short-term asset in the balance sheet) and will not be set as an expense against profit until the future period to which the expense relates.

(b)   **Consistency**

Accounting treatment of like items within each accounting period and from one period to the next should be the same, unless either a change is required by legislation or a new accounting standard, or unless circumstances change.

*Example:* Depreciation rates should remain the same from period to period unless there is clear evidence that changed circumstances require them to change.

(c)   **Prudence**

In preparing financial statements, the traditional view of prudence requires that provision should be made for all known liabilities, including those based on estimates because exact information is not available. Prudence also requires that revenue and profits should not be included in the profit and loss account until their realisation is reasonably certain. A more recent definition of prudence is a degree of caution in preparing financial information under conditions of uncertainty, so that income and assets are not overstated and expenses and liabilities are not understated.

*Example:* An allowance for doubtful debts should be created out of profits whenever the realisation of all trade debts in full is uncertain, and any increase in this allowance will be set against profits of the current period in which the increase is made. The effect of applying the prudence concept is to recognise losses in the financial statements now, even though it has not yet happened and might never happen.

# CHAPTER 2

## ACTIVITY 1

The following legal structures would be suitable:

**Piano restorer**

This should be undertaken as a sole trader. This is because:

- the initial capital investment is low and the level of working capital should also be low

- if things do not work out as planned, Charlie will be able to cease trading without incurring too many financial penalties.

Therefore, there are few benefits from operating as a limited company. The legal formalities and expenses of incorporation would not be worthwhile.

**Piano manufacturer**

This should be undertaken as a limited liability company.

This is because:

- the initial capital investment is high, and he will also be committing himself to a £36,000 lease

- the working capital tied up in construction working taking four staff for one month will also be high

- if things go wrong, Charlie will still have financial obligations to his landlord and staff. Also there is the possibility of legal action from his staff if any of them were to be injured in the factory.

Therefore, the costs of incorporation will be worth the peace of mind brought by limited liability.

## ADDITIONAL QUESTION

### LIMITED COMPANIES COMPARISONS

(a)   Trading as a limited company rather than a sole trader

**Main advantages**

(i)   Liability of shareholders is limited to the amount invested by each of them, should the company run into trading difficulties.

(ii)   Ownership is usually shared between a number of people, possibly a large number of people.

(iii)   Transfer of ownership is easy, through the sale of shares.

(iv)   Additional capital can be raised virtually at any time, by using more shares should the company framework allow.

(v)   Potentially, tax advantages.

**Main disadvantages**

(i)   Companies are governed by the requirements of the Companies Act in respect of presentation and auditing of accounts within deadlines and under specified formats.

(ii)   Costs are involved in formation.

(iii)   Greater reporting and recording requirements inevitably lead to greater running costs.

(iv)   No longer accountable to themselves only but are now accountable to the owners (shareholders).

(b)   Main types of share capital and their characteristics

There are two main types of share capital

(i)   **Ordinary share capital**

These are the most common type of share issued by limited companies. They are known as equity shares and as such carry voting rights within the company, to the holder of the shares. Shareholders are the owners of the company, receiving a dividend from profits based on the shares held, should profits be sufficient to declare a dividend. The dividend is not a fixed amount but is proposed by the directors at Annual General Meeting and voted on by the ordinary shareholders.

(ii)   **Preference share capital**

Unlike ordinary shares, preference shares are normally quoted at a fixed rate of dividend, such as 7% £1 preference shares. The preference shareholder, as the title suggests, is paid a dividend at the fixed rate, before ordinary shareholders. Usually, preference shares are cumulative which means if profits are not sufficient to allow a dividend to be paid in one financial year then that dividend is carried forward until such times as it can be paid. However, usually the preference share does not carry any voting rights.

Should the company suffer liquidation, however, they would again take preference over the return of their investment if the Articles of Association provide for this, which is usually the case.

# CHAPTER 3

## ACTIVITY 1

(a)                    **Share capital: 25 pence ordinary shares**

| | Number | £ | | Number | £ |
|---|---|---|---|---|---|
| | | | Brought forward | 900,000 | 225,000 |
| | | | New issue for cash | 500,000 | 125,000 |
| Carried down | 1,400,000 | 350,000 | | | |
| | 1,400,000 | 350,000 | | 1,400,000 | 350,000 |

**Share premium**

| | | £ | | £ |
|---|---|---|---|---|
| | | | Brought forward | 75,000 |
| | | | New issue for cash | 175,000 |
| Carried down | | 250,000 | | |
| | | 250,000 | | 250,000 |

| | Price £ | Proceeds £ |
|---|---|---|
| Nominal value | 0.25 | 125,000 |
| Share premium | 0.35 | 175,000 |
| Issue price | 0.60 | 300,000 |

500,000 shares were issued.

(b)                    **Bradawl Ltd – Balance sheet extracts**

| | | £ |
|---|---|---|
| Net assets | £456,789 + £300,000 proceeds | 756,789 |
| Capital and reserves | | |
| Called up share capital | 1,400,000 ordinary shares of 25 pence each | 350,000 |
| Share premium account | | 250,000 |
| P&L reserve | | 156,789 |
| | | 756,789 |

## ACTIVITY 2

(a)                            **Share capital**

| | £ | | £ |
|---|---|---|---|
| | | Balance b/d | |
| | | (200,000 × 50p) | 100,000 |
| | | Profit and loss account | |
| Balance c/d | 125,000 | (50,000 × 50p) | 25,000 |
| | 125,000 | | 125,000 |

**Profit and loss**

| | £ | | £ |
|---|---|---|---|
| Share capital | 25,000 | Balance b/d | 230,000 |
| Balance c/d | 205,000 | | |
| | 230,000 | | 230,000 |

(b) **Bank**

| | £ | | £ |
|---|---|---|---|
| Share capital | 25,000 | | |
| Share premium | 15,000 | | |

**Share capital**

| | £ | | £ |
|---|---|---|---|
| Balance c/d | 125,000 | Balance b/d | 100,000 |
| | | Bank | 25,000 |
| | 125,000 | | 125,000 |

**Share premium**

| | £ | | £ |
|---|---|---|---|
| Balance c/d | 15,000 | Bank | 15,000 |

## ACTIVITY 3

(a) **Profit and loss account for the year ended 31 December 20X8**

| | £ | £ |
|---|---|---|
| Operating profit | | 180,000 |
| Finance cost (60,000 × 8%) | | (4,800) |
| Profit before taxation | | 175,200 |
| Corporation tax | | 70,000 |
| Profit for the financial year | | 105,200 |

(b) **Balance sheet (extracts) as at 31 December 20X8**

| | £ |
|---|---|
| Creditors: amounts falling due within one year | |
| Corporation tax | 70,000 |
| Accrued preference dividend | 2,400 |
| | 72,400 |
| | |
| Creditors: amounts falling due after more than one year | |
| – £1 8% preference shares | 60,000 |
| | |
| Capital and reserves | |
| Called up share capital | |
| – 50p ordinary shares | 75,000 |
| Share premium account | 25,000 |
| Plant replacement reserve | 50,000 |
| Profit and loss account | 172,200 |
| | 322,200 |

**Statement of reserves**

|  | Profit and loss £ | Plant replacement £ | Share premium £ |
|---|---|---|---|
| Balance at 1 January 20X8 | 90,000 | 30,000 | 25,000 |
| Profit for the year | 105,200 | | |
| Dividends paid | (3,000) | | |
| Transfer | (20,000) | 20,000 | |
| Balance at 31 December 20X8 | 172,200 | 50,000 | 25,000 |

## ACTIVITY 4

**Profit and loss account**

|  | £000 |
|---|---|
| Profit on ordinary activities before tax | 200 |
| Tax (Note 1) | 54 |
| Profit for the year | 146 |

**Note 1 – Tax charge**

|  | £000 |
|---|---|
| Corporation tax on current year profits at X% | 56 |
| Less: over provision in previous year | (2) |
| | 54 |

**Note 2 – Dividends**

|  | £000 |
|---|---|
| Interim dividend paid | 5 |
| Final dividend proposed | 17 |
| | 22 |

## ADDITIONAL QUESTION

### RESERVES

*Tutorial note:* In practice this part of the syllabus is very unlikely to feature within an examination.

(a) (i) Reserves are balances in a company's balance sheet forming part of the equity interest and representing surpluses or gains, whether realised or not.

(ii) **Share premium account**

The surplus arising when shares are issued at a price in excess of their par value.

**Revaluation reserve**

The unrealised gain when the amount at which fixed assets are carried is increased above cost.

(Other reserves could be described.)

(b)     A **bonus issue** is the conversion of reserves into share capital, with new shares being issued to existing members in proportion to their shareholdings, without any consideration being given by the shareholders.

A **rights issue** is also an issue of new shares to existing members in proportion to their shareholdings, but with payment being made by the shareholders for the shares allotted to them.

The fundamental difference between them is that a rights issue raises funds for the company whereas a bonus issue does not.

## CHAPTER 4

### ACTIVITY 1

|  | Cost | Life | Charge |  |
|---|---|---|---|---|
|  | £m |  | £m |  |
| Land | 45.0 | 90 years | 0.5 | *over the remaining life of the lease* |
| Main building | 80.0 | 50 years | 1.6 | *over its useful life (until obsolete)* |
| Frontage | 15.0 | 10 years | 1.5 | *over its useful life* |
| Total | 140.0 |  | 3.6 |  |

### ACTIVITY 2

**Straight line method**

Annual depreciation charge $\dfrac{£(4,200 - 200)}{4} = £1,000$ pa

**Reducing balance method**

|  | £ |
|---|---|
| Cost | 1,000 |
| Year 1 (£1,000 × 50%) | (500) |
| NBV | 500 |
| Year 2 (£500 × 50%) | (250) |
| NBV | 250 |
| Year 3 (£250 × 50%) | (125) |
| NBV | 125 |
| Year 4  (£125 × 50%) | (63) |
| Final NBV | 62 |

One particular feature of the reducing balance method is that the net book value never equals zero.

## ACTIVITY 3

| | Usage | Depreciation charge |
| --- | --- | --- |
| | | £ |
| Year 1 | 12,000 hours | $\frac{12,000}{60,000} \times £1,800 = 360$ |
| Year 2 | 9,000 hours | $\frac{9,000}{60,000} \times £1,800 = 270$ |

One advantage of this method is that the original cost of the asset is allocated over accounting periods according to usage of assets. The depreciation charge becomes a function of output or usage rather than of time. Where there is variable use of the asset over time, it can be argued that this method satisfies the matching concept more satisfactorily than the earlier methods.

## ACTIVITY 4

The sum of the digits over five years is 15: (5 + 4 + 3 + 2 + 1 = 15)

The annual charges will be as follows:

| Year | Cost | Weighting | Charge |
| --- | --- | --- | --- |
| 1 | £72,000 | 5/15 | £24,000 |
| 2 | £72,000 | 4/15 | £19,200 |
| 3 | £72,000 | 3/15 | £14,400 |
| 4 | £72,000 | 2/15 | £9,600 |
| 5 | £72,000 | 1/15 | £4,800 |

## ACTIVITY 5

(a)  Prepare the T-accounts to record the disposal of this asset.

**Fixed asset at cost account   (B/S)**

| | | £ | | | £ |
| --- | --- | --- | --- | --- | --- |
| Balance b/d | | 39,000 | Disposal a/c | a | 39,000 |
| | | 39,000 | | | 39,000 |

**Fixed asset: Provision for depreciation   (B/S)**

| | | £ | | | £ |
| --- | --- | --- | --- | --- | --- |
| Disposal a/c | b | 21,000 | Balance b/d | W1 | 21,000 |
| | | 21,000 | | | 21,000 |

**Cash at bank account   (B/S)**

| | | £ | | £ |
| --- | --- | --- | --- | --- |
| Proceeds of disposal | c | 12,300 | | |

**Disposal of fixed assets account**

|  |  | £ |  |  | £ |
|---|---|---|---|---|---|
| Asset at cost | a | 39,000 | Provision for deprecation | b | 21,000 |
|  |  |  | Proceeds | c | 12,300 |
|  |  | 39,000 |  |  | 33,300 |
|  |  |  | Loss on disposal |  | 5,700 |
|  |  | 39,000 |  |  | 39,000 |

(W1) **Opening depreciation**

The annual charge was (£39,000 cost – £4,000 residual value) / 5 years = £7,000 per annum.

Depreciation will have been charged in 20X1, X2 and X3. This totals £21,000.

(b) Draft the journal to record this transaction.

| Account | Dr | Cr |
|---|---|---|
| Fixed asset disposal | 39,000 |  |
| Machine at cost |  | 39,000 |
| Fixed asset disposal |  | 21,000 |
| Machine: provision for depreciation | 21,000 |  |
| Cash at bank | 12,300 |  |
| Fixed asset disposal |  | 12,300 |
| Fixed asset disposal |  | 5,700 |
| P&L:  Loss on disposal | 5,700 |  |

# ACTIVITY 6

**Fixed assets at cost:  Elevators**

|  |  | £ |  |  | £ |
|---|---|---|---|---|---|
| Balance b/d 20X9 |  | 45,000 | Disposal a/c | a | 45,000 |
| Cost of fixed asset: Part-exchange | c | 20,000 |  |  |  |
| Cost of fixed asset:  Cash |  | 79,000 | Balance c/d |  | 99,000 |
|  |  | 144,000 |  |  | 144,000 |
| Balance b/d 20Y0 |  | 99,000 |  |  |  |

**Provision for depreciation on fixed assets:  Elevators**

|  |  | £ |  |  | £ |
|---|---|---|---|---|---|
| Disposal a/c | b | 12,000 | Balance b/d 20X9 | W1 | 12,000 |
|  |  |  | Charge for the year | W2 | 3,000 |
| Balance c/d |  | 3,000 |  |  |  |
|  |  | 15,000 |  |  | 15,000 |
|  |  |  | Balance b/d 20Y0 |  | 3,000 |

## Disposal of fixed assets account   (P&L)

| | | £ | | | £ |
|---|---|---|---|---|---|
| Elevator at cost | **a** | 45,000 | Provision for deprecation | **b** | 12,000 |
| | | | Proceeds:  Part-exchange | **c** | 20,000 |
| | | 45,000 | | | 32,000 |
| Profit on disposal | | | Loss on disposal | | 13,000 |
| | | 45,000 | | | 45,000 |

### (W1)  Opening depreciation

The annual charge was (£45,000 cost – £5,000 residual value) / 20 years = £2,000 per annum.

Depreciation will have been charged in 20X3, X4, X5, X6, X7, X8.  This totals £12,000.

### (W2)  Depreciation charge for 20X9

The annual charge is (£99,000 cost – £9,000 residual value) / 30 years = £3,000 per annum.

## ACTIVITY 7

### Buildings at cost / valuation

| | £ | | £ |
|---|---|---|---|
| Opening | 300,000 | | |
| Revaluation reserve | 420,000 | | |
| | | c/d | 720,000 |
| | 720,000 | | 720,000 |
| b/d | 720,000 | | |

### Depreciation on buildings

| | £ | | | £ |
|---|---|---|---|---|
| | | Opening | *(£300,000 × 10/50)* | 60,000 |
| Revaluation reserve | 60,000 | | | |
| | 60,000 | | | 60,000 |

### Revaluation reserve

| | £ | | £ |
|---|---|---|---|
| | | Buildings at cost | 420,000 |
| | | Accumulated depreciation | 60,000 |
| c/d | 480,000 | | |
| | 480,000 | | 480,000 |
| | | b/d | 480,000 |

The future depreciation charge will be:

$$\frac{\text{Revalued amount less residual value}}{\text{Remaining useful life of the asset}} = \frac{£720,000}{(50 \text{ years} - 10 \text{ years})} = £18,000 \text{ per annum}$$

## ACTIVITY 8

**Charlie plc – Extracts from the balance sheet – Goodwill**

| | | | 20X1 £000 | 20X2 £000 |
|---|---|---|---|---|
| Opening balance | | | – | 2,880 |
| Acquisitions | | (a) | 3,000 | – |
| Amortisation | P&L | (b) | (120) | (120) |
| Impairment | P&L | | – | – |
| Closing balance | B/S | | 2,880 | 2,760 |

Dude's business is old fashioned and well established, and so a 25-year amortisation period is considered to be appropriate. Regular impairment reviews take place to ensure that the carrying value is not in excess of the recoverable amount of the goodwill.

| (a) | Calculation of the cost and amortisation | £ |
|---|---|---|
| | Fair value of the consideration | 9,000,000 |
| | Less: Fair value of the net assets acquired | (6,000,000) |
| | Goodwill at cost | 3,000,000 |
| (b) | Annual amortisation charge over 25 years | 120,000 |

## ADDITIONAL QUESTION

### ARBALEST

(a) **Movements on reserves**

| | Share premium £000 | Revaluation reserve £000 | Retained earnings £000 | Total £000 |
|---|---|---|---|---|
| At 30 September 20X6 | 400 | | 4,060 | 4,460 |
| Rights issue | 1,000 | | | 1,000 |
| Bonus issue | (1,400) | | (600) | (2,000) |
| Revaluation of assets | | 500 | | 500 |
| Retained profit for year | | | 370 | 370 |
| At 30 September 20X7 | nil | 500 | 3,830 | 4,330 |

*Workings*

(W1)  Share premium increases on the rights issue by 2 million shares × 50 pence per share.

(W2)  The bonus issue is of 4 million shares with a nominal value of £2,000,000. The share premium will be used up entirely, leaving £600,000 to be transferred from the profit and loss reserve (retained earnings).

(b)     **Movements on fixed assets**

|  | | | Cost | |
|---|---|---|---|---|
|  | Land | Buildings | Plant and machinery | Total |
|  | £000 | £000 | £000 | £000 |
| At 30 September 20X6 | 2,000 | 1,500 | 2,800 | 6,300 |
| Additions | 600 | 2,400 | 1,600 | 4,600 |
| Disposals | | | (1,000) | (1,000) |
| Revaluation | 500 | | | 500 |
| At 30 September 20X7 | 3,100 | 3,900 | 3,400 | 10,400 |
| Depreciation | | | | |
| At 30 September 20X6 | nil | 450 | 1,000 | 1,450 |
| Charge for year | nil | 46 | 220 | 266 |
| Disposals | | | (800) | (800) |
| At 30 September 20X7 | nil | 496 | 420 | 916 |
| Net book value 30 September 20X7 | 3,100 | 3,404 | 2,980 | 9,484 |

**Calculation of depreciation charges**

|  | £000 |
|---|---|
| Buildings: | |
| 2% of 1,500,000 | 30 |
| 2% of 2,400,000 × 4/12 | 16 |
| | 46 |
| Plant and machinery: | |
| 10% of (2,800,000 − 1,000,000) | 180 |
| 10% of 1,600,000 × 3/12 | 40 |
| | 220 |

# CHAPTER 5

## ACTIVITY 1

| Range | Cost | NRV | Balance sheet value |
|---|---|---|---|
|  | £ | £ | £ |
| Alpha | 480 | 510 | 480 |
| Beta | 220 | 200 | 200 |
| Gamma | 170 | 220 | 170 |
| Delta | 150 | 200 | 150 |
| Epsilon | 600 | 450 | 450 |
| | | | 1,450 |

The stock will be valued at the lower of cost and net realisable value, which is £1,450.

## EXAM-STYLE QUESTION

**SAMPI**

(a)  **Value of stock using FIFO**

| | Opening stock units | Deliveries from factory | |
|---|---|---|---|
| | | 8 March units | 22 March units |
| | 4,000 | 3,800 | 6,000 |
| Sales | | | |
| 12 March sales | (4,000) | (1,000) | |
| | – | 2,800 | |
| 18 March sales | | (2,000) | |
| | | 800 | |
| 24 March | | (800) | (2,200) |
| | | – | 3,800 |
| 28 March | | | (2,000) |
| | | | 1,800 |

The closing stock is therefore:

| | £ |
|---|---|
| 1,800 at £18 | 32,400 |

(b)  **Value of stock using weighted average cost basis**

| | Number of units | Weighted average cost £ | Total value of closing stock £ |
|---|---|---|---|
| Opening stock | 4,000 | 13.00 | 52,000 |
| 8 March | 3,800 | 15.00 | 57,000 |
| Balance | 7,800 | 13.974 | 109,000 |
| 12 March | (5,000) | 13.974 | (69,870) |
| | 2,800 | 13.974 | 39,130 |
| 18 March | (2,000) | 13.974 | (27,948) |
| | 800 | 13.974 | 11,182 |
| 22 March | 6,000 | 18.00 | 108,000 |
| | 6,800 | 17.527 | 119,182 |
| 24 March | (3,000) | 17.527 | (52,581) |
| | 3,800 | 17.527 | 66,601 |
| 28 March | (2,000) | 17.527 | (35,054) |
| | 1,800 | 17.527 | 31,547 |

**Note:** There are some rounding differences in these calculations, because average costs are taken to just 3 decimal places.

**Summary:**

| | | £ |
|---|---|---|
| Stock value: | FIFO | 32,400 |
| | Weighted average cost | 31,547 |

# CHAPTER 6

## ACTIVITY 1

(a)     The annual charge will be 4 × £5,000 = £20,000, regardless of when it is paid.

(b)     The expense incurred by the business for the year is £1,000 + £300 = £1,300.

(c)     An estimate of the expense for the year is £820 + (1/3 × £240) = £900.

(d)     The insurance charge for the year ended 31 December 20X1 is estimated from the two bills, incorporating three months of the first bill and nine months of the second:

(3/12 × £3,000) + (9/12 × 4,200) = £3,900

A best estimate must be made of the expense that was incurred during the year, regardless of when the invoice was received or the cash paid.

## ACTIVITY 2

(a)     This bill covers June to August 20X8, and so June's electricity needs to be accrued for.  £900 × 1/3 = **£300**.

(b)     This bill covers May to July 20X8 and so two months (May and June) need to be accrued for.  £780 × 2/3 = **£520**.

(c)     The sewerage bill for June needs to be estimated on the basis of past usage.  If the quarterly bill is for £642, then the bill for one month will be about **£214**.

(d)     453 units of gas have been used but not yet invoiced.  At 10 pence per unit the accrual is **£45.30**.

## ACTIVITY 3

### Electricity

|  | £ |  | £ |
|---|---|---|---|
| PDB Invoices | 697 | Opening accrual | 172 |
| Closing accrual | 238 | **P&L charge** | **763** |
|  | 935 |  | 935 |

### Rates

|  | £ |  | £ |
|---|---|---|---|
| PDB Invoices | 756 | Opening accrual | 365 |
| Closing accrual | 28 | **P&L charge** | **419** |
|  | 784 |  | 784 |

## ACTIVITY 4

(a) This insurance is prepaid for the eight months from July 20X8 through to February 20X9. The prepayment is £2,136 × 8/12 = **£1,424**.

(b) This rent is prepaid for the month of July. £7,800 × 1/3 = **£2,600**.

## ACTIVITY 5

(a)

**Insurance**

| | £ | | £ |
|---|---|---|---|
| Opening prepayment | 3,672 | Closing prepayment | 4,107 |
| Invoices received | 7,295 | **P&L charge** | **6,860** |
| | 10,967 | | 10,967 |

(b)

**Rent**

| | £ | | £ |
|---|---|---|---|
| Opening prepayment | 3,908 | Closing prepayment | 2,798 |
| Invoices received | 19,540 | **P&L charge** | **20,650** |
| | 23,448 | | 23,448 |

## ACTIVITY 6

(a)

**P&L franchise income**

| | £ | | £ |
|---|---|---|---|
| Opening income receivable | 14,726 | Income received in 20X6 | 56,364 |
| **P&L franchise income** | **70,283** | Closing income receivable | 28,645 |
| | 85,009 | | 85,009 |

(b)

**P&L rent**

| | £ | | £ |
|---|---|---|---|
| Closing rents invoiced in advance | 23,985 | Opening rents invoiced in advance | 17,625 |
| **P&L rental income** | **68,576** | Rental invoices issued in 20X6 | 74,936 |
| | 92,561 | | 92,561 |

## ADDITIONAL QUESTIONS

1 **C** Rent for July and August is prepaid. £4,500 × 2/6 = £1,500.

2 **D**

## PRACTICE QUESTION

### RATES AND RENTALS

(a)

**Rates account**

| 20X7 | | £ | 20X7 | £ |
|---|---|---|---|---|
| 8 Mar | Purchases day book | 160 | 31 Dec P&L (bal fig) | 850 |
| 8 Apr | Purchases day book | 920 | 31 Dec Balance c/d | |
| | | | $(920 \times \frac{3}{12})$ | 230 |
| | | 1,080 | | 1,080 |
| 20X8 | | | | |
| 1 Jan | Balance b/d | 230 | | |

(b) **20X3**

As £250 cash is received in 20X3, this will be recorded (upon receipt) in the ledger accounts of the farmer.

At the year end, this amount must be removed from the accounts as it does not relate to the current year. Income has been received in advance and, therefore, to remove it a debit must be made to the income statement. The corresponding credit creates a liability in the balance sheet (known as deferred income).

**20X4**

The deferred income should be included in the 20X4 accounts as it is related to January 20X4, when the car park and field are used by the local organisation. The deferred income is a brought down balance on the credit side of the farmer's income ledger account at the start of 20X4 and therefore is automatically included in the year's income.

# CHAPTER 7

## ACTIVITY 1

See the ETB in Section 1.2 of Chapter 14.

## ACTIVITY 2

**Step 1**     Draw up a proforma extended trial balance using the account names given.

### Extended trial balance at 31 December 20X2

| Account | Trial balance | | Adjustments | | Accrued | Prepaid | Profit & loss | | Balance sheet | |
|---|---|---|---|---|---|---|---|---|---|---|
| | Dr | Cr | Dr | Cr | | | Dr | Cr | Dr | Cr |
| | £ | £ | £ | £ | £ | £ | £ | £ | £ | £ |
| Capital account | | | | | | | | | | |
| Opening stock | | | | | | | | | | |
| Sales | | | | | | | | | | |
| Purchases | | | | | | | | | | |
| Rent and rates | | | | | | | | | | |
| Drawings | | | | | | | | | | |
| Electricity | | | | | | | | | | |
| Motor van cost | | | | | | | | | | |
| Motor van Accumulated Depreciation | | | | | | | | | | |
| Bank balance | | | | | | | | | | |
| Trade debtors | | | | | | | | | | |
| Trade creditors | | | | | | | | | | |
| Sundry Expenses | | | | | | | | | | |
| Wages and Salaries | | | | | | | | | | |
| | | | | | | | | | | |
| Accrued/prepaid | | | | | | | | | | |
| Totals | | | | | | | | | | |
| Profit for year | | | | | | | | | | |
| | | | | | | | | | | |

**Step 2**   Put in the figures from the trial balance.

**Extended trial balance at 31 December 20X2**

| Account | Trial balance | | Adjustments | | Accrued | Prepaid | Profit & loss | | Balance sheet | |
|---|---|---|---|---|---|---|---|---|---|---|
| | Dr | Cr | Dr | Cr | | | Dr | Cr | Dr | Cr |
| | £ | £ | £ | £ | £ | £ | £ | £ | £ | £ |
| Capital a/c | | 12,000 | | | | | | | | |
| Opening stock | 15,000 | | | | | | | | | |
| Sales | | 100,000 | | | | | | | | |
| Purchases | 40,000 | | | | | | | | | |
| Rent and rates | 10,000 | | | | | | | | | |
| Drawings | 12,000 | | | | | | | | | |
| Electricity | 2,000 | | | | | | | | | |
| Motor van cost | 8,000 | | | | | | | | | |
| Motor van Accumulated Depreciation | | 4,000 | | | | | | | | |
| Bank balance | 4,500 | | | | | | | | | |
| Trade debtors | 20,000 | | | | | | | | | |
| Trade creditors | | 21,000 | | | | | | | | |
| Sundry Expenses | 500 | | | | | | | | | |
| Wages and Salaries | 25,000 | | | | | | | | | |
| | 137,000 | 137,000 | | | | | | | | |
| Accrued/ prepaid | | | | | | | | | | |
| Totals | | | | | | | | | | |
| Profit for year | | | | | | | | | | |

## ACTIVITY 3

**Step 1**    Produce the journals.

|  |  |  | Dr £ | Cr £ |
|---|---|---|---|---|
| (a) | Depreciation expense | | 500 | |
| | Accumulated depreciation | | | 500 |
| | Being depreciation for the year | | | |
| (b) | Irrecoverable debts expense | | 1,000 | |
| | Trade debtors | | | 1,000 |
| | Being the write off of an irrecoverable debt | | | |
| (c) | Drawings | | 200 | |
| | Sundry expenses | | | 200 |
| - | Being the transfer of an incorrect posting | | | |

**Step 2**    Enter the adjustments on to the extended trial balance.

**Step 3**    Check the debit and credit columns balance.

### Extended trial balance at 31 December 20X2

| Account | Trial balance | | Adjustments | | Accrued | Prepaid | Profit & loss | | Balance sheet | |
|---|---|---|---|---|---|---|---|---|---|---|
| | Dr | Cr | Dr | Cr | | | Dr | Cr | Dr | Cr |
| | £ | £ | £ | £ | £ | £ | £ | £ | £ | £ |
| Capital account | | 12,000 | | | | | | | | |
| Opening stock | 15,000 | | | | | | | | | |
| Sales | | 100,000 | | | | | | | | |
| Purchases | 40,000 | | | | | | | | | |
| Rent and rates | 10,000 | | | | | | | | | |
| Drawings | 12,000 | | 200 (c) | | | | | | | |
| Electricity | 2,000 | | | | | | | | | |
| Motor van cost | 8,000 | | | | | | | | | |
| Motor van Accumulated Depreciation | | 4,000 | | 500 (a) | | | | | | |
| Bank balance | 4,500 | | | | | | | | | |
| Trade debtors | 20,000 | | | 1,000 (b) | | | | | | |
| Trade creditors | | 21,000 | | | | | | | | |
| Sundry Expenses | 500 | | | 200 (c) | | | | | | |
| Wages and Salaries | 25,000 | | | | | | | | | |
| Depreciation Expense | | | 500 (a) | | | | | | | |
| Irrecov. debt Expense | | | 1,000 (b) | | | | | | | |
| Accrued/prepaid | | | | | | | | | | |
| Totals | 137,000 | 137,000 | 1,700 | 1,700 | | | | | | |
| Profit for year | | | | | | | | | | |

Note that the total of the debit and credit columns must balance, that is, the double entry has been maintained. If the column totals are not checked at this point and the columns do not balance there are two main effects. Firstly, the extended trial balance will not balance and secondly, it can be very time consuming to try to find out what has gone wrong at a later stage. Whilst it appears a little slower working through methodically, it will be a lot quicker than having to go back through the whole extended trial balance to find errors when it does not balance at the final stage.

## ACTIVITY 4

**Step 1**   Write in the accruals in the accrued column on the appropriate account line.

**Step 2**   Total up the accruals and enter the amount in the totals box at the bottom of the column.

### Extended trial balance at 31 December 20X2

| Account | Trial balance | | Adjustments | | Accrued | Prepaid | Profit & loss | | Balance sheet | |
|---|---|---|---|---|---|---|---|---|---|---|
| | Dr | Cr | Dr | Cr | | | Dr | Cr | Dr | Cr |
| | £ | £ | £ | £ | £ | £ | £ | £ | £ | £ |
| Capital account | | 12,000 | | | | | | | | |
| Opening stock | 15,000 | | | | | | | | | |
| Sales | | 100,000 | | | | | | | | |
| Purchases | 40,000 | | | | | | | | | |
| Rent and rates | 10,000 | | | | | | | | | |
| Drawings | 12,000 | | 200 | | | | | | | |
| Electricity | 2,000 | | | | 150 | | | | | |
| Motor van cost | 8,000 | | | | | | | | | |
| Motor van Accumulated Depreciation | | 4,000 | | 500 | | | | | | |
| Bank balance | 4,500 | | | | | | | | | |
| Trade debtors | 20,000 | | | 1,000 | | | | | | |
| Trade creditors | | 21,000 | | | | | | | | |
| Sundry expenses | 500 | | | 200 | 50 | | | | | |
| Wages and salaries | 25,000 | | | | | | | | | |
| Depreciation Expense | | | 500 | | | | | | | |
| Irrecov. debt expense | | | 1,000 | | | | | | | |
| Accruals/prepaid | | | | | | | | | | |
| | | | | | | | | | | |
| Totals | 137,000 | 137,000 | 1,700 | 1,700 | 200 | | | | | |
| | | | | | | | | | | |
| Profit for year | | | | | | | | | | |

## ACTIVITY 5

### Extended trial balance at 31 December 20X2

| Account | Trial balance | | Adjustments | | Accrued | Prepaid | Profit & loss | | Balance sheet | |
|---|---|---|---|---|---|---|---|---|---|---|
| | Dr | Cr | Dr | Cr | | | Dr | Cr | Dr | Cr |
| | £ | £ | £ | £ | £ | £ | £ | £ | £ | £ |
| Capital account | | 12,000 | | | | | | | | |
| Opening stock | 15,000 | | | | | | | | | |
| Sales | | 100,000 | | | | | | | | |
| Purchases | 40,000 | | | | | | | | | |
| Rent and rates | 10,000 | | | | | 800 | | | | |
| Drawings | 12,000 | | 200 | | | | | | | |
| Electricity | 2,000 | | | | 150 | | | | | |
| Motor van cost | 8,000 | | | | | | | | | |
| Motor van accumulated depreciation | | 4,000 | | 500 | | | | | | |
| Bank balance | 4,500 | | | | | | | | | |
| Trade debtors | 20,000 | | | 1,000 | | | | | | |
| Trade creditors | | 21,000 | | | | | | | | |
| Sundry expenses | 500 | | | 200 | 50 | | | | | |
| Wages and salaries | 25,000 | | | | | | | | | |
| Depreciation Expense | | | 500 | | | | | | | |
| Irrecov. debt expense | | | 1,000 | | | | | | | |
| Accruals/ prepaid | | | | | | | | | | |
| Totals | 137,000 | 137,000 | 1,700 | 1,700 | 200 | 800 | | | | |
| Profit for year | | | | | | | | | | |

When all the accruals and prepayments have been entered, total up the columns.

## ACTIVITY 6

**Step 1**     Write the new stock (closing) account in the account column.

**Step 2**     Make the closing stock entries in the adjustment columns.

### Extended trial balance at 31 December 20X2

| Account | Trial balance | | Adjustments | | Accrued | Prepaid | Profit and loss | | Balance sheet | |
|---|---|---|---|---|---|---|---|---|---|---|
| | Dr | Cr | Dr | Cr | | | Dr | Cr | Dr | Cr |
| | £ | £ | £ | £ | £ | £ | £ | £ | £ | £ |
| Capital account | | 12,000 | | | | | | | | |
| Opening stock | 15,000 | | | | | | | | | |
| Sales | | 100,000 | | | | | | | | |
| Purchases | 40,000 | | | | | | | | | |
| Rent and rates | 10,000 | | | | | 800 | | | | |
| Drawings | 12,000 | | 200 | | | | | | | |
| Electricity | 2,000 | | | | 150 | | | | | |
| Motor van cost | 8,000 | | | | | | | | | |
| Motor van accumulated depreciation | | 4,000 | | 500 | | | | | | |
| Bank balance | 4,500 | | | | | | | | | |
| Trade debtors | 20,000 | | | 1,000 | | | | | | |
| Trade creditors | | 21,000 | | | | | | | | |
| Sundry expenses | 500 | | | 200 | 50 | | | | | |
| Wages and salaries | 25,000 | | | | | | | | | |
| Depreciation Expense | | | 500 | | | | | | | |
| Irrecov. debt expense | | | 1,000 | | | | | | | |
| Closing stock | | | 17,000 | 17,000 | | | | | | |
| Accruals/prepaid | | | | | | | | | | |
| Totals | 137,000 | 137,000 | 18,700 | 18,700 | 200 | 800 | | | | |
| Profit for year | | | | | | | | | | |
| | | | | | | | | | | |

## ACTIVITY 7

**Extended trial balance at 31 December 20X2**

(see steps below for explanation)

| Account | Trial balance | | Adjustments | | Accruals | Prepaid | Profit & loss | | Balance sheet | |
|---|---|---|---|---|---|---|---|---|---|---|
| | Dr | Cr | Dr | Cr | | | Dr | Cr | Dr | Cr |
| | £ | £ | £ | £ | £ | £ | £ | £ | £ | £ |
| Capital account | | 12,000 | | | | | | | | 12,000 |
| Stock | 15,000 | | | | | | 15,000 | | | |
| Sales | | 100,000 | | | | | | 100,000 | | |
| Purchases | 40,000 | | | | | | 40,000 | | | |
| Rent and rates | 10,000 | | | | | 800 | 9,200 | | | |
| Drawings | 12,000 | | 200 | | | | | | 12,200 | |
| Electricity | 2,000 | | | | 150 | | 2,150 | | | |
| Motor van cost | 8,000 | | | | | | | | 8,000 | |
| Motor van Accumulated Depreciation | | 4,000 | | 500 | | | | | | 4,500 |
| Bank balance | 4,500 | | | | | | | | 4,500 | |
| Trade debtors | 20,000 | | | 1,000 | | | | | 19,000 | |
| Trade creditors | | 21,000 | | | | | | | | 21,000 |
| Sundry expenses | 500 | | | 200 | 50 | | 350 | | | |
| Wages and salaries | 25,000 | | | | | | 25,000 | | | |
| Depreciation Expense | | | 500 | | | | 500 | | | |
| Irrecov. debt expense | | | 1,000 | | | | 1,000 | | | |
| **Accruals** | | | | | | | | | | 200 |
| **Prepayment** | | | | | | | | | 800 | |
| Stock | | | 17,000 | 17,000 | | | | 17,000 | 17,000 | |
| Totals | 137,000 | 137,000 | 18,700 | 18,700 | 200 | 800 | | | | |
| Profit for year | | | | | | | | | | |

**Step 1**   Capital account

A balance sheet account with only one credit entry (in the trial balance column), therefore carry that figure across to the credit column of the balance sheet section.

**Step 2**   Stock

**Opening stock** – this is to become part of the cost of sales for this year, so simply carry the figure across to the debit column of the profit and loss section.

**Closing stock** – created at the bottom of the TB, with a debit and credit in the adjustments columns:

*Debit adjustment* – represents asset in the balance sheet, so carry it into the debit column of the balance sheet.

*Credit adjustment* – represents the reduction in the cost of sales, so carry it into the credit column of the profit and loss account.

**Step 3**   Sales and purchases

Single figure profit and loss account figures

**Step 4**     Rent and rates

This is a profit and loss account item with more than one figure. The debit in the trial balance is reduced by the prepayment in the 'prepaid' column.

10,000 – 800 = £9,200

**Step 5**     Drawings

This is a balance sheet item, with an original debit balance of £12,000 in the TB, along with a debit adjustment. This needs to be added together, with the resulting total being shown in the debit column of the balance sheet.

**Step 6**     Electricity

This is a profit and loss item, with a debit balance in the trial balance that needs to be increased by the accrual in the 'accrued' column.

**Step 7**     Continue down the trial balance, deciding in which column each amount should end up, and cross-casting along the line to determine the amount.

You may find it helpful to label the first six columns '+' and '–' alternatively. As you add across, treat each figure as a plus or minus according to its column heading. If the net result is positive, it represents a debit; if negative, a credit. You then just have to decide which debit or credit column it goes into!

**Step 8**     Total up the 'accrued' and 'prepaid' columns.

**Step 9**     Carry these totals across into the boxes at the bottom of the balance sheet columns. Don't forget – accruals are liabilities (thus go in the credit column) and prepayments are assets (debit column).

## ACTIVITY 8

### Extended trial balance at 31 December 20X2

| Account | Trial balance Dr £ | Trial balance Cr £ | Adjustments Dr £ | Adjustments Cr £ | Accruals £ | Prepaid £ | Profit & loss Dr £ | Profit & loss Cr £ | Balance sheet Dr £ | Balance sheet Cr £ |
|---|---|---|---|---|---|---|---|---|---|---|
| Capital account | | 12,000 | | | | | | | | 12,000 |
| Stock | 15,000 | | | | | | 15,000 | | | |
| Sales | | 100,000 | | | | | | 100,000 | | |
| Purchases | 40,000 | | | | | | 40,000 | | | |
| Rent and rates | 10,000 | | | | | 800 | 9,200 | | | |
| Drawings | 12,000 | | 200 | | | | | | 12,200 | |
| Electricity | 2,000 | | | | 150 | | 2,150 | | | |
| Motor van cost | 8,000 | | | | | | | | 8,000 | |
| Motor van accumulated depreciation | | 4,000 | | 500 | | | | | | 4,500 |
| Bank balance | 4,500 | | | | | | | | 4,500 | |
| Trade debtors | 20,000 | | | 1,000 | | | | | 19,000 | |
| Trade creditors | | 21,000 | | | | | | | | 21,000 |
| Sundry expenses | 500 | | | 200 | 50 | | 350 | | | |
| Wages and salaries | 25,000 | | | | | | 25,000 | | | |
| Depreciation expense | | | 500 | | | | 500 | | | |
| Irrecov. debt expense | | | 1,000 | | | | 1,000 | | | |
| Accruals | | | | | | | | | | 200 |
| Prepayment | | | | | | | | | 800 | |
| Stock | | | 17,000 | 17,000 | | | | 17,000 | 17,000 | |
| Totals | 137,000 | 137,000 | 18,700 | 18,700 | 200 | 800 | 93,200 | 117,000 | 61,500 | 37,700 |
| Profit for year | | | | | | | 23,800 | | | 23,800 |
| | | | | | | | 117,000 | 117,000 | 61,500 | 61,500 |

The preparation of an extended trial balance is a technique with which you must become familiar. It is quite an efficient way for the examiner to test your double entry and your understanding of how everything comes together to produce the financial statements, without getting you to draw up endless T accounts.

## PRACTICE QUESTION

**ELMDALE**

| Account | Trial balance Dr £ | Trial balance Cr £ | Adjustments Dr £ | Adjustments Cr £ | Accrued £ | Prepaid £ | Profit and loss account Dr £ | Profit and loss account Cr £ | Balance sheet Dr £ | Balance sheet Cr £ |
|---|---|---|---|---|---|---|---|---|---|---|
| Capital account | | 7,802 | | | | | | | | 7,802 |
| Stock | 2,700 | | | | | | 2,700 | | | |
| Sales | | 21,417 | | | | | | 21,417 | | |
| Purchases | 9,856 | | | | | | 9,856 | | | |
| Rates | 1,490 | | | | | 315 | 1,175 | | | |
| Drawings | 4,206 | | | | | | | | 4,206 | |
| Electricity | 379 | | | | 44 | | 423 | | | |
| Freehold shop | 7,605 | | | | | | | | 7,605 | |
| Freehold shop depreciation | | 500 | | 190 | | | | | | 690 |
| Debtors | 2,742 | | | 200 | | | | | 2,542 | |
| Allowance for debtors | | 300 | 173 | | | | | | | 127 |
| Creditors | | 3,617 | | | | | | | | 3,617 |
| Cash at bank | | 1,212 | | | | | | | | 1,212 |
| Cash in hand | 66 | | | | | | | | 66 | |
| Sundry expenses | 2,100 | | | | | | 2,100 | | | |
| Wages and salaries | 3,704 | | | | | | 3,704 | | | |
| Depreciation | | | 190 | | | | 190 | | | |
| Irrecov. debts | | | 200 | 173 | | | 27 | | | |
| Stock | | | 3,060 | 3,060 | | | | 3,060 | 3,060 | |
| Accruals/ prepayments | | | | | | | | | 315 | 44 |
| Profit/loss for the year | | | | | | | 4,302 | | | 4,302 |
| Totals | 34,848 | 34,848 | 3,623 | 3,623 | 44 | 315 | 24,477 | 24,477 | 17,794 | 17,794 |

### Working

| Required allowance for debtors | £ |
|---|---|
| Debtors | 2,742 |
| Less: Written off | 200 |
| | 2,542 |
| Allowance 5% × 2,542 | 127 |
| Opening allowance | 300 |
| Reduction in allowance | 173 |

# CHAPTER 8

## ACTIVITY 1

**Sally**
**Profit and loss account for the year ended 30 November 20X9**

|  | £ | £ |
|---|---|---|
| **Sales** |  | 756,293 |
|  |  |  |
| **Cost of sales** |  |  |
| Opening stock | 21,645 |  |
| Add: purchases | 285,365 |  |
| Less: closing stock | (24,680) |  |
|  |  | (282,330) |
| **Gross profit** |  | 473,963 |
|  |  |  |
| *Expenses* |  |  |
| Wages and salaries | 163,996 |  |
| Rent and rates | 72,000 |  |
| Motor expenses | 35,947 |  |
| Certification costs | 7,354 |  |
| Training | 14,987 |  |
| Insurance | 12,690 |  |
| Sundry expenses | 21,310 |  |
| Depreciation:  Equipment | 23,693 |  |
|                        Motors | 4,374 |  |
| Irrecoverable debt expense | 132 |  |
|  |  | (356,483) |
| **Operating profit** |  | 117,480 |
|  |  |  |
| **Interest payable** |  | (15,000) |
|  |  |  |
| **Profit for the year** |  | 102,480 |

**Balance sheet as at 30 November 20X9**

|  | Cost | Depreciation | Net book value |
|---|---|---|---|
|  | £ | £ | £ |
| **Fixed assets** |  |  |  |
| Equipment | 157,954 | 69,180 | 88,774 |
| Motor vehicles | 45,999 | 37,250 | 8,749 |
|  | 203,953 | 106,430 | 97,523 |
| **Current assets** |  |  |  |
| Stocks |  | 24,680 |  |
| Trade debtors |  | 2,253 |  |
| Prepayments |  | 29,608 |  |
| Bank and cash (145,923 + 5,750) |  | 151,673 |  |
|  |  | 208,214 |  |
| **Current liabilities** |  |  |  |
| Trade creditors |  | 32,756 |  |
| Accruals |  | 75,500 |  |
|  |  | 108,256 |  |
| **Net current assets** |  |  | 99,958 |
| **Total assets less current liabilities** |  |  | 197,481 |
| 15% loan repayable 20Y9 |  |  | (100,000) |
| Net assets |  |  | 97,481 |
| Capital |  |  |  |
| Opening capital |  |  | 250,000 |
| Add: profit for the year |  |  | 102,480 |
| Less: drawings |  |  | (254,999) |
| Closing capital |  |  | 97,481 |

**Extended trial balance for Sally at 30 November 20X9**

| | Trial balance Dr £ | Trial balance Cr £ | Adjustments Dr £ | Adjustments Cr £ | Accruals Dr to P&L £ | Prepaid Cr to P&L £ | Profit and loss Dr £ | Profit and loss Cr £ | Balance sheet Dr £ | Balance sheet Cr £ |
|---|---|---|---|---|---|---|---|---|---|---|
| Sales | | 756,293 | | | | | | 756,293 | | |
| Opening stock | 21,645 | | | | | | 21,645 | | | |
| Purchases | 285,365 | | | | | | 285,365 | | | |
| FA: Cost | | | | | | | | | | |
| Equipment | 157,954 | | | | | | | | 157,954 | |
| Motor vehicle | 45,999 | | | | | | | | 45,999 | |
| FA: Dep'n | | | | | | | | | | |
| Equipment | | 45,487 | | 23,693 | | | | | | 69,180 |
| Motor vehicles | | 32,876 | | 4,374 | | | | | | 37,250 |
| Rent | 8,000 | | | | 64,000 | | 72,000 | | | |
| Salaries and wages | 163,996 | | | | | | 163,996 | | | |
| Motor expenses | 35,947 | | | | | | 35,947 | | | |
| Certification costs | 7,354 | | | | | | 7,354 | | | |
| Training | 14,987 | | | | | | 14,987 | | | |
| Trade debtors | 2,253 | | | | | | | | 2,253 | |
| Trade creditors | | 32,756 | | | | | | | | 32,756 |
| Insurance | 14,298 | | | | | 1,608 | 12,690 | | | |
| Debts written off | 132 | | | | | | 132 | | | |
| Petty cash | 5,750 | | | | | | | | 5,750 | |
| Sundry expenditure | 49,310 | | | | | 28,000 | 21,310 | | | |
| Capital account 1-12-X8 | | 250,000 | | | | | | | | 250,000 |
| Drawings | 254,999 | | | | | | | | 254,999 | |
| 15% Loan repayable (20Y9) | | 100,000 | | | | | | | | 100,000 |
| Loan interest paid and payable | 3,500 | | | | 11,500 | | 15,000 | | | |
| Bank balance | 145,923 | | | | | | | | 145,923 | |
| | 1,217,412 | 1,217,412 | | | | | | | | |
| Closing stock (B/S, P&L) | | | 24,680 | 24,680 | | | | 24,680 | 24,680 | |
| Dep'n charge: | | | | | | | | | | |
| Equipment | | | 23,693 | | | | 23,693 | | | |
| Motors | | | 4,374 | | | | 4,374 | | | |
| Total accruals & prepayments to B/S | | | | | 75,500 | 29,608 | | | 29,608 | 75,500 |
| Sub-total | | | 52,747 | 52,747 | | | 678,493 | 780,973 | 667,166 | 564,686 |
| Profit/loss transferred to B/S | | | | | | | 102,480 | | | 102,480 |
| | | | | | | | 780,973 | 780,973 | 667,166 | 667,166 |

## ACTIVITY 2

**Step 1**   Clear net profit and drawings to the capital account.

### Capital account

|  | £ |  | £ |
|---|---|---|---|
| Drawings | 5,970 | Balance b/d | 15,258 |
| Balance c/d | 16,270 | Net profit | 6,982 |
|  | ——— |  | ——— |
|  | 22,240 |  | 22,240 |
|  | ——— |  | ——— |
|  |  | Balance b/d | 16,270 |

**Step 2**   Draw up the trial balance. Remember that all the profit and loss account items and drawings have been cleared to the capital account. The opening trial balance contains balance sheet items only.

|  | £ | £ |
|---|---|---|
| Capital |  | 16,270 |
| Allowance for debtors |  | 538 |
| Stock at 1 June 20X6 | 8,490 |  |
| Debtors | 10,760 |  |
| Creditors |  | 7,411 |
| Cash at bank | 2,534 |  |
| Cash in hand | 75 |  |
| Furniture and equipment: |  |  |
| Cost | 8,000 |  |
| Depreciation at 1 June 20X6 |  | 3,200 |
| Delivery van: |  |  |
| Cost | 3,200 |  |
| Depreciation at 1 June 20X6 |  | 640 |
| Loan account at 9% (repayable in five years) |  | 5,000 |
|  | ——— | ——— |
|  | 33,059 | 33,059 |
|  | ——— | ——— |

## PRACTICE QUESTION

### K KONG

### Requirement 1

**Extended trial balance for the year ended 31 December 20X6**

| Account | Trial balance Dr £ | Trial balance Cr £ | Adjustments Dr £ | Adjustments Cr £ | Accrued £ | Prepaid £ | Profit and loss account Dr £ | Profit and loss account Cr £ | Balance sheet Dr £ | Balance sheet Cr £ |
|---|---|---|---|---|---|---|---|---|---|---|
| Sales | | 9,000 | | | | | | 9,000 | | |
| Purchases | 6,900 | | | | | | 6,900 | | | |
| Rent | 300 | | | | 100 | | 400 | | | |
| Stationery | 70 | | | | | | 70 | | | |
| Insurance | 50 | | | | | 10 | 40 | | | |
| Fixtures and fittings, cost | 700 | | | | | | | | 700 | |
| Debtors | 2,500 | | | | | | | | 2,500 | |
| Creditors | | 900 | | | | | | | | 900 |
| Cash at bank | 1,100 | | | | | | | | 1,100 | |
| Drawings | 1,020 | | | | | | | | 1,020 | |
| Capital introduced | | 2,740 | | | | | | | | 2,740 |
| Stock | | | 750 | 750 | | | | 750 | 750 | |
| Depreciation expense | | | 65 | | | | 65 | | | |
| Acc depreciation | | | | 65 | | | | | | 65 |
| Prov for debtors | | | | 100 | | | | | | 100 |
| Irrecov. debts | | | 100 | | | | 100 | | | |
| Accruals/ prepayments | | | | | | | | | 10 | 100 |
| Profit/loss for period | | | | | | | 2,175 | | | 2,175 |
| Totals | 12,640 | 12,640 | 915 | 915 | 100 | 10 | 9,750 | 9,750 | 6,080 | 6,080 |

**Requirement 2**

**Trading and profit and loss account
for year ended 31 December 20X6**

| | £ | £ |
|---|---:|---:|
| Sales | | 9,000 |
| Purchases | 6,900 | |
| Less: Closing stock | (750) | |
| | | |
| Cost of sales | | (6,150) |
| | | |
| Gross profit | | 2,850 |
| Rent | 400 | |
| Stationery | 70 | |
| Insurance | 40 | |
| Depreciation | 65 | |
| Irrecoverable debts | 100 | |
| | | |
| | | (675) |
| | | |
| Net profit, transferred to capital account | | 2,175 |

*Workings*

Depreciation expense $= \dfrac{700 - 50}{10}$

$= £65$

**Balance sheet as at 31 December 20X6**

| | Cost | Dep'n | |
|---|---:|---:|---:|
| | £ | £ | £ |
| Fixed assets | | | |
| Fixtures and fittings | 700 | 65 | 635 |
| | | | |
| Current assets | | | |
| Stock | | 750 | |
| Debtors | 2,500 | | |
| Less: Allowance for debtors | (100) | | |
| | | | |
| | | 2,400 | |
| Prepayments | | 10 | |
| Cash at bank | | 1,100 | |
| | | | |
| | | 4,260 | |
| Less: Current liabilities | | | |
| Creditors | 900 | | |
| Accrued expenses | 100 | | |
| | | | |
| | | (1,000) | |
| | | | 3,260 |
| | | | 3,895 |
| | | | |
| Capital account | | | |
| Capital introduced | | | 2,740 |
| Add: Net profit | | | 2,175 |
| | | | |
| | | | 4,915 |
| Less: Drawings | | | (1,020) |
| | | | |
| | | | 3,895 |

# CHAPTER 9

## ACTIVITY 1

|  | 1 Jan 20X5 | 31 Dec 20X6 | |
|---|---|---|---|
|  | Assets | Liabilities | Assets |
| Statement of affairs at: | | | |
|  | £ | £ | £ |
| Shop premises | 14,000 | | 14,000 |
| Shop depreciation 2% × £14,000 × 2 years | | | (560) |
| Fittings | 2,000 | | 2,000 |
| Fittings depreciation 5% × £2,000 × 2 years | | | (200) |
| Cash | 4,000 | | 2,500 |
| Stock | | | 6,000 |
| Debtors | | | 1,040 |
| Motor lorry | | | 8,000 |
| Motor lorry depreciation 20% × £8,000 × 6 months | | | (800) |
| Trade creditors | | 1,400 | |
| Loan | | 10,000 | |
| Accrued interest | | 200 | |
|  | | 11,600 | 31,980 |
|  | | | (11,600) |
| Capital | 20,000 | | 20,380 |

### Capital account

|  | £ |  | £ |
|---|---|---|---|
| Drawings 24 × £300 | 7,200 | Opening capital | 20,000 |
| Closing capital | 20,380 | Net profit (bal fig) | 7,580 |
|  | 27,580 | | 27,580 |

## ACTIVITY 2

### Cash

|  | £ |  | £ |
|---|---|---|---|
| Balance b/d | 100 | Expenses | 750 |
| Sales | 2,500 | Bank (bankings) | 4,220 |
| Cash from debtors – sales control | | Drawings | 1,200 |
| (bal fig) | 3,620 | Balance c/d | 50 |
|  | 6,220 | | 6,220 |

### Sales control

|  | £ |  | £ |
|---|---|---|---|
| Balance b/d | 460 | Irrecoverable debt | 50 |
| Sales | 3,700 | Discounts allowed | 70 |
|  | | Cash received | 3,620 |
|  | | Balance c/d | 420 |
|  | 4,160 | | 4,160 |

## PRACTICE QUESTION

### B LETITSLIDE

**Trading and profit and loss account for
year ended 31 December 20X5**

|  | £ | £ |
|---|---|---|
| Credit sales (W2) |  | 1,560 |
| Cash sales (W2) |  | 4,317 |
|  |  | 5,877 |
| Opening stock | 1,310 |  |
| Add: Purchases (W3) | 3,133 |  |
|  | 4,443 |  |
| Less: Closing stock | 1,623 |  |
|  |  | 2,820 |
|  |  | 3,057 |
| Gross profit |  |  |
| Expenses (W4) | 1,090 |  |
| Irrecoverable debts (W6) | 49 |  |
| Depreciation (W7) | 60 |  |
|  |  | 1,199 |
| Net profit |  | 1,858 |

**Balance sheet as at 31 December 20X5**

Fixed asset:

| | | | |
|---|---|---|---|
| Delivery van, at cost | | | 900 |
| Less: Depreciation (W7) | | | 60 |
| | | | 840 |

Current assets:

| | | | |
|---|---|---|---|
| Stock | | 1,623 | |
| Debtors | 382 | | |
| Less: Allowance for doubtful debts (W6) | 19 | | |
| Cash at bank | | 363 | |
| Cash in hand | | 572 | |
| | | 29 | |
| | | 2,587 | |

| | | | |
|---|---|---|---|
| Less: Current liabilities: | | | |
| Trade creditors | 914 | | |
| Accruals | 103 | | |
| | | 1,017 | |
| | | | 1,570 |
| | | | 2,410 |

| | | |
|---|---|---|
| Capital account: | | |
| At 1 Jan 20X5 (W1) | | 1,652 |
| Add: Profit for year | | 1,858 |
| | | 3,510 |
| Less: Drawings (W5) | | 1,100 |
| | | 2,410 |

*Note:* As the cash account and bank account have already been summarised it is only necessary to post the other side of the cash and bank entries to the relevant accounts. Some information may be inserted immediately into the final accounts, so leave a page for each of the final accounts. Information can then be inserted as soon as it is available. For example, opening and closing stock can be put straight to the final accounts.

*Workings*

(W1) **Opening statement of affairs**

| | £ |
|---|---|
| Stock | 1,310 |
| Debtors | 268 |
| Cash | 62 |
| Bank | 840 |
| | 2,480 |
| Less: Creditors (£712 + 116) | 828 |
| Capital at 1 Jan 20X5 | 1,652 |

*Note:* There is no need to complete this working before proceeding to post the transactions for the year. It is better to add the items as and when you find them in the question.

(W2)

**Sales ledger control**

| | £ | | £ |
|---|---|---|---|
| Debtors b/d | 268 | Cheques for sales | 1,416 |
| Sales for year (bal fig) | 5,877 | Irrecoverable debt written off | 30 |
| | | Cash takings | 4,317 |
| | | Debtors c/d | 382 |
| | 6,145 | | 6,145 |
| Balance b/d | 382 | | |

*Note:* The sales control account has been used to find total sales. An alternative approach would be to post the 'shop takings' straight to the trading account as cash sales and the balancing figure in the sales control account would then be £1,560, i.e. the credit sales.

(W3)

**Purchases control**

| | £ | | £ |
|---|---|---|---|
| Cash | 316 | Creditors b/d | 712 |
| Bank | 2,715 | Drawings | 100 |
| Balance c/d | 914 | Purchases | 3,133 |
| | 3,945 | | 3,945 |
| | | Balance b/d | 914 |

(W4)

**Expenses**

| | £ | | £ |
|---|---|---|---|
| Cash | 584 | Creditors b/d | 116 |
| Bank | 519 | Profit and loss account | 1,090 |
| Balance c/d | 103 | | |
| | 1,206 | | 1,206 |
| | | Balance b/d | 103 |

(W5) **Drawings**

| | £ |
|---|---|
| Purchases | 100 |
| Cash account | 600 |
| Bank account | 400 |
| | 1,100 |

(W6)

**Irrecoverable debts account**

| | £ | | £ |
|---|---|---|---|
| Irrecoverable debt | 30 | Profit and loss account | 49 |
| Sales control account | | | |
| Allowance for doubtful | | | |
| debts account 5% × 382 | 19 | | |
| | 49 | | 49 |

*Note:* As there is no opening allowance for doubtful debts, there is no need to show that account. The £19 can be inserted into the balance sheet.

(W7) **Depreciation**

$20\% \times 900 \times 4/12 = £60.$

---

## ADDITIONAL QUESTION 1

**CYGNUS**

*Tutorial note:* Exam questions will almost certainly feature a partnership, rather than a sole trader. However, the technique of preparing accounts from incomplete records is exactly the same for all types of organisation. This question is exam standard.

### Capital as at 1 February 20X0

| | £ | £ |
|---|---|---|
| Assets | | |
| Shop equipment | | 7,900 |
| Stock | | 146,400 |
| Trade debtors | | 14,400 |
| Rent in advance | | 1,000 |
| Cash in hand | | 800 |
| | | 170,500 |
| | | |
| *Less:* Liabilities | | |
| Loan – Draco | 24,000 | |
| Trade creditors | 12,100 | |
| Accrued expenses | 2,300 | |
| Bank overdraft | 2,600 | 41,000 |
| Opening capital | | 129,500 |

### Trading and profit and loss account for the year ended 31 January 20X1

| | Reference to workings | £ | £ |
|---|---|---|---|
| Sales revenue | 2 | | 202,400 |
| *Less:* Cost of sales | | | |
| Opening stock | | 146,400 | |
| Purchases | 1 | 83,500 | |
| | | 229,900 | |
| *Less:* Closing stock | | 128,700 | |
| | | | 101,200 |
| | | | |
| Gross profit | | | 101,200 |
| *Less:* Expenses | 3 | | |
| Rent (8,250 + 1,000 – 1,500) | | 7,750 | |
| Sundry expenses (18,600 – 2,100 + 3,300) | 4 | 19,800 | |
| Depreciation | | 1,490 | |
| Profit on sale of equipment (300 – 200) | 5 | (100) | |
| Interest on loan (2,400 – 200 + 100) | | 2,300 | |
| Net profit | | | 31,240 |
| | | | 69,960 |

**Balance sheet as at 31 January 20X1**

|  | £ | £ |
|---|---|---|
| *Fixed assets* |  |  |
| Cost (W4) | 15,800 |  |
| Accumulated depreciation (6,900 – 600 + 1,490) (W4) | 7,790 |  |
|  |  | 8,010 |
| *Current assets* |  |  |
| Stock | 128,700 |  |
| Trade debtors | 15,700 |  |
| Prepayment: rent in advance (W3) | 1,500 |  |
| Cash at bank | 4,850 |  |
| Cash in hand | 900 |  |
|  | 151,650 |  |
| *Current liabilities* |  |  |
| Trade creditors | 14,200 |  |
| Accrued expenses (3,300 + 100) | 3,400 |  |
|  | 17,600 |  |
| Net current assets |  | 134,050 |
| *Total assets less current liabilities* |  | 142,060 |
| *Long-term creditors* |  |  |
| Loan – Draco |  | (12,000) |
|  |  | 130,060 |
| *Capital* |  |  |
| As at 1 February 20X0 (see above) |  | 129,500 |
| Profit for year to date |  | 69,960 |
|  |  | 199,460 |
| *Less:* Drawings (W6) |  | 69,400 |
| As at 31 January 20X1 |  | 130,060 |

### *Workings*

### (W1)  **Calculation of purchases**

**Purchases total account**

|  | £ |  | £ |
|---|---|---|---|
| Cash paid for purchases | 81,400 | Opening balance | 12,100 |
| Closing balance | 14,200 | Purchases (balancing figure) | 83,500 |
|  | 95,600 |  | 95,600 |

### (W2)  **Calculation of sales revenue**

Sales prices are fixed by doubling cost – sales revenue is therefore double the cost of sales = £101,200 × 2 = £202,400.

### (W3)  **Calculation of rent expense**

Rent went up in July 20X0 from £500 each month to £750 each month. The prepayment at the year end is for two months of rent (February and March). At 31 January 20X1 the prepayment is therefore 2 × £750 = £1,500. The rent expense for the year is £8,250 rent paid + £1,000 opening prepayment – £1,500 closing prepayment = £7,750.

**(W4)** **Fixed assets and depreciation**

|  | Cost | Accumulated depreciation |
|---|---|---|
|  | £ | £ |
| As at 1 February 20X0 | 14,800 | 6,900 |
| *Less:* Items sold | (800) | (600) |
|  | 14,000 | 6,300 |
| Additions | 1,800 |  |
|  | 15,800 |  |
| Depreciation for year |  |  |
| £14,000 at 10% |  | 1,400 |
| £1,800 at 10% for six months |  | 90 |
| As at 31 January 20X1 | 15,800 | 7,790 |

**(W5)** **Interest**

Accrued interest at the year end = 1 month of interest = $1/12 \times 10\% \times £12,000 = £100$. Interest expense for the year = Interest paid £2,400 – opening accrual £200 + closing accrual £100 = £2,300.

**(W6)** **Calculation of drawings**

A figure for cash from customers is needed to establish how much cash has been taken in drawings.

**Sales total account**

|  | £ |  | £ |
|---|---|---|---|
| Opening balance | 14,400 | Cash for sales (balancing figure) | 201,100 |
| Sales (W2) | 202,400 | Closing balance | 15,700 |
|  | 216,800 |  | 216,800 |

**Cash summary**

|  | £ |  | £ |
|---|---|---|---|
| Opening balance | 800 | Banked | 131,600 |
| Cash from customers (see above) | 201,100 | Drawings (balancing figure) | 69,400 |
|  |  | Closing balance | 900 |
|  | 201,900 |  | 201,900 |

## ADDITIONAL QUESTION 2

**AMY AND BARBARA**

(a)  **Trading and profit and loss account for the year ended 31 December 20X6**

|  | £ | £ |
|---|---:|---:|
| Sales (W1) |  | 592,500 |
| Opening stock | 37,500 |  |
| Purchases (W2) | 292,500 |  |
| Carriage inwards | 6,750 |  |
|  | 336,750 |  |
| Closing stock | (55,500) |  |
|  |  | (281,250) |
| Gross profit |  | 311,250 |
| Less:  Expenses |  |  |
| Vehicle running expenses | 20,250 |  |
| Insurance (6,000 + 7,500 – 1,500) | 12,000 |  |
| Heating and lighting  (4,500 – 10,500 + 3,375) | 9,375 |  |
| Telephone | 5,250 |  |
| Advertising (3,000 + 3,375) | 6,375 |  |
| Rent and rates (22,500 – 1,500) | 21,000 |  |
| Office supplies | 1,875 |  |
| Irrecoverable debts | 22,500 |  |
| Discounts allowed | 7,500 |  |
| Depreciation: |  |  |
| Vehicles (48,000 – 12,000 × 25%) | 9,000 |  |
| Equipment (90,000 × 20%) | 18,000 |  |
|  |  | (133,125) |
| Net profit |  | 178,125 |

**Appropriation account**

|  | Total £ | Amy £ | Barbara £ |
|---|---:|---:|---:|
| Net profit for the year | 178,125 |  |  |
| Interest on capital (10%) | (19,500) | 12,000 | 7,500 |
| Interest on drawings | 4,500 | (3,000) | (1,500) |
| Profit appropriation (2:1) | 163,125 | 108,750 | 54,375 |
|  | – | 117,750 | 60,375 |

(b)
## Partners' current accounts

|  | Amy £ | Barbara £ |  | Amy £ | Barbara £ |
|---|---|---|---|---|---|
| Drawings | 90,000 | 45,000 | Balance b/d | 34,500 | 31,500 |
| Interest on drawings | 3,000 | 1,500 | Interest on capital | 12,000 | 7,500 |
| Balance c/d | 62,250 | 46,875 | Profit | 108,750 | 54,375 |
|  | 155,250 | 93,375 |  | 155,250 | 93,375 |

(c)
## Balance sheet at 31 December 20X6

|  | Cost £ | Accumulated depreciation £ | Net book value £ |
|---|---|---|---|
| Non-current assets: |  |  |  |
| Vehicles (W3) | 48,000 | 21,000 | 27,000 |
| Equipment (W3) | 90,000 | 36,000 | 54,000 |
|  | 138,000 | 57,000 | 81,000 |
| Current assets: |  |  |  |
| Stock |  | 55,500 |  |
| Trade debtors |  | 82,500 |  |
| Prepayments |  | 1,500 |  |
| Cash at bank (W4) |  | 102,000 |  |
|  |  | 241,500 |  |
| Current liabilities: |  |  |  |
| Trade creditors |  | 15,000 |  |
| Accruals |  | 3,375 |  |
|  |  | 18,375 |  |
| Net current assets |  |  | 223,125 |
|  |  |  | 304,125 |
| Partners' capital accounts: |  |  |  |
| Amy |  | 120,000 |  |
| Barbara |  | 75,000 |  |
|  |  |  | 195,000 |
| Partners' current accounts: |  |  |  |
| Amy |  | 62,250 |  |
| Barbara |  | 46,875 |  |
|  |  |  | 109,125 |
|  |  |  | 304,125 |

*Workings*

(W1)                                        **Trade debtors**

| | £ | | £ |
|---|---|---|---|
| Balance b/d | 120,000 | Cash received | 600,000 |
| Sales (bal fig) | 592,500 | Irrecoverable debts | 22,500 |
| | | Discounts allowed | 7,500 |
| | | Balance c/d | 82,500 |
| | 712,500 | | 712,500 |

(W2)                                        **Trade creditors**

| | £ | | £ |
|---|---|---|---|
| Cash paid | 300,000 | Balance b/d | 22,500 |
| Balance c/d | 15,000 | Purchases (bal fig) | 292,500 |
| | 315,000 | | 315,000 |

(W3)    **Fixed assets**

| | *Vehicles* £ | *Equipment* £ | *Total* £ |
|---|---|---|---|
| Cost | 48,000 | 90,000 | 138,000 |
| Accumulated depreciation | | | |
| At 1 January 20X6 | 12,000 | 18,000 | 30,000 |
| Charge for year | 9,000 | 18,000 | 27,000 |
| At 31 December 20X6 | 21,000 | 36,000 | 57,000 |
| Net book value | 27,000 | 54,000 | 81,000 |

(W4)                                        **Cash at bank**

| | £ | | £ |
|---|---|---|---|
| Balance b/d | 15,000 | Payments | 378,000 |
| Receipts | 600,000 | Drawings: | |
| | | Amy | 90,000 |
| | | Barbara | 45,000 |
| | | Balance c/d | 102,000 |
| | 615,000 | | 615,000 |

# CHAPTER 10

## ACTIVITY 1

**Current accounts**

|  |  | Tor £ | Hill £ |  |  | Tor £ | Hill £ |
|---|---|---|---|---|---|---|---|
| *20X4* |  |  |  | *20X4* |  |  |  |
|  | Drawings | 2,000 | 1,500 |  | Share of profit | 6,000 | 3,000 |
| 31 Dec | Balance c/d | 4,000 | 1,500 |  |  |  |  |
|  |  | 6,000 | 3,000 |  |  | 6,000 | 3,000 |
| *20X5* |  |  |  | *20X5* |  |  |  |
| 31 Dec | Drawings | 2,500 | 1,500 | 1 Jan | Balance b/d | 4,000 | 1,500 |
|  | Balance c/d | 9,500 | 4,000 |  | Share of profit | 8,000 | 4,000 |
|  |  | 12,000 | 5,500 |  |  | 12,000 | 5,500 |
| *20X6* |  |  |  | *20X6* |  |  |  |
|  |  |  |  | 1 Jan | Balance b/d | 9,500 | 4,000 |

## ACTIVITY 2

**Allocation of net profit of £3,680**

|  | Flame £ | Smoke £ | Total £ |
|---|---|---|---|
| Interest on capital | 480 | 320 | 800 |
| Salaries | 6,000 | 8,000 | 14,000 |
| Balance of loss £3,680 − £14,800 |  |  |  |
| = (£11,120) to be shared in ratio 3 : 2 | (6,672) | (4,448) | (11,120) |
| Totals | (192) | 3,872 | 3,680 |

The double entry in this case would be:

| Debit | Credit | With |
|---|---|---|
| Profit and loss appropriation account | Smoke's current account | £3,872 |
| Flame's current account | Profit and loss appropriation account | £192 |

The relevant part of the profit and loss account would show:

|  | £ | £ |
|---|---|---|
| Net profit |  | 3,680 |
| Allocated to: |  |  |
| Smoke | 3,872 |  |
| Flame | (192) |  |
|  |  | 3,680 |

## ADDITIONAL QUESTION

### OWEN AND GRIFFITHS

(a) **Trial balance as at 31 December**

|  | Dr £ | Cr £ |
|---|---|---|
| Capital account: |  |  |
| Owen |  | 9,000 |
| Griffiths |  | 10,000 |
| 10% loan account: |  |  |
| Griffiths |  | 5,000 |
| Williams |  | 6,000 |
| Current account balance on 1 January: |  |  |
| Owen |  | 1,000 |
| Griffiths |  | 2,000 |
| Drawings: | 6,500 |  |
| Owen | 5,500 |  |
| Griffiths |  |  |
| Sales |  | 113,100 |
| Sales returns | 3,000 |  |
| Closing stock | 17,000 |  |
| Cost of goods sold | 70,000 |  |
| Sales ledger control account | 30,000 |  |
| Purchase ledger control account |  | 25,000 |
| Operating expenses | 26,100 |  |
| Fixed assets at cost | 37,000 |  |
| Provision for depreciation |  | 18,000 |
| Bank overdraft |  | 3,000 |
| Suspense (bal fig) |  | 3,000 |
|  | 195,100 | 195,100 |

*Tutorial note:* The question requires a trial balance to be drawn up before any adjustments are made. Many candidates attempted to make adjustments before the extraction of the trial balance but this was not what was required.

The information in the question refers to 'closing stock' and 'cost of goods sold'. Both of these imply that the year-end adjustments for stock have already been made.

(b) *Tutorial note:* There is no set format per part (b). The key thing to remember is that parts (b) and (c) of the question are the normal parts of an accounts preparation from a trial balance question.

## Adjustments to trial balance

| Ref to question | | | Dr £ | Cr £ |
|---|---|---|---|---|
| (i) | (a) | Sales returns | 100 | |
| | | Sales ledger control | | 100 |
| | (b) | Purchase ledger control | 200 | |
| | | Sales ledger control | | 200 |
| | (c) | Sales ledger control | 1,800 | |
| | | Sales | | 1,800 |
| (ii) | | Disposal | 5,000 | |
| | | Fixed asset cost | | 5,000 |
| | | Accumulated depreciation | 5,000 | |
| | | Disposal | | 5,000 |
| | | Suspense | 1,000 | |
| | | Disposal | | 1,000 |

*Tutorial note:* The last entry arises as the transaction was originally inserted into the books as a one-sided transaction (Dr Bank). The missing credit entry must therefore make up part of the £3,000 suspense account balance.

| | | | | |
|---|---|---|---|---|
| (iii) | | Expenses | 500 | |
| | | Drawings – Griffiths | | 500 |
| | | Drawings – Owen | 1,000 | |
| | | Cost of goods sold | | 1,000 |
| (iv) | | Interest expense | 1,100 | |
| | | Interest accrual | | 1,100 |

(c) 
## Profit and loss account for the year

| | £ | £ |
|---|---|---|
| Sales (113,100 + 1,800) | | 114,900 |
| Less: Returns (3,000 + 100) | | 3,100 |
| | | 111,800 |
| Cost of sales (70,000 – 1,000) | | (69,000) |
| Gross profit | | 42,800 |
| Operating expenses (26,100 – 1,000 + 500) | 25,600 | |
| Loan interest | 1,100 | |
| | | (26,700) |
| Net profit for year | | 16,100 |
| | | |
| Appropriations: | | |
| Interest | | |
| Owen | 900 | |
| Griffiths | 1,000 | |
| | | (1,900) |
| | | (5,000) |
| Salary – Owen | | 9,200 |
| Balance of profit: | | |
| Owen | 4,600 | |
| Griffiths | 4,600 | |
| | | (9,200) |

**Balance sheet as at 31 December**

|  | £ | £ | £ |
|---|---|---|---|
| Fixed assets: | | | |
| Cost (37,000 – 5,000) | | 32,000 | |
| Depreciation (18,000 – 5,000) | | 13,000 | |
| | | | 19,000 |
| Current assets: | | | |
| Stock | | 17,000 | |
| Debtors (30,000 – 100 – 200 + 1,800) | | 31,500 | |
| | | 48,500 | |
| Current liabilities: | | | |
| Creditors (25,000 – 200) | 24,800 | | |
| Interest | 1,100 | | |
| Bank overdraft | 3,000 | | |
| Suspense account | 2,000 | | |
| | | 30,900 | |
| Net current assets | | | 17,600 |
| | | | 36,600 |
| Loans | | | (11,000) |
| | | | 25,600 |

|  | Capital £ | Current £ | Total £ |
|---|---|---|---|
| Owen (see working) | 9,000 | 4,000 | 13,000 |
| Griffiths (see working) | 10,000 | 2,600 | 12,600 |
| | 19,000 | 6,600 | 25,600 |

**Working**

### Current accounts

|  | Owen £ | Griffiths £ |  | Owen £ | Griffiths £ |
|---|---|---|---|---|---|
| Drawings | 6,500 | 5,500 | Balance b/d | 1,000 | 2,000 |
| Adjustment to drawings | 1,000 |  | Adjustment to drawings |  | 500 |
|  |  |  | Interest on capital | 900 | 1,000 |
|  |  |  | Salary | 5,000 |  |
| Balance c/d | 4,000 | 2,600 | Profit | 4,600 | 4,600 |
|  | 11,500 | 8,100 |  | 11,500 | 8,100 |

# CHAPTER 11

## ACTIVITY 1

4 months to 30 April 20X8

|  | £ | £ |
|---|---|---|
| Gross profit (3/18) |  | 15,000 |
| Less:  Selling and distribution expenses (3/18) | 2,000 |  |
| Administration expenses (4/12) | 1,000 |  |
|  |  | 3,000 |
|  |  | 12,000 |
| Share of profits:      Harry (2/3) |  | 8,000 |
| Barry (1/3) |  | 4,000 |
|  |  | 12,000 |

8 months to 31 December 20X8

|  | £ | £ |
|---|---|---|
| Gross profit (15/18) |  | 75,000 |
| Less:    Selling and distribution expenses (15/18) | 10,000 |  |
| Administrative expenses (8/12) | 2,000 |  |
|  |  | 12,000 |
|  |  | 63,000 |
| Share of profits:    Harry (2/4) |  | 31,500 |
| Barry (1/4) |  | 15,750 |
| Gary (1/4) |  | 15,750 |
|  |  | 63,000 |

Each partner's share of profit for the year will be:

|  |  | £ |
|---|---|---|
| Harry | (8,000 + 31,500) | 39,500 |
| Barry | (4,000 + 15,750) | 19,750 |
| Gary |  | 15,750 |
|  |  | 75,000 |

## ACTIVITY 2

### Revaluation account

| | £ | | £ |
|---|---|---|---|
| Debtors | 1,000 | Plant and Machinery | 5,000 |
| Stock | 1,000 | Property | 17,000 |
| Profit on revaluation | | | |
| Blagden | 12,000 | | |
| MacDonald | 8,000 | | |
| | 20,000 | | |
| | 22,000 | | 22,000 |

## ACTIVITY 3

### Faldo, Woosnam and Newcomer
### Balance sheet as at 1 July 20X6

| | £ |
|---|---|
| Goodwill | 280,000 |
| Other net assets (45,000 + 90,000) | 135,000 |
| | 415,000 |

| Partners' accounts | Capital | Current | Total |
|---|---|---|---|
| | £ | £ | £ |
| Faldo | 230,000 | 8,000 | 238,000 |
| Woosnam | 82,000 | 5,000 | 87,000 |
| Newcomer | 90,000 | – | 90,000 |
| | 402,000 | 13,000 | 415,000 |

**Workings**

### Goodwill

| | £ | | £ |
|---|---|---|---|
| Valuation to | | | |
| capital accounts | 280,000 | | |

### Capital accounts

| | Faldo | Woosnam | Newcomer | | Faldo | Woosnam | Newcomer |
|---|---|---|---|---|---|---|---|
| | £ | £ | £ | | £ | £ | £ |
| Balance c/d | 230,000 | 82,000 | 90,000 | Balance b/d | 20,000 | 12,000 | |
| | | | | Goodwill 3 : 1 | 210,000 | 70,000 | |
| | | | | Cash | | | 90,000 |
| | 230,000 | 82,000 | 90,000 | | 230,000 | 82,000 | 90,000 |

## ACTIVITY 4

### Capital accounts

|  | Ratner £ | Hogg £ | Friar £ |  | Ratner £ | Hogg £ | Friar £ |
|---|---|---|---|---|---|---|---|
|  |  |  |  | Balance b/d | 12,500 | 8,600 |  |
|  |  |  |  | Cash |  |  | 10,000 |
| Balance c/d | 22,500 | 18,600 | 10,000 | Goodwill | 10,000 | 10,000 |  |
|  | 22,500 | 18,600 | 10,000 |  | 22,500 | 18,600 | 10,000 |
|  |  |  |  | Balance b/d | 22,500 | 18,600 | 10,000 |

### Goodwill account

|  | £ |  | £ |
|---|---|---|---|
| Capital  Ratner | 10,000 |  |  |
|         Hogg | 10,000 | Balance c/d | 20,000 |
|  | 20,000 |  | 20,000 |

## ADDITIONAL QUESTION 1

### AL, BERT AND HALL

(a) and (b)

### Capital accounts

|  |  | Al £ | Bert £ | Hall £ |  |  | Al £ | Bert £ | Hall £ |
|---|---|---|---|---|---|---|---|---|---|
|  |  |  |  |  | 30 June | Balances b/d | 12,000 | 15,000 |  |
|  |  |  |  |  |  | Cash |  |  | 20,000 |
|  |  |  |  |  |  | Goodwill written up (0.5 × |  |  |  |
| 1 July | Balance c/d | 21,000 | 24,000 | 20,000 |  | (18,000) | 9,000 | 9,000 |  |
|  |  | 21,000 | 24,000 | 20,000 |  |  | 21,000 | 24,000 | 20,000 |
|  | Goodwill written down |  |  |  | 1 July | balance b/d | 21,000 | 24,000 | 20,000 |
|  | (⅓ × 18,000) | 6,000 | 6,000 | 6,000 |  |  |  |  |  |
|  | Balances c/d | 15,000 | 18,000 | 14,000 |  |  |  |  |  |
|  |  | 21,000 | 24,000 | 20,000 |  |  | 21,000 | 24,000 | 20,000 |

(c)    Goodwill is the difference between the value of a business as a whole and the value of the tangible and other identifiable intangible assets less liabilities.

It is thus a balancing item rather than an item which can be objectively valued in its own right.

Adjustments are required when a new partner joins a business as the new partner is entitled to a share in the future growth of all the partnership assets. His entitlement arises either because he makes a payment to enter the partnership or the other partners consider he will enhance the future profitability of the firm.

His entitlement, is, however, to a share in future growth not past growth. Thus goodwill which has been built up by the existing partners needs to be credited to them.

## ADDITIONAL QUESTION 2

### RED, BLUE AND YELLOW

(a) **Partners' capital accounts**

|  | Red | Blue | Yellow |  | Red | Blue | Yellow |
| --- | --- | --- | --- | --- | --- | --- | --- |
|  | £ | £ | £ |  | £ | £ | £ |
| Goodwill | – | 27,000 | 18,000 | Balance b/d 1.4.X8 | 14,000 | 13,000 | 11,000 |
| (6:4) |  |  |  | Cash |  | 20,000 |  |
| Loan account |  |  |  | Revaluation (L&B) (W) | 8,000 | 6,000 | 6,000 |
| (bal fig) | 42,930 |  |  | Goodwill | 18,000 | 13,500 | 13,500 |
| Balance c/d 31.3.X9 |  | 25,500 | 12,500 | (4:3:3) |  |  |  |
|  |  |  |  | Current a/c | 2,930 |  |  |
|  | 42,930 | 52,500 | 30,500 |  | 42,930 | 52,500 | 30,500 |

***Working:*** Revaluation account

|  | £ |  | £ |
| --- | --- | --- | --- |
| Receivables | 5,000 | Land and buildings | 25,000 |
| Profit on revaluation: |  |  |  |
| Red 4/10 | 8,000 |  |  |
| Blue 3/10 | 6,000 |  |  |
| Yellow 3/10 | 6,000 |  |  |
|  | 25,000 |  | 25,000 |

(b)     **Red, Blue and Yellow: Appropriation account for the year ended 31 March 20X9**

|  | £ | £ |
|---|---|---|
| Net profit | | 53,060 |
| Less partners' salaries | | |
| Red | 9,000 | |
| Blue | 8,000 | |
| Yellow | 6,500 | |
| | | 23,500 |
| Less interest on capital | | |
| Red (14,000 × 12%) | 1,680 | |
| Blue (13,000 × 12%) | 1,560 | |
| Yellow (11,000 × 12%) | 1,320 | |
| | | 4,560 |
| Net profit available for appropriation | | 25,000 |
| | | |
| Balance of profits shared | | |
| Red 4/10 | 10,000 | |
| Blue 3/10 | 7,500 | |
| Yellow 3/10 | 7,500 | |
| | | 25,000 |

(c)     **Partners' current accounts**

|  | Red £ | Blue £ | Yellow £ |  | Red £ | Blue £ | Yellow £ |
|---|---|---|---|---|---|---|---|
| Drawings | 19,000 | 15,000 | 14,500 | Balance b/d 1.4.X8 | 1,250 | 1,080 | 935 |
| | | | | Interest on capital | 1,680 | 1,560 | 1,320 |
| Capital a/c | 2,930 | | | | | | |
| Balance c/d 31.3.X9 | – | 3,140 | 1,755 | Salaries | 9,000 | 8,000 | 6,500 |
| | | | | Profit | 10,000 | 7,500 | 7,500 |
| | 21,930 | 18,140 | 16,255 | | 21,930 | 18,140 | 16,255 |

(d)     **Red: Loan account**

|  |  |  |  |  |
|---|---|---|---|---|
| Balance c/f 31.3.X9 | 42,930 | Capital a/c | 42,930 | |
| | 42,930 | Current a/c | | |
| | | | 42,930 | |

# CHAPTER 12

## ACTIVITY 1

(a)

### Profitability:

| | | | 20X5 | 20X6 |
|---|---|---|---|---|
| (1) | Net profit margin | | | |

(1)  Net profit margin     *20X5*       *20X6*

$$\frac{\text{Net profit before tax}}{\text{Sales}} \qquad \frac{21{,}500}{202{,}900} \times 100 \qquad \frac{37{,}500}{490{,}700} \times 100$$

$$= 10.6\% \qquad = 7.6\%$$

(2)  Return on capital employed:

$$\frac{\text{Net profit before taxation}}{\text{Net assets employed}} \qquad \frac{21{,}500}{119{,}200} \times 100 \qquad \frac{37{,}500}{326{,}600} \times 100$$

$$= 18.0\% \qquad = 11.5\%$$

### Liquidity:

(3)  Current ratio:

$$\frac{\text{Current assets}}{\text{Current liabilities}} \qquad \frac{66{,}500}{52{,}300} \qquad \frac{152{,}500}{85{,}900}$$

$$= 1.3 \qquad = 1.8$$

(4)  Quick ratio:

$$\frac{\text{Current assets - Stock}}{\text{Current liabilities}} \qquad \frac{35{,}500}{52{,}300} \qquad \frac{57{,}200}{85{,}900}$$

$$= 0.7 \qquad = 0.7$$

### Financial stability:

(5)  Gearing:

$$\frac{\text{Long - term debt}}{\text{Net assets employed}} \qquad \text{Nil} \qquad \frac{100{,}500}{326{,}600} \times 100$$

$$= 30.6\%$$

(6)  $$\frac{\text{Liabilities}}{\text{Shareholders' funds}} \qquad \frac{52{,}300}{119{,}200} \qquad \frac{185{,}900}{226{,}600}$$

$$= 0.4 \qquad = 0.8$$

(b)  **Comment**

*Tutorial note*: Comments need not be long. It is better that they are short and to the point. It is a good idea to state whether each ratio is showing a better or worse position compared to last year.

### Profitability

Profitability in relation to sales and capital employed has fallen. However, the fall has occurred in a period of sales increasing two and a half times and capital increasing due to the issue of loan stock.

It will take time to invest the additional capital efficiently.

The decline in the profitability compared to sales may also be a short-term problem. For example overheads are not being kept under control in the period of rapid expansion. Alternatively the sales volume may have been achieved by cutting gross profit margins.

### Liquidity

The current ratio has increased to give a comfortable level of cover for short-term creditors. Most of the increase, however, is derived from higher stocks. The quick ratio is constant.

Whether these two ratios are good or bad depends on what is normal/efficient in the type of business that Nantred is in.

### Financial stability

There has been a major injection of long-term finance during the year, producing a gearing ratio of 30%. The business is thus in a riskier position than last year but the expansion of the business may be necessary to protect the existing business (by becoming larger it may be better able to protect itself).

The liabilities to shareholders' funds show a similar position as the gearing (and for the same reasons).

## PRACTICE QUESTION

### ELECTRICAL ENGINEERING

*Tutorial note:*

Fairly straightforward ratio analysis question. Ensure calculations are shown clearly and note that ROOE is based only on capital and reserves, while ROCE includes long-term creditors.

For part (b) comment on the liquidity position of the company, the declining profitability and effect of gearing and interest payable.

|  | | *20X1* | *20X0* |
|---|---|---|---|
| (a) | Current ratio | 30,500: 24,000 = 1.3:1 | 28,500: 20,000 = 1.4:1 |
|  | Quick ratio | 16,500: 24,000 = .7:1 | 15,500: 20,000 = .8:1 |

Stock turnover in days

$$\frac{14,000}{42,000} \times 365 = 122 \text{ days}$$

$$\frac{13,000}{34,000} \times 365 = 140 \text{ days}$$

Debtors turnover in days

$$\frac{16,000}{60,000} \times 365 \text{ days} = 97 \text{ days}$$

$$\frac{15,000}{50,000} \times 365 = 110 \text{ days}$$

| Creditors turnover in days | $\dfrac{24,000}{42,000+15,500}$ | $\dfrac{20,000}{34,000+13,000}$ |
|---|---|---|

(assume operating expenses incurred on credit terms)

|  | $\times 365 = 152$ days | $\times 365 = 155$ days |
|---|---|---|

| Gross profit % | $\dfrac{18,000}{60,000} \times 100 = 30\%$ |  |
|---|---|---|
|  |  | $\dfrac{16,000}{50,000} \times 100 = 32\%$ |

| Net profit % (before tax) | $\dfrac{300}{60,000} \times 100 = 0.5\%$ |  |
|---|---|---|
|  |  | $\dfrac{1,700}{50,000} \times 100 = 3.4\%$ |

| Interest cover | $\dfrac{2,500}{2,200} = 1.1\,\text{times}$ | $\dfrac{3,000}{1,300} = 2.3\,\text{times}$ |
|---|---|---|

| Dividend cover | $\dfrac{(50)}{600} = (0.8)\,\text{times}$ |  |
|---|---|---|
| $\dfrac{1,100}{600} = 1.8\,\text{times}$ |  |  |
|  | (No cover) |  |

| ROOE (before taxation) | $\dfrac{300}{13,000} \times 100 = 2.3\%$ |  |
|---|---|---|
|  |  | $\dfrac{1,700}{14,000} \times 100 = 12.1\%$ |

| ROCE | $\dfrac{2,500}{13,000+6,000} \times 100 = 13.2\%$ |  |
|---|---|---|
|  |  | $\dfrac{3,000}{14,000+5,500} \times 100 = 15.4\%$ |

| Gearing | $\dfrac{6,000}{13,000+6,000} \times 100 = 31.6\%$ |  |
|---|---|---|
|  |  | $\dfrac{5,500}{14,000+5,500} = 28.2\%$ |

(b) There has been a decline in the liquidity position of the business. The 'weak' position in 20X0 where quick assets (debtors and bank) do not cover the immediate liabilities has deteriorated even further in 20X1. If this trend were to continue the going concern ability of the business would probably be in question. In addition the cover provided by profits over interest payable has more than halved; this would be considered a poor indicator by the interest bearing creditors. Such creditors may question the decision to declare the same level of dividend for 20X1 as for 20X0, even though the business made an after tax loss.

The business's profitability shows only a small 2% drop at the gross profit level but because of the significant levels of operating expenses and interest payable the net profit percentage in 20X1 is only one seventh of its 20X0 level. Clearly improvements are required if the business is to continue to report positive profit after tax figures.

Finally, management has increased the level of fixed assets; with such poor trading results they should be asked if such expansion was necessary and when the benefits from the use of such resources can be expected to accrue.

## ADDITIONAL QUESTION

### HAWK

(a)

#### Year ended 31 March

|       |                                                | 20X1      | 20X2      |
|-------|------------------------------------------------|-----------|-----------|
| (i)   | Gross profit as percentage of sales            |           |           |
|       | 600/1,800 × 100                                | 33.3%     |           |
|       | 700/2,500 × 100                                |           | 28.0%     |
| (ii)  | Operating profit as percentage of sales revenue |           |           |
|       | 240/1,800 × 100                                | 13.3%     |           |
|       | 250/2,500 × 100                                |           | 10.0%     |
| (iii) | Return on capital employed                     |           |           |
|       | 190/1,568 × 100                                | 12.1%     |           |
|       | 200/2,122 × 100                                |           | 9.4%      |
|       | Valid alternative calculations also acceptable |           |           |
| (iv)  | Current ratio                                  |           |           |
|       | 700 : 518                                      | 1.35:1    |           |
|       | 1,230 : 860                                    |           | 1.43:1    |
| (v)   | Quick ratio                                    |           |           |
|       | 500 : 518                                      | 0.96:1    |           |
|       | 870 : 860                                      |           | 1.01:1    |
| (vi)  | Stock turnover (days)                          |           |           |
|       | 200/1,200 × 365                                | 60.8 days |           |
|       | 360/1,800 × 365                                |           | 73.0 days |

(vii)   Trade debtors – sales (days)

      400/1,440 × 365                        101.4 days

      750/2,000 × 365                                      136.9 days

(viii)  Trade creditors – purchases (days)

      210/1,220 × 365                        62.8 days

      380/1,960 × 365                                      70.8 days

(b)   **Comments on ratios**

(i)   Gross profit percentage on sales has declined from 33.3% to 28.0%, a substantial drop. This could possibly be due to a decision to lower prices in order to increase sales revenue, which has risen by 38.9%. A drop in the gross profit percentage might be an indicator of possible error or fraud if another explanation such as a lowering of prices cannot be found.

(ii)   Net profit to sales is down from 13.3% to 10%, which is also a large drop, but not as large as the drop in the gross profit percentage. A large rise in distribution costs as a percentage of sales helps to explain this poor result.

(iii)   Return on capital employed has declined from 12.1% to 9.4%. This is a reflection of the decline in profitability as shown by ratio (ii) above.

(iv) & (v) The two ratios measuring liquidity have changed little between the two periods, suggesting that the liquidity position is satisfactory at both dates.

(vi)   The stock turnover ratio has increased because the stock level has risen faster than the increases in cost of sales and sales. The higher stock could be a reflection of slowing demand for the company's goods towards the end of the period and/or slackness in the company's stock control procedures.

(vii)   The debtors days have increased considerably from 101.4 days, a high level, to the even higher level of 136.9 days. The increase suggests slackness in the company's credit control procedures.

(viii)   There has been a relatively small increase in the number of days' purchases in trade creditors. The increase is perhaps caused by pressure on the company's liquid resources as a result of the increased stock and trade debtors.

KAPLAN PUBLISHING

# INDEX

KAPLAN PUBLISHING